HEALTH AND HEALING
THE NATURAL WAY

EXERCISE AND
YOUR HEALTH

HEALTH AND HEALING
THE NATURAL WAY

EXERCISE
AND YOUR
HEALTH

Reader's
Digest

PUBLISHED BY

THE READER'S DIGEST ASSOCIATION LIMITED

LONDON NEW YORK SYDNEY MONTREAL CAPE TOWN

EXERCISE AND YOUR HEALTH
was created and produced by
Carroll & Brown Limited
5 Lonsdale Road, London NW6 6RA
for The Reader's Digest Association Limited, London

CARROLL & BROWN

Publishing Director Denis Kennedy
Art Director Chrissie Lloyd

Managing Editor Sandra Rigby
Managing Art Editor Tracy Timson

Project Coordinator Laura Price

Editor Richard Emerson

Design Mercedes Morgan,
Rachel Goldsmith, Simon Daley

Photographers Jules Selmes, David Murray

Production Wendy Rogers, Karen Kloot

Computer Management John Clifford, Paul Stradling

Reproduced by Colourscan, Singapore
Printing and binding: Printer Industria Gráfica S.A., Barcelona

CONSULTANTS

Bob Smith MA, BEd Hons, Cert Ed
*Department of Physical Education, Sports Science and
Recreation Management, Loughborough University*

Dr Amanda Roberts MB, BChir

CONTRIBUTORS

Professor Ron Maughan BSc, PhD
Professor of Human Physiology

Dr Lorraine Cale BSc, MSc, PhD
Lecturer in Physical Education

Dr Briony Thomas BSc, PhD, SRD
Nutritionist

Tim Cable PhD
Reader in Exercise Physiology

Penny Hunking SRD
Accredited Sports Dietitian

Rozalind Gruben Prof AHSI, RSA
Health and Fitness Consultant

Kelly Hosking BEd Hons
Fitness Consultant

Fiona Hayes
Fitness Consultant

FOR THE READER'S DIGEST

Series Editor Christine Noble
Editorial Assistant Chloë Garrow

READER'S DIGEST GENERAL BOOKS

Editorial Director Cortina Butler
Art Director Nick Clark

The information in this book is for reference only;
it is not intended as a substitute for a doctor's diagnosis and care.
The editors urge anyone with continuing medical problems
or symptoms to consult a doctor.

EXERCISE AND YOUR HEALTH

More and more people today are choosing to take greater responsibility for their own health rather than relying on the doctor to step in with a cure when something goes wrong. We now recognise that we can influence our health by making an improvement in lifestyle – a better diet, more exercise and reduced stress. People are also becoming increasingly aware that there are other healing methods – some new, others very ancient – that can help to prevent illness or be used as a complement to orthodox medicine.

The series *Health and Healing the Natural Way* will help you to make your own health choices by giving you clear, comprehensive, straightforward and encouraging information and advice about methods of improving your health. The series explains the many different natural therapies now available – aromatherapy, herbalism, acupressure and many others – and the circumstances in which they may be of benefit when used in conjunction with conventional medicine.

For those who have led rather sedentary lives up to now, or who are moderately active but just want to increase their fitness levels, exercise can seem daunting. Health clubs and gym workouts, aerobics and jogging can be intimidating to the uninitiated when all they really want is to feel healthier and better able to cope with day-to-day activities. *EXERCISE AND YOUR HEALTH* demystifies the subject of exercise and shows how getting fitter does not have to involve major alterations to your lifestyle or a gruelling training routine. It shows how to build up exercise levels safely as your fitness improves and how to assess your progress. Everyone can incorporate healthy exercise into their daily lives with surprisingly little effort and disruption. In return you will reap major health benefits such as reduced chance of illness, increased stamina and strength, and a more positive outlook – and discover how enjoyable exercise can be.

CONTENTS

FIT FOR LIFE

Regular healthy exercise doing an activity that you enjoy not only offers a satisfying pastime but can also greatly enhance your quality of life.

Most of us are aware of the extent to which exercise can improve health, but it still seems difficult to overcome entrenched habits and attitudes to make the change towards a more active lifestyle. Yet exercise needn't be intimidating, or a chore. There are plenty of ways to exercise that are fun and rewarding in their own right. Exercise can be a good opportunity for socialising – activities like team sports or dancing are great ways to meet people, as well as helping you to get fit. Exercise can also be a means of relieving stress in your daily life. Yoga and t'ai chi are calming and relaxing, and also build strength and flexibility.

Exercise need not involve long sessions of physical activity. Short spells of exercise carried out three or four times a day, which most people can easily fit into an average day, can be just as effective. A study from the University of Pittsburgh found the same level of fitness benefit for women who did 10 minutes of exercise four times a day as those who did 40-minute once-a-day sessions. But why aren't we getting enough exercise? And why, in recent years, has there been so much focus on the link between fitness and health?

THE DECLINE OF EXERCISE

For our grandparents' and great-grandparents' generations, physical effort was an inescapable part of daily life. Until earlier this century most men and many women worked in physically demanding manual trades, while for the majority of women housework and child rearing, without the benefit of labour-saving devices, was a constant round of physical work. Even leisure periods were likely to involve some effort. Dancing was one of the most popular pastimes for all ages, and most people expected to walk at least part of the way to their social venues. The average person's basic calorie intake has actually altered little over the last century. Yet obesity was not a major issue 100 years ago. The reason for the difference is that, with Western society's more sedentary lifestyle today, the calories consumed are not burned up at the same rate in fuelling the average person's current level of physical activity. The advent of television, cars, and modern household appliances, and the switch from manual labour to automated or clerical jobs, mean that people are far less active than in the past. And when someone used to very low levels of activity attempts something more strenuous, such as running to catch a bus, or DIY, it can lead to a range of medical problems, from strains and sprains to heart attack and stroke.

ALL WORK
In the past, people got enough daily exercise from their occupations, but now most people do sedentary jobs.

EXERCISE AND HEALTH

While no one advocates a return to back-breaking manual labour and dawn-to-dusk household drudgery, health experts do feel that the pendulum has swung too far towards inactivity and many people now have too little physical effort in their lives. Researchers are constantly finding new evidence of the health benefits that exercise provides. For example, it is known that sustained exercise such as brisk walking, jogging or cycling, that raises the pulse and breathing rate for at least 20 minutes, three times a week, can help to protect the heart and circulatory system from the major killers of the developed world – heart and artery disease, and stroke.

Regular exercise, provided it is not taken to extremes, also boosts the body's immune system, helping to guard against cancer and other diseases. Weight-bearing exercise can strengthen the bones, and so help to guard against osteoporosis, the brittle-bone condition that afflicts many people in later life.

THE STRENGTH TO COPE
Weight training is not just about building bigger muscles, regular strength exercises can help you to cope much better with everyday tasks, such as decorating, housework, DIY and looking after children.

STRESS RELIEF

Exercise brings many important psychological benefits too. There is evidence to show that regular energetic exercise can increase the production of naturally occurring 'feel-good' chemicals in the body, called endorphins, which help to counteract anxiety and depression and enhance a feeling of general well-being. Exercise can also help to alleviate another major scourge of the modern age – stress. Many people suffer levels of mental stress that are severe enough to cause physical symptoms, such as sleeplessness and tension headaches, and may lead to serious disorders such as ulcers and high blood pressure. In large part such problems result from the body's natural response to stress, which is to produce hormones that prepare it for a physical reaction. This so-called 'fight or flight' response helps us to counter physical threats – an essential attribute for our ancient ancestors – but is less appropriate for dealing with many modern causes of stress, such as relationship difficulties and work pressures. Exercise helps to dissipate these stress hormones by channelling nervous energy into healthy physical activity.

THE PEOPLE'S RACE

Once you become more active, you will be amazed by the exercise feats that become attainable. Most people think of the marathon as the supreme test of fitness, but with careful training more and more amateurs are now taking part in this race. The contest evolved from the achievement of the Greek messenger Pheidippides, who, in 490 BC, ran non-stop from Marathon to Athens to announce a decisive victory by the Athenians over the Persian army. The Battle of Marathon is now largely forgotten, but the race which commemorates that remarkable run is known worldwide.

The marathon was one of the main events at the first modern Olympic Games held in Athens in 1896. The first 'city' marathon was held in Boston, USA, in 1897 and comprised just 15 runners. A century later, 40 000 runners took part in the Boston Marathon and, for many of them, it was just one of several appearances they make at marathons in the world's major cities, including Tokyo, Paris, and the most famous venues, London and New York. For the majority, the joy of the marathon is in completing the course, no matter how long it takes. Participants come from a wide range of ages and backgrounds. In a recent London Marathon, runners included a 73-year-old woman who had been sedentary up to the age of 62 (see page 59).

Not all forms of exercise are as demanding as marathon running, of course. Whether the activity involves a competitive event, a keep fit session at the local sports centre, or a brisk walk in the countryside, there is a leisure pursuit to suit the fitness level, commitment and personal interests of everyone. By far the most important issue is to find an activity that you will enjoy and that you will be able to sustain.

MARATHON MAN
According to legend, the Athenian Pheidippides ran non-stop to announce victory in the Battle of Marathon and collapsed with the words 'Rejoice, we conquer!'.

FIND YOUR OWN LEVEL OF EXERCISE
You don't have to go to marathon levels to benefit from exercise. Many forms of physical activity, such as walking the dog every day or regular gardening, can aid health and mental well-being and make daily tasks much easier to cope with.

EXERCISE FOR ALL AGES

It is vitally important to acquire the exercise habit at an early age. Young children are naturally energetic, but for older children and adolescents the attractions of such sedentary pastimes as television and computer games can prove a more powerful draw than active leisure pursuits. In addition schools tend to place less emphasis on physical activities than was the case in the past, and many parents now drive their children to school, rather than letting them walk, which further reduces the opportunities for exercise. By helping children to find an activity that they can enjoy at an early age, and encouraging them to continue with it, parents can ensure that their children reap the health benefits of exercise well into old age.

Exercise is not, of course, the sole province of the young. People of all ages and fitness levels can find active leisure pursuits that are both a source of enjoyment and an aid to better health. Swimming, for example, can be enjoyed at many levels and can be especially useful for elderly people by exercising the limbs, heart and lungs while the water provides support for weakened muscles and painful joints. Research shows that, for sedentary people, the greatest health benefits are achieved through quite a modest increase in activity levels, such as a daily walk of 10 to 20 minutes.

IMPORTANCE OF PLAYTIME
By encouraging young children to take part in physical games you can aid their physical development and also promote hand and eye coordination.

KEEPING FIT AND HAVING FUN

For many people, however, the primary purpose of an active leisure pursuit is to have fun, and keeping fit is a bonus. It has never been easier to find a sport or activity to suit each individual's interests, finances and commitment. Most people are within easy travelling distance of a leisure centre offering a range of activities at a price that they can afford. In addition, golf courses and health clubs are springing up at an ever-increasing rate, and many firms are starting company sports clubs or sponsoring their own sports teams.

Sport and exercise also provide important social opportunities, such as the friendly outings of a rambling group, the close bond between badminton or tennis doubles partners, and the boisterous camaraderie of a soccer or rugby team. For many, such social interaction gives shape and purpose to their lives, while the support and encouragement of others enables them to push themselves further than might otherwise have been possible.

VALUE FOR MONEY
Taking up a new sport may mean an initial investment in a few items of equipment and comfortable shoes. However, in the long term, exercise is one of the most economical forms of entertainment.

HOW TO USE THIS BOOK

The purpose of *Exercise and Your Health* is to encourage an active lifestyle and to give advice on how to derive more enjoyment and greater health benefits from exercise. Chapter 1 looks at the effects of exercise on the body and shows how exercise can improve the quality of life – physically, mentally and emotionally. As well as bringing about physical changes that make it much easier to carry out ordinary tasks, exercise can also aid disorders such as high blood pressure, arthritis and asthma.

Chapter 2 covers the different types of exercise and explains what each one achieves in terms of enhancing general fitness, boosting strength, and aiding flexibility. It looks at the various components of a well-balanced fitness programme and compares different activities to show what type of exercise each one provides.

The important link between exercise and diet is dealt with in Chapter 3. This chapter examines the various roles that different nutrients play in exercise and fitness and shows how to plan your diet to ensure that you get the most out of an exercise programme.

ENERGY FOR EXERCISE
Increasing your intake of starchy foods such as bread and rice, while limiting your intake of fats and refined sugar, will give you more energy without leading to unwanted weight gain.

To monitor your progress during your fitness programme you need to know how to recognise and measure the improvements you are making. Chapter 4 looks at ways of testing your current physical status, depending upon whether you are concentrating on stamina, flexibility or strength, and explains how to set attainable goals. Safety is a vital part of sport and exercise, and Chapter 5 looks at the most suitable clothing to wear, how to avoid injury or other ill effects during exercise and what to do if injury occurs. The chapter also looks at situations that require extra caution when exercising, such as pregnancy, illness or surgery.

There is a wide range of leisure pursuits to choose from and Chapter 6 aims to help you to select the one that is right for you. It describes how to decide what your personal aspirations are, taking into account your age, budget and level of commitment. Chapter 7 shows how you can incorporate more exercise into your daily life. It explains how to set up a home gym, describes exercises you can do both at home and at work, and suggests how you can involve the family and stay motivated. Finally, Chapter 8 shows what to look for in a health club or leisure centre, how to make the best use of the facilities and how to choose a good instructor.

ARE YOU GETTING ENOUGH EXERCISE?

You may feel that you get enough exercise each week by simply going for a leisurely stroll on a Sunday, if the weather is fine. But if this is all the physical activity you get it will not go very far towards protecting you against heart disease or avoiding strains and sprains resulting from, say, lifting a heavy object. A regular exercise routine can make a big difference to both your health and quality of life.

Q **IS IT A LONG TIME SINCE YOU EXERCISED? DO YOU FEEL THAT IT'S TOO LATE TO START NOW?**

It is never too late to begin some form of exercise programme, no matter what your age or fitness level. In fact, research shows that for those who have been inactive for a long time, major health benefits can be achieved through a quite modest increase in exercise. Going for a gentle walk each day for just 20 minutes, for example, can greatly reduce the risk of heart disease. As your fitness improves you can increase your level of exertion to, say, a brisk 20-30 minute walk three times a week. It will not be long before you feel a dramatic improvement in your general health and fitness. There are also many sports clubs that cater for senior team members, allowing you to restart a sport you may have enjoyed when you were younger and get back into the game at your own pace.

Q **DO YOU WANT TO GET FIT BUT DISLIKE THE IDEA OF JOGGING OR GOING TO THE GYM?**

There is a wide range of activities available that are within the reach of most people, so you are bound to find one or more pursuits that you'll enjoy. Whether you are interested in running or rambling, kayaking or karate, baseball or ballroom dancing they all bring their own particular fitness benefits as well as providing great opportunities to have fun. Some sports are best suited to those who prefer a mainly solitary activity while others have a highly social element. Chapter 6 has some suggestions, and you could ask at your local library or sports centre for a list of the leisure activities on offer in your neighbourhood. It is also worth checking in the sports pages or the advertising section of your local newspaper to see if sports groups in your area are looking for new members. Try a few activities until you find ones that you like. You may find that you need a little general fitness training as well. Chapters 7 and 8 have lots of exercise ideas for you to try.

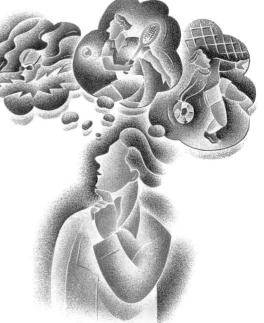

Q DO YOU FEEL YOUR LIFE IS SIMPLY TOO BUSY
FOR YOU TO FIT IN REGULAR EXERCISE?

With a little planning you can fit exercise into the busiest of
schedules. For short journeys, walk instead of taking the car or bus – by
the time you have waited for the bus or parked the car, you may find it's
actually quicker on foot. Make an effort twice a week to exercise in your
lunch hour. Going for a brisk walk is simple enough, but if there is a gym
or swimming pool nearby you can fit in a 20-minute work-out. This is not
wasted time, as some people seem to think. Regular exercise will sharpen
your responses and actually make you more efficient at work, so you gain
time in the long run. In the evening and at weekends, instead of watching
television, go for a cycle or a country ramble: if you have children, take
them with you and you can all enjoy the benefits of healthy exercise.

Q HAS YOUR CHRONIC BACKACHE OR JOINT PAIN
BECOME AN EXCUSE TO AVOID EXERCISE?

Many people with chronic joint or muscle problems find that the
thought of going to the gym or taking up jogging is just too painful to
consider. In fact, there are many forms of exercise that can be tailored to
allow for injury and often help to relieve chronic pain. Some sports, such as
aerobics, can be carried out in water to relieve pressure on joints and
muscles. Others, such as yoga, can be practised in conjunction with a
variety of sports to strengthen muscles and joints. It is important that you
do not exacerbate a problem with the wrong sorts of exercise, but there is
no need to avoid it altogether. Check with a qualified trainer or fitness
instructor, so that he or she can modify a work-out to meet your needs.

Q DO YOU HATE FEELING HUNGRY ALL THE TIME
WHEN YOU DIET AND EXERCISE?

A common mistake that many people make is to think that the only
way to lose weight is to starve yourself. If you are trying to follow a regular
fitness programme and yet keep to a very low-calorie diet there is a risk
that you will not get enough energy from your meals to meet your
increased activity levels and you quickly become fatigued. In Chapter 3 we
show that a planned regular fitness programme combined with a diet that
is low in fat but high in complex carbohydrates will provide all the energy
you need and yet still help you to lose weight. As you become fitter your
body will start to burn up the calories more efficiently, so you may end up
eating more than you did before your diet, yet still stay slim.

CHAPTER 1

HOW EXERCISE IMPROVES YOUR HEALTH

Exercise brings many benefits. It not only improves the physical condition of your body – your fitness, stamina and strength – it also brings a feeling of mental well-being and increases your self-confidence. Regular exercise can pave the way for a healthy, independent life well into old age.

WHY YOU SHOULD EXERCISE

The key to a healthy lifestyle, which will incorporate both physical and mental well-being, is to find a level of exercise that you find stimulating and can easily sustain on a regular basis.

The association between good health and exercise has been convincingly established by doctors over the years, and yet it is clear that, from a health point of view, the current lifestyle of the average person is still far from ideal. Although many people do exercise regularly, most of us operate at the lowest possible level – where it cannot be avoided, it must be endured.

This picture, however, is slowly changing. As the physical demands of most occupations are reduced and information regarding the various benefits of exercise becomes more readily accessible, so more people are taking up exercise on a recreational basis.

HEALTH AND FITNESS

In general terms, there are two clear benefits that can be obtained from regular exercise. The first is an improvement in health,

the second is an improvement in fitness. The concepts of 'health' and 'fitness' are often used as if they were interchangeable, but there is a clear distinction between the two. The *Oxford English Dictionary* defines health as 'soundness of body'. More specifically, good health signifies the absence of illness and the efficient functioning of all the systems of the body. Regular sensible exercise can improve the efficiency of many of the body's systems, in particular the cardiovascular and respiratory systems. It can also boost your immune system making you less susceptible to colds and flu.

In contrast, fitness means different things to different people. It can be broadly defined as an ability to perform everyday physical activities with vigour. The aim of the average person should be to achieve a level of fitness appropriate to his or her own requirements. At a basic level this may mean being able to walk to the shops and back without getting out of breath, or being able to play football in the park with your grandchildren. At a high level, fitness for a serious athlete may mean pushing yourself to the limit either in competition with other athletes, or the record books, or the elements.

Low levels of fitness are now recognised as an extremely serious problem, perhaps the leading risk to general health, and are particularly linked to a susceptibility to cardiovascular diseases. The Framingham study, which was begun in America in 1948, lasted over 40 years and involved 5000 people, has provided powerful evidence of this. The results of the study confirmed that people with very low levels of activity were over five times more likely to die from heart disease than those who incorporated moderate levels of exercise into their daily lives.

FAMILY EXERCISE
Simple games such as tug-of-war can be enjoyed almost anywhere and provide a good way to encourage the whole family to include more healthy physical activity in their day.

Mental and emotional fitness

In the case of mental and emotional rather than physical fitness, the same arguments apply – it is not enough just to be free of specific disorders. Just as exercise produces direct benefits to your physical health, it also improves your emotional and psychological health. Perhaps one of the most important benefits of exercise is its effectiveness in reducing stress, the long-term risks of which are now established.

A HEALTHY LIFESTYLE

Exercise plays an important part in a healthy lifestyle. As you exercise you burn up energy so you can enjoy your food without worrying about putting on weight. You also build strength, stamina and muscle tone, gain confidence and reduce stress, in addition to the other important health benefits.

The case for regular exercise seems overwhelmingly convincing. Yet the trend in recent years has been towards a less active lifestyle. In particular, children now spend more time engaged in sedentary pursuits such as watching television than in activities involving physical exercise. About half of the population aged 12–21 in the UK take no vigorous exercise on a regular basis, with adolescent girls less active than boys.

HEALTH OF A NATION

The Department of Health recently published alarming figures on the population's current lifestyle and its effect on the state of health in Britain.

▶ *74 per cent of British men and 83 per cent of British women over 50 years of age do not take part in enough physical activity to improve their health.*

▶ *13 per cent of British men are obese, while 43 per cent are overweight.*

▶ *16 per cent of British women are obese while 24 per cent are overweight.*

If this trend continues it is likely to lead to serious health problems in the future. Yet exercise opportunities are more accessible than ever before, with gyms, health clubs and community sports facilities now widely available. Even for those who cannot easily attend organised fitness sessions, or who do not like the idea, possibilities for increasing the level of physical activity in their daily lives are all around. By re-discovering the physical potential of your body, you may discover how enjoyable exercise can be, and reap the health benefits of physical fitness.

SIMPLE STRESS RELIEF

Regular exercise not only conditions and strengthens the body and improves your fitness, it also provides relief from many of life's everyday stresses.

Stress can lead to a range of specific diseases and illnesses, as well as contributing to negative emotional states such as depression. Exercise provides an excellent release for the nervous tension produced by stress, and helps you to cope more effectively with everyday life.

The simple stretching exercise shown here will help to relieve stress if practised on a regular basis. It stretches the chest muscles, allowing the lungs to fill with oxygen and relieving stress-induced pressure across the chest.

1 *Stand with your feet together and arms by your sides.*

2 *Take a deep breath and raise your arms slowly.*

3 *Rise up onto your toes as you raise your arms to meet above your head. Repeat twice.*

PHYSICAL BENEFITS OF EXERCISE

Regular exercise provides a wide range of physical benefits that both help the body to work more efficiently and reduce the likelihood of developing a number of life-threatening diseases.

The major health benefits of regular physical activity were spelt out in a 1995 report from the Department of Health and Human Services in the United States. Exercise reduces the risk of various diseases, including heart disease, diabetes, high blood pressure and cancer of the colon, and also raises the level of life expectancy, improving the likelihood of longevity.

Exercise improves posture, strengthens the back, and helps to maintain healthy bones, muscles and joints, reducing the risk of arthritis and helping older adults become stronger and better able to move about safely and independently. It also helps to speed up the recovery process following childbirth and various illnesses, builds up your energy levels, and helps to control your weight.

THE CARDIOVASCULAR SYSTEM

The most basic measure of health and fitness is the efficiency of the cardiovascular system, the network of blood vessels with the heart at its centre. The heart pumps blood through the arteries, circulating oxygen throughout the body, then blood returns via the veins. During exercise the muscles demand more oxygen, which forces the heart to work harder and pump more blood around the body. Over time, this improves the heart's strength and efficiency: regular training helps the heart to beat more strongly, which, in turn, allows it to beat more slowly. A slow heartbeat is a sign of a healthy heart as it doesn't have to work so hard to pump the blood the body needs.

Comparing the heart rate of a sedentary person with a physically trained person shows some major differences. At rest, the average adult needs about 5 litres (8¾ pints) of blood per minute to be pumped around the body. In a sedentary person, this could demand a heart rate of 80 or more beats per minute, and the stroke volume (the amount of blood ejected from the heart per beat) would be about 70 millilitres (2½ fluid ounces) or less. By contrast, in a physically

HOW YOUR HEART WORKS

Your heart is divided into four chambers – the two atria and the two ventricles – and acts as a pump. The two chambers on the right side of the heart receive blood from the body's tissues after it is depleted of oxygen and pump it to the lungs where the oxygen is replaced. The chambers on the left side of the heart receive the oxygen-rich blood from the lungs and then pump it back round the body.

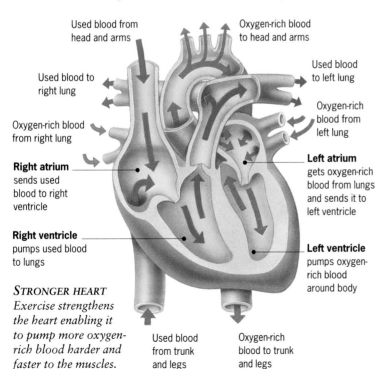

Used blood from head and arms

Oxygen-rich blood to head and arms

Used blood to right lung

Used blood to left lung

Oxygen-rich blood from left lung

Oxygen-rich blood from right lung

Right atrium sends used blood to right ventricle

Left atrium gets oxygen-rich blood from lungs and sends it to left ventricle

Right ventricle pumps used blood to lungs

Left ventricle pumps oxygen-rich blood around body

STRONGER HEART
Exercise strengthens the heart enabling it to pump more oxygen-rich blood harder and faster to the muscles.

Used blood from trunk and legs

Oxygen-rich blood to trunk and legs

ASTHMA AND EXERCISE

Many people who suffer from asthma think that exercise in any form is bad for them and that it would only exacerbate their condition. This, however is untrue. Although breathlessness and wheezing cannot be eradicated through exercise alone, the deep breathing techniques and the controlled regular breaths required by exercises such as yoga or swimming can help to improve lung function. These exercises will help to ease tense muscles, widen the airways and promote overall relaxation which will in turn lower your stress levels and help to minimise attacks.

TAKE THE PLUNGE
Swimming is an excellent exercise that also strengthens the respiratory system and allows the practice of controlled breathing.

Boost your lungs
Many people use only a quarter of their lung capacity and quickly run out of breath. Exercise can improve the elasticity of the lungs and so make your respiratory system more efficient.

SHALLOW BREATHING
During normal breathing the lungs move just 500 millilitres (17 fluid ounces) of air with each breath.

trained person the stroke volume would be much greater, about 100–200 millilitres (3½–7 fluid ounces), and the heart rate much lower at 40–50 beats per minute. This means that the heart is pumping out more blood with each beat and working less hard to deliver the blood the body needs.

Top long-distance runners have a greatly enlarged heart size, and can achieve a cardiac output as high as 40 litres (70 pints) per minute. They may have a resting heart rate of 30 beats per minute or even less.

THE RESPIRATORY SYSTEM

Exercise can improve the efficiency of the respiratory system by improving your lung capacity. This is because in normal daily life, only a small part of the total lung capacity is used (see right).

Training during adolescence, when the lungs are still developing, can significantly increase their dimensions, improving their capacity for delivering oxygen to the blood. These improvements can then be maintained throughout adult life, even after training has ceased. Activities that require the development of enhanced breathing capacity lead to the greatest increases in lung volume: divers and people who learnt to play a wind instrument when young will usually have the largest lungs.

Available lung volume usually begins to decline after about the age of 30 owing to a loss of tissue elasticity. However, most tissues respond to the demands placed upon them and the lungs are no exception. The age-related decline in lung function can be slowed by exercise.

THE LYMPHATIC SYSTEM

The lymphatic system is the cornerstone of your immunity. It is a barrier to the spread of infection and harmful bacteria – the more efficiently it works, the healthier you are. The system is a series of connected vessels containing lymph fluid, a watery substance that bathes all the tissues of the body. This fluid contains the white cells that help to combat infection, along with any harmful microorganisms that might be present.

Unlike blood, which is pumped by the heart muscle, lymph relies solely on physical movement for its circulation. Activity therefore improves lymph activity. For example, the repeated waves of gravitational pull exerted on your body when bouncing on a trampet (a mini trampoline) act like a pump and promote better lymphatic functioning.

THE BRAIN

Doctors and scientists have long been interested in the changes in the cardiovascular and muscular systems brought about by exercise. More recently, however, there has been a growing realisation that changes in psychological function also accompany regular exercise. The study of these adaptations is still in its infancy, partly due to the practical difficulties of measuring the changes, but also because our understanding of normal brain function is still relatively poor.

What is clear, however, is that most people who engage in regular exercise report an improved sense of well-being. This probably has a chemical basis and there is now some evidence to suggest that exercise produces changes in the sensitivity of some of

DEEP BREATHS
During hard exercise, lung capacity increases to about 2.5–3.5 litres (4½–6 pints).

CASE STUDY

Returning to Exercise

As people age, many find that they begin to gain a disproportionately large amount of weight. This is not because they are eating more than before, but because their lifestyle has become more sedentary without a corresponding reduction in food intake. The best way to tackle this weight gain is to take up exercise again, but returning to exercise after a break needs planning and preparation.

Joe is 48 and married with three children, the eldest, Paul, being married with five-year-old twins. Joe was a keen amateur footballer when younger, but he hasn't played for ten years and now takes little exercise. More recently, his job as a sales manager has become more demanding. Because he spends long hours in the office he often misses the family evening meal and snacks on chips, takeaways and pastries instead.

Although he won't admit it, he's becoming extremely conscious of his expanding waistline. As a starting point to improving his health, he decided to play a game of football with his grandchildren one weekend and was horrified to find himself breathless after only a few minutes.

WHAT SHOULD JOE DO?

Joe went to see his doctor, who told him that he was overweight, that his blood pressure was a little on the high side and his cholesterol level was raised. However, the doctor found no medical reason why Joe should not embark on an exercise programme. He advised him to start gradually, with a less strenuous form of exercise than football. Joe was also advised to try to lose weight by improving his diet, cutting back on high fat food and eating more vegetables, fruit and complex carbohydrate meals.

The doctor recommended that Joe start a programme of gentle walking for the first few weeks, gradually building up in intensity to a slow jog within a month.

Action Plan

HEALTH
Have regular check-ups to monitor cholesterol and blood pressure levels.

DIET
Cut down on fatty foods, eat more fresh fruit, vegetables and high carbohydrate foods such as pasta, brown rice, potatoes and brown bread.

FITNESS
Start a fitness programme initially involving gentle exercise. Gradually build up its intensity and time until fit enough to carry out more strenuous forms of exercise.

HEALTH
Lack of exercise can aggravate many health problems such as high cholesterol and high blood pressure.

HOW THINGS TURNED OUT FOR JOE

Joe started to take a 30-minute walk every lunchtime which helped with both his weight and his breathlessness. His new diet improved his energy levels and after three months a medical check-up revealed a slight improvement in his cholesterol levels and blood pressure. A recent game of football with his grandchildren left him pleasantly tired and relaxed, rather than breathless, and he is considering joining a football team for older players.

DIET
The wrong type of food combined with a sedentary lifestyle is a recipe for ill health and a lack of general fitness.

FITNESS
Undertaking strenuous exercise after a long break can bring on unpleasant physical symptoms.

MUSCLE CHANGES THROUGH USE AND DISUSE

Muscle is one of the most elastic of all the body's tissues. It is designed to expand to cope with increased physical activity and so rapidly adapts to exercise. Changes in the structure and function of muscle are apparent after as little as one week of a training programme involving a gradually increasing training load.

Unused muscles do not turn to fat, but if a muscle is not used, it will atrophy, or decrease in size as the muscle fibres waste away. A reduced level of activity will mean a reduced energy expenditure, but, unfortunately, the appetite does not shrink accordingly, and if food intake continues at the previous level, there will be an increase in body fat that will occur alongside the loss of muscle mass. The good news is that these changes are easily reversed by a return to the previous level of activity.

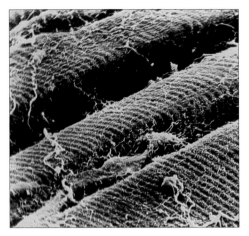

SKELETAL MUSCLE
Muscle that is responsible for physical action is known as skeletal or striated (striped) muscle (above). Skeletal muscle is in a constant state of tension, called muscle tone, and needs to be kept active or it will shrink and start to be covered by a layer of fat.

the brain cells to neurotransmitter agents (the chemical messengers that enable brain cells to communicate with each other). These changes may have implications for enhancing mood and coping with stress.

THE MUSCLES

Some of the characteristics of your muscles are determined by genetic makeup, but major changes can be produced by training.

The response of the muscles to exercise depends on the form of training undertaken which can increase muscle size, strength or endurance, or a combination of these. A bodybuilder's training programme results in large, well-defined muscles; training like a weightlifter will not result in such increase in size, but will produce strong muscles capable of generating greater force; and a marathon runner's training does not develop muscle size, but results in muscles that keep active for long periods without tiring.

Training regimes for the average person are designed to improve health and well-being by increasing both strength and endurance, but they usually focus on the cardiovascular benefits that accompany aerobic training (see page 35). Strength training should not be neglected, however. Muscular strength can be significantly improved without a large increase in muscle size. Muscle strength usually declines with age, but this is largely due to the reduced activity that normally occurs as we get older. Remaining active will preserve muscle strength, helping you to keep your independence into old age.

BONES

After early middle age, there is a progressive loss of the mineral calcium from the bones which results in a loss of bone strength. This affects both men and women, but is a more serious concern for women. There are two reasons for this. First, on average women live longer than men and so are more likely to live to an age where the loss of bone mineral becomes very serious. Second, the hormone oestrogen plays an important role in maintaining bone density in women. After the menopause, the level of oestrogen in the blood reduces, leading to a higher rate of calcium loss and increased demineralisation.

An adequate intake of calcium and vitamin D in the diet is essential for providing the raw minerals for building bones, but regular exercise is also important because it ensures these minerals are converted into bone. When a bone is put under stress during exercise, it responds by becoming thicker and stronger, that is it increases the bone mass. Exercise during the early years of life

A STRONGER LEANER LOOK WITH TRAINING
The 1970s tennis star Chris Evert illustrated the dramatic changes possible in muscle tone and strength through a combination of aerobic and anaerobic training. She developed a leaner and more defined physical appearance by changing her training to build up muscle and reduce excess body fat.

is particularly important as it increases the peak bone mass, which is normally reached between the ages of 20 to 30 years.

Continuing exercise after this point will slow the rate of bone loss. The most effective types of exercise are those that place stress on the bones, such as jogging and high-impact aerobics. If you are just starting out on an exercise programme, however, begin these activities at a moderate level and increase slowly so that the bones, muscles and joints have time to adjust.

METABOLIC ADAPTATIONS TO EXERCISE

Regular exercise has a direct effect on your body's metabolic rate – that is the amount of energy your body needs to fuel all bodily functions. Your metabolic rate rises during exercise and falls shortly afterwards. There is evidence to suggest that it remains above the resting level for between 12 and 24 hours if the exercise is prolonged and close to the maximum intensity that can be sustained. This applies more to the distance runner, cyclist or swimmer engaged in hard training than to moderate exercise.

For the recreational exerciser, however, the cumulative effect of even small elevations in metabolic rate may be important over the longer term.

Weight loss and weight control

One of the biggest metabolic changes that occurs with regular aerobic exercise is a switch in the fuel mixture that the body uses to power the muscles during exercise. Muscles are normally fuelled by a mixture of fat and carbohydrate, which is broken down in the presence of oxygen to produce carbon dioxide and water. The energy released during combustion is then available for the muscles to use.

At low exercise intensities, only a small contribution comes from carbohydrates while fat is the major fuel. Some of the fat that is used comes from the small stores within working muscles, but most comes via the blood from the large stores that are contained in the adipose tissue underneath the skin and around internal organs such as the kidneys. As the exercise intensity increases, however, there is a gradual increase in the proportion of energy that carbohydrate supplies and a decreased contribution from fat. This is good news if you are overweight as

*YOU'RE NEVER TOO OLD TO EXERCISE
A carefully structured exercise regime designed for older people has been shown to improve mobility and flexibility and strengthen bones.*

Origins

A research team at the UK's Medical Research Council, led by Professor Jerry Morris, was the first to prove a link between inactivity and the risk of heart attack. In a long-term study into the lifestyles of thousands of civil servants they found that those who did active leisure pursuits such as brisk walking, swimming and badminton, even if only at the weekend, had a third of the risk of heart attack as those who led completely sedentary lives.

*ROUTE TO GOOD HEALTH
A link between exercise and health was first discovered during research into jobs conducted in the late 1940s. Postmen, for example, were found to be at less risk of heart disease than office-based colleagues.*

it means that you need not feel pressured into performing high-intensity exercise because low-intensity exercise, such as regular walking, is the best way to lose fat.

EXERCISE AND AGEING

Exercise not only helps prevent or relieve age-related illnesses such as osteoporosis and arthritis, it also leads to greater independence in old age. A 1994 study of residents in a nursing home with an average age of 98 years showed that they could improve their fitness with a graded weight training programme. Using elastic training straps that provided gentle resistance, they were able to increase their muscular strength significantly. Not only did this increase their independence, allowing them to do things for themselves that had previously been impossible, such as getting up from a chair unaided, but the improved strength was accompanied by a better sense of balance and a reduced risk of falling.

PSYCHOLOGICAL BENEFITS

Regular exercise provides clearly discernible improvements in self-confidence and mental alertness, and can positively influence mood disorders such as anxiety and depression.

The psychological benefits of exercise can be just as valid and important as the physical ones; for some people, they may even be the most rewarding aspect of their training. Exercise produces these beneficial effects in two general ways: first, it counteracts the negative effects of emotional factors such as stress; and second, it acts as a mood enhancer, creating an emotional 'high' for the exerciser.

STRESS REDUCTION

Perhaps the most important and best understood psychological benefit of exercise is its role in reducing negative stress. Although it is a psychological phenomenon, stress has pronounced physical effects. A certain degree of stress is inevitable, and even desirable in everyday life, as it can act as a spur towards greater achievements and also improve physical performance by accelerating the metabolism. Reaction to stress varies from person to person, with some people able to cope with far higher levels than others. However, excess levels of stress are harmful and in extreme cases could even provoke a heart attack.

Your body's stress response is designed to help you deal with physical danger. In a stressful situation, adrenaline and noradrenaline are released giving you extra energy; your heart rate speeds up and your blood pressure rises, your liver releases glucose sugar for energy and all your senses are sharpened as your body experiences a state of extreme alertness.

These physiological changes require a physical release – if stress is not released, physical damage and mental tension can follow. High levels of stress hormones in the blood increase your heart rate and blood pressure, putting strain on the heart. In the long term, these same hormones raise blood fat and cholesterol levels and cause the arteries to become clogged with fatty deposits, which also go to increase the likelihood of heart disease.

Long-term stress can weaken the immune system making you more prone to infection, and it can lead to depression as unrelieved tension and anxiety combined with fatigue

STRESS THROUGH HISTORY

The stress response is partly a throwback to more violent times in human history. It is designed to ensure that your body is at its peak of physical efficiency and so increase your chances of survival when threatened. In the days of our distant ancestors, the problems that triggered a stress response, such as attack by wild animals or enemies, could only be resolved by violent action or rapid escape – in other words, fight or flight. But the causes of stress today are more likely to involve mental pressures such as overwork or financial worries and to require a non-physical solution. Exercise provides a vital release valve to avoid a harmful build-up of unresolved physical tension.

FIGHT OR FLIGHT
The ancient Greeks recognised that people under stress can achieve amazing feats in sport and battle. Many Greek vase paintings celebrate the prowess of athletes and warriors, and the stress factor still plays a part in competition today, as is shown by athletes who break records during major events.

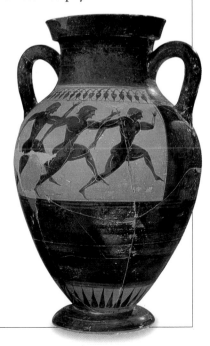

STRESS RELIEF
Sport does not have to be strenuous to improve mood and relieve stress. Activities such as bowls provide many beneficial emotional effects, both through the physical activity involved in the sport and the important social opportunities that they afford.

affects the balance of chemicals in the brain. However, this physiological stress reaction is ideal for exercise: your body is prepared for extreme exertion and a challenging game of tennis, or simply a very brisk walk, will utilise your body's additional energy reserves. The effectiveness of exercise in releasing stress has been measured in athletes and other physically fit people. The results show that people who regularly exercise have lower pulse rates under stressful conditions than those who are unfit.

IMPROVED MOOD

As tension and anxiety are released, a state of relaxation will follow leading to a positive sense of well-being and euphoria. Explanations for this lift in mood vary. Stress relief is probably responsible for much of the improvement in mood that most people report when exercising. But one of the most widely accepted explanations is the theory of the 'runner's high', whereby prolonged exercise brings about the release of mood-enhancing chemicals called endorphins which induce a state of euphoria. However, there are other theories to explain this change.

The thermogenic theory attributes lower levels of tension to an increase in body temperature, which in turn affects brain waves. The neurotransmitter theory suggests that exercise increases the sensitivity of serotonin receptors in the brain, making these naturally produced chemical messengers more effective at reducing pain. An experiment on mood and exercise conducted in 1993 showed that after exercise, brain serotonin was increased, followed by a reduction in appetite and relief from depression.

In addition to its effect on a person's emotional state, regular exercise promotes a rise in self-esteem through an increasingly improved body image and greater self-confidence. As well as providing 'time out' from daily concerns and stresses, completing an exercise and improving upon a physical skill confers a sense of self-empowerment, which in turn promotes emotional stability and self-sufficiency.

SOCIAL OPPORTUNITIES

There is a longstanding image of the athlete as a solitary individual, treading a lonely road in pursuit of physical excellence. However, although there are undoubtedly some people who prefer to exercise alone, exercise in general offers many social opportunities, both during the activity itself and afterwards.

Whatever your favoured choice of sport or exercise, there will probably be a club or centre associated with it where participants can meet. The shared goals and sense of achievement of fellow sports people can create powerful bonds, and membership of a club brings a realisation that there are many others with similar ambitions to your own. Joining a club often makes an important contribution in the early stages of an exercise programme, when the encouragement of others who have been through the same experiences can be of great help, and can save a beginner from many mistakes.

EXERCISE AND ENDORPHINS

Many people who exercise regularly report that they achieve a feeling of euphoria, or a meditative, trance-like state of altered consciousness. There is still much that is not clearly understood about this effect, which is often referred to as a 'runner's high', but it has been linked to the release of endorphins – the body's natural painkilling chemicals.

Most recent studies indicate that 30 to 60 minutes of constant moderate to intense exercise does indeed increase endorphin levels, which in turn reduces anxiety, depression, stress and sensitivity to pain, although this still remains a controversial subject.

The Grieving Widower

Losing a loved one or encountering any of life's major stresses, such as moving house, can have a profound effect not only on your mental health but also on your physical well-being. Rather than turning to conventional medicine and drugs as an antidote to the problems of stress, depression and anguish, many people find that regular exercise offers a far more attractive alternative.

Ted is a 62-year-old ex-teacher who took early retirement, feeling burned out and unable to cope with another term in the classroom. He was looking forward to a long retirement with his wife, Sue, and was devastated when she developed breast cancer and died less than a year later. The trauma of loss was gradually replaced by an acute sense of loneliness which was accompanied by growing isolation and depression. As Ted and Sue had been content to be together, they had never felt the need for other friends. While Sue had been a keen cook, Ted now eats ready-made meals from the supermarket. After three years on his own, Ted began to experience recurring chest pains and was forced to see his doctor.

WHAT SHOULD TED DO?

After a thorough physical examination, the doctor said that Ted was in reasonable physical shape. His electrocardiogram was fine and his blood cholesterol was normal. His blood pressure was slightly above the recommended range, but he was not overweight. While discussing these results the doctor realised that Ted's chest pains were probably a manifestation of his unhappiness.

Ted expected his doctor to prescribe medication and was going to resist this suggestion. He was very surprised when instead the doctor told him that he just needed to get some exercise. He gave Ted the name of a fitness instructor at the local leisure centre to contact.

Action Plan

STRESS
Looking forward to physical exercise, especially with other people, helps focus your attention away from continually thinking about how lonely you are.

DIET
Start looking at cookery books and learn how to prepare and cook food. Have people over to share in it.

EXERCISE
Take up some form of social exercise or fitness programme where there will be contact and interaction with other people.

STRESS
Emotional turmoil and tension can increase blood pressure and heart rate. Worrying about it simply adds to the burden.

DIET
A monotonous and poor diet will deplete the body of vitamins and minerals needed to maintain your emotional and physical health.

EXERCISE
Lack of regular exercise can block the release of pent-up emotions and intensify stress levels.

HOW THINGS TURNED OUT FOR TED

Ted joined a senior's aerobics class, which he attended twice a week. As he became fitter and began to exercise harder, his chest pains disappeared and he started to take more interest in his meals. He made a point of selecting healthy, low-fat options and also learned some cooking skills. He was able to put these to good use during his aerobics class's social evenings where members took turns preparing meals for others in the group.

PREVENTING DISEASE WITH EXERCISE

While regular exercise provides many general health benefits, there are a number of specific illnesses and diseases that can be prevented or relieved directly by taking exercise.

RISK FACTORS FOR HEART DISEASE
According to a recent US survey, inactivity is the most significant factor in the development of heart disease, affecting 59% of the population. The next most harmful factor was smoking (18%), followed by high cholesterol (10%); all other factors grouped together totalled 13%.

Much recent research has focused on the major contribution that regular exercise can make to the onset or severity of a number of serious disorders. These include coronary heart disease, high cholesterol levels, high blood pressure and diabetes mellitus.

CORONARY HEART DISEASE
The major cause of death in most of the industrialised countries of the world, coronary heart disease accounts for twice as many deaths as cancer, which is the second most common cause. Even in young adults, coronary heart disease is a major killer. American statistics show that in the age range 25 to 44, only accidents rank higher as a cause of death. Death rates from coronary heart disease are largely related to lifestyle factors, including diet, smoking, stress and habitual low levels of exercise. Although much emphasis is always placed on the first three, the evidence now available shows that physical inactivity may in fact be the most significant factor contributing to heart disease.

There is compelling evidence that regular physical activity, even in modest amounts, can help to lower blood pressure and cholesterol, and contribute to a decreased risk of dying prematurely from a heart attack. People who exercise regularly also have a reduced tendency to form blood clots, and it is these clots that often precipitate heart attacks and strokes.

HIGH BLOOD CHOLESTEROL
A high blood cholesterol level has been linked with an increased likelihood of suffering a heart attack. The main risk comes from excess levels of a substance called low density lipoprotein (LDL) which deposits cholesterol in the arteries often resulting in heart disease and stroke. Another substance, called high density lipoprotein (HDL), is more beneficial because it tends to prevent the build-up of cholesterol in the arteries. It is important for good health, therefore, to have low overall cholesterol levels in the blood and, in particular, a blood profile that is low in LDL and relatively high in HDL.

Evidence suggests that exercise reduces overall cholesterol levels and produces a favourable shift in the blood profile from LDLs to HDLs. The overall picture, however, is slightly confused because there is also a link between the degree of body fat and blood cholesterol levels. Those who exercise on a regular basis tend to be leaner than average and thus the finding of low LDL

BLOOD PRESSURE AND EXERCISE

Blood pressure readings show the elasticity of the arteries, which can harden and narrow as a result of age and disease. Abnormally high blood pressure indicates an increased risk of heart disease, stroke and kidney disease. Exercise helps to keep arteries healthier and more elastic, resulting in lower blood pressure and a reduced risk of illness.

MEASURING BLOOD PRESSURE
Blood pressure monitoring involves taking two readings registered in millimetres of mercury, or mm Hg – systolic, or maximum, pressure and diastolic, or minimum, pressure. A very unfit person may have a reading of 170/105 mm Hg or higher, while a regular exerciser will have a lower reading, such as 120/85 mm Hg.

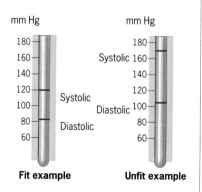

CHOLESTEROL AND EXERCISE

A substance in the blood called low density lipoprotein (LDL) is partly responsible for depositing fatty plaques on artery walls, causing them to narrow and to restrict blood flow, leading to heart attacks and stroke. High density lipoprotein (HDL), however, helps carry cholesterol away from the artery walls to the liver where it is turned into bile and used in digestion or removed from the body.

BLOOD CHOLESTEROL
Exercise encourages a shift from the development of 'bad' LDL to 'good' HDL in the body.

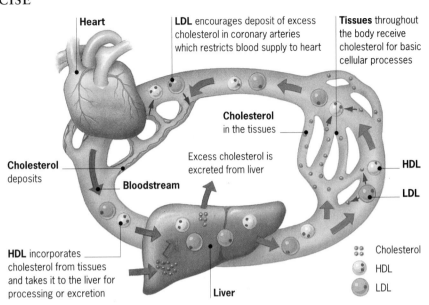

Heart

LDL encourages deposit of excess cholesterol in coronary arteries which restricts blood supply to heart

Tissues throughout the body receive cholesterol for basic cellular processes

Cholesterol in the tissues

Excess cholesterol is excreted from liver

HDL

LDL

Cholesterol deposits

Bloodstream

HDL incorporates cholesterol from tissues and takes it to the liver for processing or excretion

Liver

Cholesterol
HDL
LDL

---

and high HDL levels is to be expected. However, even after differences in body fat content are accounted for, the evidence still indicates that those who exercise have a more favourable blood cholesterol profile.

OBESITY

There is overwhelming evidence that obesity is a contributing cause to a number of the most common diseases, including coronary heart disease, diabetes and high blood pressure. Statistics show that obese people are twice as likely to die of heart disease as their slimmer counterparts. In addition, many overweight people are dissatisfied with their condition, and in extreme cases this can lead to psychological and emotional problems.

The usual approach to losing weight is to reduce food intake, but the weight losses that result are generally small and in many cases prove to be temporary. Severe dieting is often accompanied by feelings of weakness and tiredness that discourage physical activity, but without exercise the body will lose muscle tissue during periods of restricted energy intake. This loss of muscle leads to a lowered metabolic rate, which further reduces energy requirements.

A better approach to weight control is to increase energy expenditure through exercise while restricting the types of food eaten. A diet which is low in fat and high in complex carbohydrate such as rice, potatoes and pasta, together with regular exercise, will maintain muscle while reducing weight. Choose a form of exercise that is within your capabilities and does not place undue stress on the joints – swimming and walking are ideal. The energy used by walking is proportional to body weight, so even walking a short distance is effective when your body weight is high. Inevitably, your capacity will be limited at first, but increasing levels of fitness will allow more exercise to be performed without discomfort.

DIABETES MELLITUS

Diabetes mellitus is the result of a failure of the body to produce or use the hormone insulin in sufficient amounts to regulate the supply of glucose to the tissues. This leads to large swings in blood sugar levels. There are two main forms of diabetes. Type I or insulin-dependent diabetes usually develops in young people aged under 16 years and is controlled by regular insulin injections. Type II or non-insulin-dependent diabetes mainly develops in adults over 40 and may require oral medication to control.

With suitable attention to diet, and perhaps some alteration to the medication regimen, diabetic individuals can usually take part in sport and exercise. Indeed, a number of top sportsmen and women are diabetic. Many diabetics who exercise report better control of their blood sugar levels and reductions in the amount of insulin needed.

continued on page 30

LOSING WEIGHT
Cycling is a good form of exercise for overweight people: it is aerobic, so it helps to burn up calories, but it is non impact, so minimises joint strain.

Using Exercise and Diet to Treat

Diabetes Mellitus

The disorder diabetes mellitus is due to a problem with insulin, the hormone that enables the tissues to utilise glucose for energy. There is no cure, but a healthy diet and regular exercise can help diabetics to manage the condition and lead healthy, active lives.

ESSENTIAL EQUIPMENT
An identification bracelet, medication, and emergency carbohydrate are essential items for diabetics to carry with them.

DIABETES AND TOP-CLASS SPORT

Top footballer Gary Mabbutt has had insulin-dependent diabetes since he was 17 years old. He needs to monitor his blood sugar levels regularly, have insulin injections four times a day and follow a controlled high-carbohydrate diet. Nevertheless, diabetes has not hindered his training or sporting success and he has had a long career in premier football having captained Tottenham Hotspur for over 10 years and played 16 games for England.

GARY MABBUTT
Diabetic sports stars such as Gary Mabbutt must check their blood glucose before and after a game and at half time and, if necessary, have a snack to top up sugar levels.

Exercise is of enormous benefit to all diabetes sufferers. Diabetics often have abnormally high blood pressure and cholesterol, and are at increased risk of heart disease. Many are also overweight. Regular moderate exercise can aid diabetic control, reduce blood pressure and cholesterol levels, assist weight loss and protect against heart disease. For some sufferers exercise can even help to restore blood glucose to normal, or near normal, levels.

There are two main types of diabetes and each requires different forms of treatment. Most diabetes sufferers manage the condition with diet and tablets, or diet alone. However, 25 per cent of sufferers have a more severe form of diabetes and must have daily insulin injections. How you introduce exercise into your life will depend on

what form of diabetes you have. If you are insulin-dependent you must seek the advice of your doctor as exercise will rapidly lower blood glucose levels, and can cause hypoglycaemia. This occurs when blood glucose falls too low. The symptoms of hypoglycaemia – a 'hypo' – include shaking, sweating, blurred or double vision and slurred speech. In this situation, extra sugar in the form of glucose tablets, sugar lumps, chocolate or sweet tea will relieve the symptoms. In severe cases the sufferer may lose consciousness and require emergency treatment.

It is also important to take the advice of your doctor if you are taking tablets rather than insulin. While you are not at as much risk of hypoglycaemia as insulin-dependent diabetics, exercise can still lower blood glucose to dangerous levels.

A SENSIBLE EATING PLAN FOR DIABETICS

Diabetics require individual advice from a dietitian or other diabetes specialist. But the principles are the same for all diabetics and are similar to the healthy eating guidelines recommended for everyone.

Starchy foods such as bread, potatoes, rice and pasta should form the bulk of the diet. Your nutritionist will advise you on the amount of carbohydrate that is safe for you to consume at each meal.

Sugary foods and drinks cause a rapid rise in a diabetic's blood glucose levels and so should be consumed sparingly and usually

combined with a complex carbohydrate (unless you need to take some in an emergency to counteract a sudden drop in blood glucose levels).

Aim to reduce your daily sugar intake – without going to extremes. For example, spreading a little marmalade on toast is perfectly OK.

Eating healthy, regular meals helps avoid wide swings in blood glucose levels. It is important to eat in the morning, at midday and in the evening. People on insulin or tablets also need snacks at mid-morning, mid-afternoon and bedtime.

EXERCISE FOR DIABETICS

If you are managing your diabetes with dietary measures alone there is no risk of hypoglycaemia so no special precautions are necessary when exercising. However, it is advisable to discuss your plans with your doctor or dietitian in case you need to adjust your diet to ensure that it contains enough energy for the level of activity you are doing. If you are unused to exercise, choose an aerobic activity that you can easily incorporate into your lifestyle. Start with 5 minutes a day and, as your fitness improves, gradually extend the sessions to 20–30 minutes three to five days a week.

Diabetes treated with tablets

Diabetic medication and exercise both reduce blood glucose, so levels can drop too low. Try to exercise when blood glucose levels are at their highest (usually an hour after a meal) and have your next scheduled meal or snack shortly after strenuous exercise. Monitor your blood glucose levels before and after exercise. If the levels are persistently low, ask your doctor to reduce your dosage. Carry diabetic identification and emergency carbohydrate with you at all times.

insulin about an hour before exercise but don't inject into a muscle that will be exerted, as this may alter the effect of the insulin. Always carry diabetic identification and emergency carbohydrate, such as glucose tablets, and ensure people with you know what to do in an emergency. Many diabetics carry glucagon with them. This hormone, available on prescription, will boost sugar levels and rouse an unconscious diabetic.

BLOOD GLUCOSE MONITORING
Electronic devices are available to make it easier for diabetics to monitor their blood glucose levels before, after, and sometimes during an exercise session.

Diabetes treated with insulin

Exercise quickly lowers glucose levels in insulin-dependent diabetics, so you may be advised to eat extra carbohydrate before, during and after exercise. What and how much depends on the type and duration of the activity. Short bursts of activity may require a rapid source of energy such as a chocolate bar or glucose tablets. For more prolonged exercise you may need starchy carbohydrate, such as a peanut butter sandwich. Extra carbohydrate 'top-ups' such as sweetmeal biscuits may also be needed during and after exercise.

Monitor your blood glucose before and after exercising and, if necessary, during the session as well. Regular exercise may require a reduction in your insulin dosage. Administer

ESSENTIAL FOOT CARE

Everyone should follow good hygiene practices in the changing room, but it is especially vital for diabetics to do so. Poor foot care, in particular, can lead to serious complications as diabetics are prone to foot infections, foot ulcers and, in extreme cases, gangrene (tissue death). To avoid infection, follow scrupulous daily hygiene, wear sandals in the shower and never walk barefoot. Do not cut corns or calluses and, to avoid blisters, wear cushioned socks and comfortable shoes. Seek immediate treatment if a foot infection develops.

PREVENTING FOOT INFECTIONS
Always dry the feet carefully and use foot creams and powders to keep the skin supple and avoid cracking.

Exercise for relieving PMT symptoms

Regular exercise helps reduce the symptoms of PMT, including headache, fatigue and general discomfort. The main reason for this is that exercise helps to prevent fluid retention by relocating any excess fluid from the tissues back into the bloodstream.

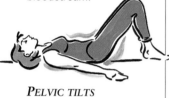

PELVIC TILTS
Lie on the floor with your knees bent about a hip-width apart. Breathe out, tucking your chin in, and push your lower back against the floor while raising your pubic bone. Repeat ten times.

ABDOMINAL CURLS
Start as for the pelvic tilts but rest your hands on your thighs. As you breathe out and perform a pelvic tilt, curl your head and shoulders off the floor, sliding your hands up your thighs. Count to four then slide back slowly. Repeat ten times.

The tissues of an athlete are more sensitive to the effects of insulin than those of an untrained person, so less insulin is needed to regulate the responses of the body to ingested food. Provided that sensible precautions are taken and that the programme builds up gradually, every individual who is diagnosed as diabetic should be encouraged to become more active.

LUNG DISORDERS

People with lung disorders, whether a permanent condition such as chronic lung disease or an intermittent condition such as asthma, have limited tolerance to exercise. Nevertheless, exercise can bring about major physical and psychological benefits. Exercise tolerance can be increased by medication, by increasing muscular strength and endurance through exercise, and by conscious control of the breathing pattern. A training programme of regular aerobic exercise is in itself beneficial because it will increase the general level of fitness, thus reducing the need for strenuous breathing at lower levels of exercise.

OSTEOPOROSIS

The incidence of osteoporosis among older women is becoming much more widespread. Fractures, particularly of the hip or wrist as a consequence of falls, are a major cause of hospitalisation and can lead to further complications. There is normally a progressive loss of bone in later life. If this continues over a prolonged period, the bone may eventually deteriorate to the point where fractures occur easily. Exercise cannot completely prevent the gradual loss of bone in later life, but vigorous exercise during childhood and up to the age of around 35 years ensures a high peak bone mass, so the bone has further to deteriorate before it becomes brittle. In addition, a sensible exercise programme from your late thirties onwards will slow the rate of demineralisation.

OTHER BENEFITS

Exercise improves the blood circulation to the brain, so improving brain function. This is particularly important in the elderly where there is evidence that regular exercise may slow the decline in mental performance that can accompany old age.

Patients with kidney disease have reported improvements in kidney function after beginning exercise, and the mental attitude of patients also improved.

There is convincing evidence of a reduced risk of developing cancer of the colon among regular exercisers, and some surveys have shown a direct relationship between physical fitness levels and death rates from all types of cancer. The major benefit in this respect may be a secondary one in that regular exercise may help promote lifestyle changes, such as stopping smoking, leading in turn to a reduced risk of lung cancer.

OSTEOPOROSIS PREVENTION EXERCISES

Regular exercise helps to maintain bone density. Many of the stresses imposed on bones during exercise strengthen the bones making them more resistant to weakening. The spine strengthening exercises shown below will help to reduce the potential for osteoporosis-related curvature of the spine.

1 *Lie on your back, and bring both knees as close as possible to your chest, hold for 5 seconds and lower your legs back down. Then using only one leg at a time, repeat the stretch ten times.*

2 *Lie on your back with your knees bent. Raise your head and shoulders off the floor and push the small of your back as hard as you can against the floor. Hold for 5 seconds and repeat ten times.*

CHAPTER 2

EXERCISE FACTS

While you do not need a comprehensive knowledge of the physiology of exercise in order to get fit, an understanding of the basics, such as the components of fitness and the difference between aerobic and anaerobic exercise, will allow you to tailor your fitness programme specifically to your personal needs.

DIFFERENT TYPES OF EXERCISE

There are two main types of exercise – anaerobic and aerobic. Because they utilise different energy systems in the body, they each offer a different range of physical benefits.

Every movement that your muscles make will draw on their reserves of energy. In order to meet this demand, your body must continually replenish the muscles' energy stores. Energy can be supplied to the muscles using one of three systems: the creatine phosphate system, the lactic acid system and the aerobic system. Which system comes into play depends on the intensity and the duration of the exercise being undertaken.

Intense exercise performed for 3 minutes or less, such as sprinting, demands that your body uses the first two forms of energy production, the creatine phosphate system and the lactic acid system, which require no oxygen. Together they are known as the anaerobic (without oxygen) systems.

Low intensity exercise lasting more than 3 minutes draws on a form of energy production involving oxygen. This is the aerobic (with oxygen) system. When muscles are at rest – although they are never totally inactive – their energy reserves are topped up at a steady rate from all three systems.

ANAEROBIC SYSTEMS

Anaerobic systems can deliver energy very quickly so they provide the power needed for short bursts of sudden activity, for instance if you were to jump up out of your chair and dash upstairs. Energy provided anaerobically is quickly used up by the body, however, so these systems cannot maintain the fuel supplies needed for sustained exercise, such as a 20-minute run.

AEROBIC VS. ANAEROBIC EXERCISE

Having a good general level of fitness means undertaking both aerobic and anaerobic exercise. Aerobic exercise helps to improve overall cardiovascular fitness, while anaerobic exercise helps to build strength. The amount of each form of exercise that you do depends on your current fitness levels and exercise goals.

DIFFERENT TYPES OF EXERCISE	ADVANTAGES	DISADVANTAGES
Aerobic exercise (swimming, walking, jogging, cycling) can be sustained for long periods	Level of intensity can gradually be increased making this suitable for all fitness levels Improves cardiovascular function – your basic measure of fitness Low intensity aerobic exercise utilises fat as an energy source, making it useful as part of a weight reduction programme	Exercise needs to be sustained for at least 12 minutes and performed regularly to be effective
Anaerobic exercise (weight-lifting, sprinting, ballet, sports involving sudden movement, such as cricket)	Can help build strength and power to carry out everyday activities Increased strength leads to lower risk of injury Increased speed, strength and power improves ability to enjoy sport	Needs a high level of fitness Can place sudden strain on the body Lactic acid produced as side effect causes pain and fatigue

Creatine phosphate

This system is the first to be drawn on for energy. It breaks down a high-energy storage molecule called creatine phosphate, which is held in the muscles. It is very responsive to the muscles' needs for energy and is capable of supplying large amounts of energy very quickly, but lasts only briefly. For example, it will supply the energy used when a person runs for a bus.

The creatine phosphate system is sometimes thought of as the start-up system. Like the battery of a car which supplies a sudden burst of energy to start the car, it supplies a sudden burst of energy to start the muscles moving. The system is also called on when high intensity activity demands more energy than the other energy systems can meet, for instance, when a person is sprinting or lifting an extremely heavy weight.

Also like the car battery, the creatine phosphate system can become drained very quickly. Just as running a car at a steady pace for a while will utilise energy from the fuel system to recharge the battery, in the same way, energy produced aerobically recharges the creatine phosphate system.

In general, stored creatine phosphate has the capacity to supply the body with enough energy to walk quickly for about 1 minute, to run for around 20–30 seconds, or to sprint flat out for 6 seconds.

Lactic acid

Carbohydrate is stored as glycogen in the liver and muscles. The lactic acid system breaks down glycogen to release energy. This is the best form of energy for more sustained periods of high intensity activity because, unlike the aerobic system, it is not

ENERGY PRODUCTION SYSTEMS

The energy to power the muscles can either come from processes that do not use oxygen, called anaerobic systems, or from one that does, the aerobic system. The anaerobic systems quickly supply high intensity energy but cannot sustain it for long periods. The aerobic system, on the other hand, supplies low-intensity sustainable energy. One of the anaerobic systems produces the waste product lactic acid which builds up to the point where muscular activity is no longer possible. Once the high intensity activity stops, oxygen can be made available to remove the lactic acid by converting it into glucose and carbon dioxide.

ANAEROBIC SYSTEMS (WITHOUT OXYGEN)

AEROBIC SYSTEM (WITH OXYGEN)

CREATINE PHOSPHATE SYSTEM

Creatine phosphate is broken down to release rapid energy

Energy produced is of high intensity but short duration

LACTIC ACID SYSTEM

Glycogen is broken down to release more energy along with unwanted **lactic acid**

Lactic acid build-up causes pain and fatigue

Glycogen and fatty acids are broken down using **oxygen**

Energy produced is of low intensity but can be sustained

ENERGY FOR SPRINT RACES
A sprint race requires anaerobic energy because the blood cannot supply oxygen fast enough for the aerobic system to operate. The waste product lactic acid builds up in the muscles causing fatigue and pain until it is impossible to go on.

ENERGY FOR DISTANCE RACES
A distance race is lower intensity so oxygen can be supplied fast enough for the aerobic system to work. The waste product carbon dioxide is easily removed from the body.

THE ENERGY SYSTEMS
Running at a steady pace for 20 minutes, then jogging up a hill for 30 seconds, and then sprinting for 1 minute demands shifting between the three different energy systems. The aerobic system is used for the constant, moderate endurance phase; the creatine phosphate system is called on for the high-energy hill climb; and the lactic acid system comes into play for the quick minute of sprint-power.

limited by the speed at which the blood circulation can supply oxygen to the muscles in order to operate. However, in breaking down, glycogen releases lactate which builds up in the muscles in the form of the waste product lactic acid. Lactic acid build-up blocks muscle contraction, causing a burning sensation and pain. This acts as a safety valve, forcing the body to slow down or stop when the intensity is too great. At high intensities it takes between 45 seconds and 3 minutes for lactic acid to build up to a level that causes pain.

Although the lactic acid system is anaerobic, once we stop high-intensity exercise oxygen is required in a process that removes lactic acid by breaking it down into glucose and carbon dioxide. This requirement is called the oxygen debt and is the reason why we pant for breath after sprinting.

THE AEROBIC SYSTEM

The aerobic system takes over the task of supplying energy to the muscles when exercise is sustained for longer periods. Aerobic fitness describes the body's ability to take in, transport and use oxygen to meet the energy demands of the muscles. Improved aerobic fitness allows you to carry out moderate intensity exercise for longer periods of time with less effort.

Both carbohydrate and fat are broken down in the aerobic system in a process involving oxygen called oxidation. The oxidation of carbohydrate in the form of glycogen supplies most of your energy needs.

Low intensity, long duration exercise, however, relies much more on fat as a fuel. Although fat is a very dense energy source – 1 gram of fat supplies about 9 calories of energy – its breakdown requires large amounts of oxygen, which limits the intensity of exercise that it can fuel. This is why more intense exercise is fuelled by carbohydrate breakdown and creatine phosphate.

CHOOSING AN EXERCISE TO MAKE YOU FIT

The question of which form of exercise is best for promoting fitness depends on the individual's definition of 'fit', which can mean many things to many people. To one person it may mean carrying out everyday tasks without needing help. To others it may mean being able to go windsurfing, cycling or hill walking every weekend without feeling tired and sore, or performing well in competition in their chosen sport.

Whichever definition is applied, fitness involves a mixture of anaerobic and aerobic activities. The decisions people make about what they want to achieve by being fit will determine the balance of anaerobic activities (high intensity) and aerobic activities (low to moderate intensity) in their chosen exercise programme.

A sprinter will need mainly high intensity activity, whereas a marathon runner will need a much greater mix of low and moderate intensity activities. For general improvements in health, a build up from low to moderate intensity is recommended.

HIGH OR LOW INTENSITY?

People often think that only high intensity exercise promotes true physical fitness. However, a Californian study produced some surprising results. Three groups of men and women aged 50 to 60, all of whom had previously been sedentary, were given exercise programmes to do at different levels of intensity. The first group did high intensity exercise in an exercise class, the second did high intensity exercise at home, and the third did lower intensity exercise at home. All three groups significantly improved their fitness levels regardless of the intensity level.

GETTING THE BALANCE RIGHT
Finding the right balance of high and low intensity exercise depends on your goals. In most cases, low to moderate intensity is best.

COMPONENTS OF FITNESS

All-round fitness involves three components – stamina, strength and flexibility. To achieve your fitness goals you may need to concentrate more on some areas than others.

When you begin a new fitness programme it is important to give some thought to what you want to achieve, that is, which aspects of your fitness and health you wish to improve upon. If your sole concern is to lose some weight, then an intense course of strength training alone would not do you a great deal of good, whereas a low-fat diet combined with regular aerobic exercise and some strength exercises would produce a clearly noticeable difference in a matter of weeks.

Most people find that they have strengths and weaknesses in different areas, and they need to take these into account when they plan an exercise programme.

STAMINA

Stamina is given a variety of names such as cardiovascular endurance, cardiopulmonary endurance, or aerobic fitness. All of these refer to the capacity of the heart and lungs to supply oxygen to the working muscles, and the ability of the muscles to extract that oxygen and use it to release energy from stored carbohydrate and fat.

With regular stamina training, the body develops stronger, more elastic blood vessels and a bigger, stronger heart which is able to pump a larger volume of blood with each beat. This improves the blood supply both to the heart itself and to the muscles around the body that are being worked.

MASTER OF THE DECATHLON
The decathlon involves ten different events and requires stamina, strength and flexibility. This means that competitors must excel at all aspects of physical fitness. In the 1980s, decathlon world record holder Daley Thompson was called 'the world's greatest all-round athlete'.

CROSS-TRAINING

Cross-training means working on all the components of fitness in one session by doing aerobic exercises, strength training and stretches. This gives a thorough workout and also brings variety to the routine, which helps to maintain interest. The amount of each type of exercise that you do depends on your personal goals.

STAMINA
Aerobic step exercises help to build cardiovascular stamina for all-round fitness.

STRENGTH
Strength training using dumbbells will build muscular strength and endurance.

FLEXIBILITY
Stretches enhance the suppleness and flexibility of the muscles and joints.

Belly dancing for muscle strength

You don't need to use weights to build muscular strength and endurance. There are many surprising forms of exercise that provide excellent ways to enhance your strength. Belly dancing, for example, is a good exercise for developing flexibility and muscular strength, especially in the abdominal and lower back muscles. It is also great fun to do, and you don't need a high level of fitness to begin with.

DANCE OF THE EAST
Belly dancing originated in the Middle East but is becoming increasingly popular in the West where it is taught in evening classes and leisure centres.

WORKING AT THE CORRECT INTENSITY?

This table shows how to use your own responses to judge the intensity of your exercise. Beginners should train at levels 1 and 2, which are fairly easy and leave you only slightly breathless. Healthy active people should train at levels 1 and 2, but also include some at level 3, which should make you breathless but still able to talk. Serious sports people usually aim to train at all levels of intensity.

Level 1	Easy – I could keep going at this level for a long time
Level 2	I am slightly breathless but I can still keep going at this level
Level 3	I am somewhat breathless but I can still manage to talk
Level 4	I am so breathless that I don't want to talk any more
Level 5	I couldn't talk even if I tried

Stamina training improves lung capacity, increasing the volume of air that is moved in and out of the lungs with each breath. It also improves the body's ability to extract oxygen from the air, resulting in easier breathing at any given level of exertion.

Forms of stamina training

Any form of aerobic exercise will enhance your stamina. Brisk walking, swimming, skating, jogging, running, cycling, dancing, rowing, and aerobic step and dance classes are all effective. Chapter 7 looks at home exercises you can try and illustrates an aerobic routine which can be done anywhere to improve cardiovascular fitness.

Training intensity

The intensity of stamina training is directly related to heart rate. Your maximum heart rate potential is the uppermost level at which your heart should beat during exercise, and this varies according to age.

A safe way of estimating your maximum heart rate is to subtract your age from 220 to give the number of beats per minute. For a 30-year-old man, for example, this would be 220 minus 30, which equals 190, thus 190 is his maximum heart rate.

A newcomer to exercise needs to start training at a lower intensity – around 65 per cent of maximum heart rate (see page 61). Healthy people who are regular exercisers need never train above 85 per cent of their maximum heart rate. Only serious athletes, particularly those involved in competitive sports, need to include some exercise activity at 85–90 per cent of maximum heart rate in their training programme.

Training duration

When training to improve stamina, the same benefits can be gained from carrying out low intensity activities of longer duration as from more vigorous activities of shorter duration. Current medical opinion recommends that for improved health we should do at least 20 minutes of moderate intensity activity, such as brisk walking, a minimum of three times a week. For greater aerobic fitness, however, longer periods of a more vigorous activity, such as running, three or more times a week is necessary.

MUSCULAR STRENGTH AND ENDURANCE

At its most basic level, muscular strength and endurance training ensures that muscles are able to meet the physical demands that everyday life puts on them, such as getting in and out of the bath, carrying shopping and maintaining good posture, without getting unduly fatigued or sustaining injury. It can also help to ensure that you maintain a good level of strength throughout your life.

Weight training is the best known type of strength and endurance training, but it conjures up images of competitive bodybuilders which can be off-putting to many people. But improved strength and endurance can be achieved through many other forms of exercise, including dance.

Benefits of strength training

The health benefits of strength training include reducing the risk of serious injury, making it easier to carry out everyday activities and improving your resting metabolic rate and body composition. It also increases or maintains bone density, depending on your age, which reduces the risk of osteoporosis in later life.

However, if you have high blood pressure you should seek medical advice before starting high intensity weight training as this can increase blood pressure to unsafe levels.

Isometric and isotonic movements

In any activity, some muscles will be causing movement while others will be checking movement in order to stabilise the body. The muscles causing movement are working isotonically and those checking movement are working isometrically. Take care when training isometrically, such as supporting a heavy weight or your own body weight for several seconds without moving, as this increases blood pressure dramatically.

Strength training without weights

Muscular strength and endurance training can be carried out without weights. One method is callisthenics, which involves gymnastic exercises that boost strength and encourage graceful movement. Many techniques used in aerobic step or circuit training also increase strength and endurance.

Muscles must be pushed beyond their previous levels in order to stimulate them to improve. They can be worked with the same weight, or 'resistance', but for a longer duration in order to improve muscular endurance, or with a greater weight but the same duration to improve strength.

FLEXIBILITY AND STRETCHING

Flexibility is crucial to ensure a complete range of movement, good posture, reduced muscle stiffness and lower risk of injury. The key to developing and keeping flexibility is to stretch often. However, stretches should only be performed after the muscles of the body are warmed up. In sports such as swimming that involve a lot of stretching it is important to warm up and do stretching exercises before participating.

Active and passive stretching

There are two main types of stretching: active and passive. Active stretches are movements in which one muscle is extended while its opposing muscle is contracted. This performs two exercise functions at once: it not only develops the flexibility of the muscle being stretched but also strengthens the muscle that is being contracted.

Passive stretching is when gravity or some other outside influence exerts pressure to stretch the target muscle. This is a safe way of stretching as it does not involve any sudden movement, and performed gradually it gives the muscles and connective tissue time to adapt to the stretch.

MUSCLE MOVEMENT
When walking and carrying an object, such as a bag, the muscles in your legs are working isotonically, propelling you forwards, while the muscles of your torso and arms are working isometrically, keeping you upright and gripping the bag.

FLEXIBILITY AND STRETCHING

Flexibility and stretching movements should be performed before exercise, to warm and stretch the muscles; after exercise, when the muscles are warm and can be lengthened more easily; and at any time during the day, to give yourself a reviving stretch and keep supple.

ACTIVE STRETCHING
An example of active stretching is to stand up straight and reach towards the ceiling. In this instance the shoulder muscles contract in order to stretch (extend) the large muscles of the upper back.

PASSIVE STRETCHING
One example of passive stretching is sitting on the floor with your legs straight out in front of you, then leaning forwards. This stretches the muscles at the back of the leg (hamstrings) and the lower back.

PNF
Proprioceptive neuromuscular facilitation, PNF for short, is an advanced form of stretching used by athletes and therapists to increase their range of motion. It involves alternately stretching, contracting and relaxing a muscle. It can be carried out with a partner.

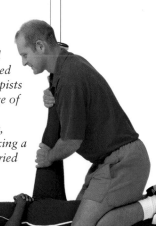

HOW MUCH EXERCISE AND WHEN?

Lack of physical activity is now seen as a major contributing factor in many Western diseases, and much research has focused on how much exercise is needed to maintain good health.

TIME VERSUS INTENSITY
Physical activity takes various forms. The best type of activity to select would be one that you enjoy and that fits readily into your day. Moderate physical activity is roughly defined as using about 150 calories of energy per day – each of the activities below burns approximately this amount. However, the less vigorous the exercise the more time you need to spend doing it in order to burn up the same number of calories.

Medical experts throughout the world are now issuing statements regarding the amount of physical activity necessary to keep a person fit and healthy. Many of these concentrate on cardiovascular activity, though more recent reports also discuss the benefits of muscular strength and endurance.

HOW OFTEN?

All health researchers agree that physical inactivity is a precursor to ill-health and a major contributing factor to cardiovascular disease. Doctors now recommend that exercise should be performed on a regular basis to help prevent a wide range of illnesses and diseases. People should try to get in as much exercise throughout the week as they possibly can, working at a level appropriate to their needs and capabilities.

Twenty minutes or more of moderate exercise at least three times a week is the recommended minimum amount for all children and adults to live a healthier lifestyle. This amount of exercise will maintain your cardiovascular health and your aerobic fitness. If you already exercise at this level you can gain additional benefits by becoming even more active or by increasing the intensity of your exercising. In any case, it is advisable, particularly for older people, to be active every day in some way, even if it is just walking to the local shops.

No particular exercise or sport is singled out as being a more effective form of getting fit, so long as it is performed at an intensity which raises and sustains your metabolic rate for the entire duration. In short, whatever exercise, activity or sport you choose to participate in will be beneficial.

45–60 minutes
Washing and waxing a car

35–45 minutes
Gardening, such as light digging or clipping hedges

35 minutes
Brisk walking for 3 km (2 miles) on a level surface

CHOOSING THE BEST TIME TO EXERCISE

Whenever you feel comfortable exercising and whenever you can fit it into your daily routine is undoubtedly the best time to exercise. It takes a very dedicated exerciser to assign specific times for training. Serious sports people may try to ensure that they exercise at the time of day at which their competitions will take place. The triathlon, for instance, is often held in the early morning, thus many triathletes will ensure that they swim in the early morning so they get used to being active at this time of day.

For most people, however, it is more a question of 'when can I fit exercise into my day on a regular basis?' This may be before or after work, or while the children are at school, or at lunch time. The most important thing is to exercise on a regular basis.

Vigorous exercise is not advisable immediately after a heavy meal, as it is likely to cause severe stomach cramps. Light exercise undertaken after a meal can be beneficial, however, as it has been shown to increase the uptake and usage of fat by the muscles.

Exercising vigorously or for long periods of time without eating is not advisable as the muscles become depleted of carbohydrate. This will result in feelings of fatigue, loss of power, and finally light-headedness and an inability to concentrate.

Vigorous exercise is usually more effective if undertaken later in the day, after you have had time to eat and digest a meal, and after your body has had time to really 'wake up and get going'. During long duration exercises, such as a full day spent rambling or cycling, the muscles need to be refuelled by eating high carbohydrate foods at regular intervals. It is possible to eat something and then carry on with the activity straight away so long as the exercise is at a low intensity for the period immediately after eating and the food is easily digested (see page 50).

For beginners, short bouts of 10 or 15 minutes of exercise carried out several times a day is likely to be easier to cope with than one longer exercise session.

Pathway to health

The more exercise you do the more important it is to ensure that your energy intake (in food) is adequate, otherwise you will find yourself becoming fatigued. In addition, you must make sure that you drink plenty of liquid every time you exercise in order to replace lost fluids, whether you feel thirsty or not, otherwise you will get dehydrated.

Safe exercise also entails resting any strained muscles. The old adage 'no pain, no gain' is definitely not something to aim for as it is likely to lead to injury. If you feel pain stop. If, after an injury, pain persists for more than two days, see your doctor.

HIDDEN EXERCISE OPPORTUNITIES
There are opportunities for you to exercise without having to don shorts or a tracksuit. Window cleaning, for example, builds muscle, stamina and flexibility, especially when it involves moving and climbing a ladder.

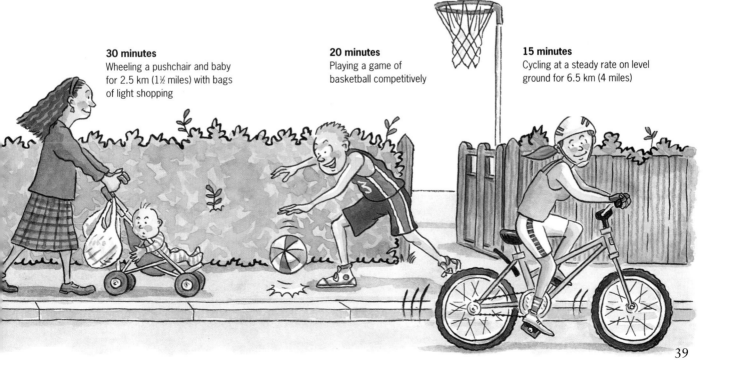

30 minutes
Wheeling a pushchair and baby for 2.5 km (1½ miles) with bags of light shopping

20 minutes
Playing a game of basketball competitively

15 minutes
Cycling at a steady rate on level ground for 6.5 km (4 miles)

High Blood Pressure

Being overweight is often the cause of high blood pressure. Couple this with a sedentary lifestyle and the ramifications can be even more serious. By cutting back on high-fat foods and those high in cholesterol, you are taking a step in the right direction, but for maximum benefit, regular exercise is also needed.

Sarah is 48 years old and married with two teenage children. She works as a secretary in a busy office just 5 minutes from her house. After a recent routine check-up her doctor said that her blood pressure was too high. Sarah currently does no exercise at all and is overweight. She eats well enough during the day but tends to pick at high-sugar, high-fat snacks during the evening while she watches television. After Sarah had described her daily regime, the doctor told her that in order to lose weight and lower her blood pressure, all she needed to do was to moderate her snacking in the evenings and take up some form of low-impact aerobic exercise. Ideally, Sarah should exercise two to three times a week to begin with.

WHAT SHOULD SARAH DO?

Sarah needs to find an activity that she will enjoy and that will fit into her lifestyle without too much disruption. If she took up exercise in the evenings, this would have the added bonus of occupying some of the time she spends watching television and snacking.

As Sarah enjoyed swimming when she was at college, a good option for her would be to take it up again. However, although she won't have forgotten how to swim, she will find that she isn't capable of doing as much as she used to and will need to build up gradually. Sarah also needs to cut out the high-sugar and high-fat snacks and replace these with healthy options such as fruit or raw vegetable dips.

Action Plan

LIFESTYLE
Find ways of introducing exercise into everyday life, such as taking a walk at lunch times instead of sitting in the canteen.

FITNESS
Exercise for 30 minutes a couple of nights a week to begin with, gradually building this up to three or more sessions a week.

DIET
Allow snacks only one day a week while watching television. Limit snacks for the rest of the week or choose healthy options instead, such as toast or fruit.

DIET
Frequent high-fat snacks can quickly pile on the calories.

LIFESTYLE
A sedentary lifestyle can quickly cause weight gain and lack of fitness.

FITNESS
Lack of regular exercise contributes to obesity and high blood pressure as well as many other diseases and general poor health.

HOW THINGS TURNED OUT FOR SARAH

As Sarah's confidence returned in the water, she found that she was still quite a good swimmer and now visits the pool regularly. She managed to wean herself off the unhealthy snacks with surprising ease and now looks on them as an occasional indulgence rather than a regular habit. After two months Sarah had lost 6.5 kilos (14 pounds) and a check-up at the doctor's showed that her blood pressure was back within acceptable levels.

CHOOSING A HEALTHY ACTIVITY

Taking up a sport or other physical pursuit that you enjoy offers an excellent way to enhance your health and fitness, while providing the motivation to keep to a regular exercise regime.

All forms of sport and other active leisure pursuits provide their own unique combination of health benefits. Some activities, such as chess, fishing or snooker, aid stimulation, relaxation and stress relief but do little to improve aspects of physical conditioning. Some activities enhance a particular physical attribute, such as speed, strength, power or flexibility, while others provide a mixture of these.

By taking part in two or three different pursuits rather than concentrating on a single activity you can get a wide range of health benefits. If you prefer to concentrate on a single pursuit, you can aim to maintain all-round physical fitness by training for those components of fitness that are not developed by your chosen activity. For example, road cyclists could include some strength and endurance exercises for their upper body. Racquet sports players could add strength and endurance work for the arm that does not hold the racquet. Distance runners could include strength exercises and some flexibility training.

If you have not been active for some time, you should work up to your maximum output only gradually, building up your time and intensity according to your capabilities. To get up suddenly and play badminton for an hour, or walk briskly for 5 kilometres (3 miles), will give you sore muscles and discourage you from taking part again. How quickly you become comfortable in a new

FUN ON ICE
Ice skating is enjoyed at all levels of commitment, from an occasional visit to the rink with family and friends, to daily training sessions to reach competition standard.

WHAT IS SPORT?

People often have a restrictive view of sport, tending to think of stereotypes of highly competitive sports people. Interestingly, the dictionary defines sport not only as 'a game or competitive activity involving physical exertion' but also as 'amusement, diversion or fun'. Sport can also be a form of artistic expression. For example, gymnastic floor exercises, ice skating, dancing and synchronised swimming are sports which involve a high level of artistry. When thinking about sport options, consider your personal likes and dislikes and your temperament. Sports can offer you the chance to express your creativity, challenge your skill, give you opportunities to socialise, or provide you with time for relaxation and reflection.

GET FIT TO HAVE FUN
Training for, and taking part in, sport throughout the year will keep you fit enough to take advantage of an active holiday pursuit that may unexpectedly arise, such as the opportunity to spend a day sailing.

GONE FISHING
Relaxing pastimes, such as fishing, can be very beneficial for reducing stress and promoting relaxation.

activity, or get back into playing sport, will depend on your age, number of years of inactivity and psychological make-up.

THE FUN OF COMPETITION

Many people are attracted to activities that involve strong competition against other people, while others prefer to compete against the elements or against themselves. Few ramblers or hill-walkers would consider themselves in competition with others. Rather their achievement is in finishing the walk and enjoying the peace and beauty of the natural surroundings.

Likewise many marathon runners take part in events knowing that they will never win the race, but are content to compete against themselves, striving to improve their personal best time. Members of sports teams continue to turn out week after week and do their best because they enjoy the game, even after a long run of losses has ruled out any likelihood of trophies or league promotion. In choosing a sport, the aim should be to compete at a level that will extend you a little but is not so demanding that you get discouraged.

Any leisure pursuit can be made competitive for those who prefer it. Aerobics has championships, health clubs have 'ultra-fit competitions', and ballroom dancers compete all over the world. Challenge walking involves completing set routes, varying from a few kilometres to many hundreds of kilometres, within a time limit. There is no prize for finishing first and the last person home is as much a winner as the first. The competition is between the individual and the conditions. Audax cycling provides the same challenge but on a bicycle. Participants still need to train, however, to ensure that they are fit enough to complete the challenge.

For many people, competitive sport provides the incentive to train regularly and increase their activity levels beyond the minimum necessary for health. In some sports it is the training rather than the competition that is of particular value to your health.

FITNESS COMPONENTS OF DIFFERENT ACTIVITIES

Choosing a sport or exercise activity to take up can initially be a daunting task. However, if you know what areas of fitness you want to develop, the table below can help you decide which is the right sport or exercise activity for you.

SPORT	MUSCULAR STRENGTH	AEROBIC STAMINA	MUSCULAR STAMINA	FLEXIBILITY
Aerobics class		✔	✔	✔
Dancing	✔	✔	✔	✔
Circuit training	✔	✔	✔	✔
Walking		✔	✔	
Running		✔	✔	
Rowing	✔	✔	✔	✔
Swimming	✔	✔	✔	✔
Martial arts	✔		✔	✔
Downhill skiing			✔	
Gymnastics	✔		✔	✔
Racquet sports		✔	✔	✔
Golf		✔		
Cycling		✔	✔	

CHAPTER 3

EXERCISE AND DIET

An exercise programme will bring the most benefits if it is underpinned by a healthy diet. To perform effectively during exercise, your body needs to be supplied with the right food, in the right amounts, at the right time. Exactly what this 'right' diet is can vary for different forms of exercise.

COMBINING EXERCISE AND DIET

One of the most important requirements for an effective exercise programme is to ensure that your body receives the correct fuel to sustain your chosen type and intensity of exercise.

THE RIGHT COMBINATION
In order to maximise exercise performance and ensure good health, the bulk of your diet should be made up of complex carbohydrates (50%), followed by fruit and vegetables (22%). Dairy products and protein should comprise the next largest constituents (13% each), and the smallest percentage should be fats, oils and refined sugars (2%).

The fuel to power your body comes from converting the food you eat into the energy you need for exercising effectively. In order to understand your energy needs during exercise you must first understand your body's basic daily requirements and the process by which exercise increases those requirements.

THE BASICS OF HEALTHY EATING
Regardless of your level of physical activity, everyone should be aware of the basic elements of healthy eating. Once you understand these you can then make adaptations to suit your specific exercise needs. The most important aspect of diet is getting the right balance of the various food groups.

Complex carbohydrates supply the basic fuel your body needs, so this food group should form the largest part of your diet. Good sources of complex carbohydrates include wholemeal bread, cereals, pasta, rice and potatoes. The next largest constituent in the diet should be vegetables and fruit. As well as being a rich energy source, these foods provide you with many of the vitamins, minerals and other micronutrients essential for the healthy functioning of your body. The next most important food group is protein, which is needed for growth, especially muscle growth, the repair and replacement of tissues, and the manufacture of hormones and enzymes. Good sources include pulses such as peas, beans and lentils, meat, fish, soya, and dairy products such as milk and cheese. For most adults, meat and dairy foods should be eaten more sparingly. Although these foods provide protein necessary for growth, they are often high in fat. Choose lean meats and low-fat forms of dairy food where possible. The foods you should keep to a minimum are fats, especially saturated fats, such as full-fat dairy products, and refined sugars, found in butter, crisps and cakes.

You should ensure that your diet contains plenty of fibre, which is mainly obtained from the first two food groups – complex carbohydrates, particularly cereals and grains, and fruits and vegetables. There are two types or fibre. Insoluble fibre, which is also known as roughage, absorbs water and provides the bulk needed to carry waste products through the body quickly. The other type, soluble fibre, prevents the digestive system reabsorbing fats and helps keep blood cholesterol levels low. Lack of fibre has been linked to health problems ranging from chronic constipation to bowel cancer.

Finally, make sure that you drink plenty of water every day – at least seven glasses, on average. Water has many important uses including carrying nutrients around the body, lubricating joints and aiding food digestion and absorption.

Eating a diet based on these principles will ensure that you gain all the essential nutrients for good health. Exercise, however, places extra demands on your body that may require changes in your diet.

RAISING METABOLIC RATE THROUGH REGULAR EXERCISE

Regular exercise strengthens the heart, lungs and muscles so that food is converted more efficiently into energy, which raises your metabolic rate. In order to exercise efficiently and to keep your weight down, you must ensure that your daily intake of calories matches your energy output. The charts below show the recommended calorie intake for men and women according to their level of activity.

Male   Female

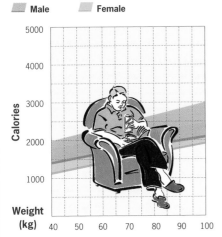

SEDENTARY LIFESTYLE
When you are mainly inactive, your heart and lungs are less efficient and you have little muscle growth, so your metabolic rate remains low.

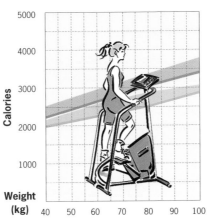

REGULAR EXERCISE
Once you start to exercise regularly, your heart rate rises, your lungs work harder, your muscles increase in size and your metabolic rate rises.

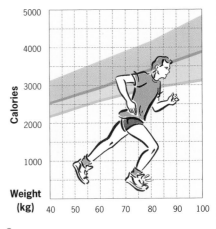

INCREASED EXERCISE
Following a fitness regime, your heart and lungs work more efficiently, and your muscles need more energy, resulting in a high metabolic rate.

BASAL METABOLIC RATE

Your basal metabolic rate (BMR) is the amount of energy required to keep the body's basic physiological processes operating, such as breathing, circulation and heart beat. This is separate from the energy required for physical activities, such as walking. BMR accounts for a large proportion of total daily energy expenditure – up to 75 per cent in mainly sedentary people.

BMR is determined by many factors, including genetic make-up, age, sex, body size and body composition. Men tend to have a higher BMR than women because they generally have a higher proportion of muscle tissue to fat. Muscle is metabolically active, that is, it burns calories even when you are at rest, so increases in muscle mass resulting from exercise are reflected in an increase in BMR.

Periods of energy imbalance or a shortage of calories can trigger a drop in BMR. This is an important consideration when assessing your food intake, as your body will attempt to overcome any shortfall in calorie consumption by conserving energy, which may leave you feeling tired and lethargic.

Activity and metabolism

Any activity raises your energy expenditure and metabolic rate above BMR. Washing, ironing, even sitting reading will have an effect, but the increase is more dramatic with more energetic exercise such as running or cycling. Activity levels can alter dramatically from person to person, and from day to day in the same person, but in an average sedentary person, activity above BMR accounts for between 15–30 per cent of total daily energy expenditure. In athletes this figure can rise to 50 per cent.

The most important factor affecting the metabolic rate is the intensity of exercise – the increase will become more pronounced as the intensity of training increases.

Increasing your level of activity will require an increase in food intake, not only to fuel the added energy expended in exercise, but also because, over time, regular exercise actually raises your BMR so you expend more energy even when resting. You should look carefully at your current diet as well as at the fuel demands of your chosen exercise to see whether you need to make any dietary changes.

MUSCLE MATTERS
You do not have to lift heavy weights to put on more muscle. Activities such as dancing and swimming will also increase muscle bulk.

GLYCAEMIC INDEX

All the foods below contain 50 grammes of carbohydrate. Those on the left, with a high glycaemic index (GI), will provide a quick energy top-up for intense exercise. Those on the right, with a low GI, release energy more slowly for sustained exercise.

HIGH GI FOODS		
FOOD GROUP	**FOOD ITEM**	**SERVING**
Cereals	Wholemeal bread	120g
	Bagel	90g
	Rice	195g
Breakfast cereals	Cornflakes	60g
	Muesli	75g
	Weetabix	70g
Biscuits and confectionery	Sweet-meal biscuits	75g
	Crispbread – rye	70g
	Plain cracker	65g
Vegetables	Sweetcorn	220g
	Parsnips	370g
	Potato (baked)	200g
Fruit	Banana	260g

LOW GI FOODS		
FOOD GROUP	**FOOD ITEM**	**SERVING**
Fruits	Apples	400g
	Cherries	420g
	Dates (dried)	80g
	Grapefruit (canned)	300g
	Peaches	450–560g
Legumes	Butter beans	290g
	Baked beans	485g
	Chick peas	305g
Dairy products	Milk (skimmed)	800g
	Yoghurt (plain,low fat)	800g
	Yoghurt (fruit, low fat)	280g
Soup	Tomato	735ml

ENERGY REQUIREMENTS DURING EXERCISE

When you embark on an exercise programme it is important to maximise your nutritional intake in order to compensate for the increased energy demands being made on the body and the increase in your basal metabolic rate. The increase in BMR is mainly a result of the extra muscle mass which you develop and use during exercise. If you do not ensure you are getting enough energy in your diet to satisfy the demands made by exercise it will result in a loss of body mass and strength, and rapid fatigue.

Carbohydrate, fat and protein all provide fuel for exercise, but only carbohydrate and fat play a significant role. The choice of fuel during exercise is influenced by many factors including intensity, duration, training status and diet. As exercise becomes more intense there is a greater reliance on carbohydrate, but as exercise duration increases there is a reduction in the role that carbohydrate plays in providing energy and an increase in the contribution from fat.

CARBOHYDRATE

Carbohydrate is the major fuel used in exercise, particularly intense exercise, but body stores are limited – about 300 grams (11 oz)

in sedentary people, and up to 500 grams (18 oz) in trained athletes. Energy from carbohydrate is released within exercising muscles up to three times faster than the energy from fat. Carbohydrate is converted by the body into glycogen and glucose. Glycogen is the long-term storage form of glucose. It is held in the liver and muscles where it is quickly converted into glucose for energy.

When the level of glucose becomes depleted fatigue sets in and so the liver compensates by converting more glycogen into glucose to restore the balance. To maximise glycogen storage it is important to eat adequate quantities of carbohydrate. Current recommendations are that sedentary people eat a minimum of 4.5 grams of carbohydrate per kilogram of body weight per day, or 50 per cent of their daily diet. So for someone weighing 63.5 kilograms (10 stone) this would mean an intake of 285 grams (10½ oz) of carbohydrate per day. Athletes in training require double this amount, around 8-10 grams of carbohydrate per kilogram of body weight per day.

Carbohydrates exist in complex forms, such as starch, and simple forms, such as sugar. The rate at which different carbohydrate foods can be broken down to provide glucose for the body can be used to classify them, on a scale known as the glycaemic index (GI). Many complex carbohydrates such as pasta have a low GI which means they supply glucose to the bloodstream very slowly. This is because they have to be broken down into a simple carbohydrate form before they can be used to provide energy. Foods containing simple carbohydrates, on the other hand, such as raisins or carrots, often have a high GI as they reach the bloodstream more quickly and so offer a rapid energy source.

However, it is not a simple equation of complex equals low and simple equals high GI. Some simple carbohydrate foods also contain fibre or fat which slows their rate of digestion and absorption. These may have a low GI and act like a complex carbohydrate. The table opposite gives examples of foods with high or low GI rates which can help you better prepare for exercise.

FAT

Fat is the body's principal energy reserve. It is mainly stored in the muscles and as adipose tissue around the body. It is broken down into free fatty acids (FFAs) which can be released for use as an energy source. Only FFAs are used to provide muscle energy. They are stored as triglycerides in fat cells and in muscle fibres for use by the muscles, after being broken down.

The rate at which triglycerides are broken down may, in part, determine the rate at which muscles use fat as fuel during exercise. More oxygen is required to release energy from fat than from carbohydrate, and there appears to be a metabolic limit to the ability of fat to generate energy, so fat alone cannot be used to sustain exercise at higher levels of intensity. While even the leanest athletes have enough fat stored within their body to exercise for long periods of time, they simply cannot convert all of it for effective use during intensive exercise and must rely on their carbohydrate reserves.

You must have some fat in your diet to provide your requirement of nutrients called essential fatty acids which are needed for basic physiological processes. But excess fat leads to obesity and health disorders and so should be limited in the diet (see page 44).

PROTEIN

Protein is essential for many of the body's vital functions including tissue repair and growth. It is found throughout the body, but primarily in muscle. Protein requirements can be influenced by diet, the form of exercise undertaken, gender and age, but a protein intake of 12–15 per cent of total energy intake is usually sufficient. Higher intakes are thought to be superfluous, even for trained athletes. Protein is not usually a major source of energy, but it can be broken down and utilised by the body when carbohydrate and fat stores are depleted.

FLUID REPLACEMENT

The body is losing water all the time, but especially during periods of intense exercise. At least 75 per cent of the energy expended in exercise is released as heat and the evaporation of sweat is the primary mechanism to dissipate this heat. Sweat rates vary according to factors such as the intensity of the activity, environmental conditions and the
continued on page 50

Protein-building

The issue of how much protein is necessary for athletic performance is a topic of huge debate. Many bodybuilders and weightlifters believe that a high protein consumption will increase muscle mass and maximise strength. However, it is now thought that a daily intake of just 1.2–1.7 grams of protein per kilogram of body weight is sufficient for both speed and strength, providing enough carbohydrate is consumed. In practice, sports people routinely consume more protein than this and so are unlikely to need any extra.

STAYING TOPPED-UP
Studies involving cyclists show that performance quickly falls if body fluid and blood sugar levels drop below normal levels. Isotonic drinks provide a handy source of both energy and fluid.

ENERGY-GIVING SPORTS DRINKS

Sports drinks usually contain some carbohydrate in the form of sugar so as well as replacing lost fluid they can provide a rapid source of energy. They come in three types, hypertonic, isotonic and hypotonic according to how concentrated the drink is in relation to the blood's own density. Their concentration level determines how quickly the fluid they contain can be absorbed by the body.

HYPERTONIC DRINKS	ISOTONIC DRINKS	HYPOTONIC DRINKS
These have a high carbohydrate content and are more dense than the blood, so they are absorbed slowly by the body. They are formulated to provide energy rather than replace fluid.	These contain carbohydrate at a level of concentration on a par with the blood and so can be drunk before, during and after exercise both to replace lost fluids and to provide extra energy.	These contain only a small amount of carbohydrate and are less dense than the blood. They are taken to provide quick fluid replacement rather than for an energy boost.

Improving Exercise with Increased

Carbohydrate

One of the most common reasons for failing to complete an exercise session is fatigue. This listlessness is often the result of poor nutritional practice and a failure to refuel your body with enough carbohydrates and other nutrients.

FOOD FOR ACTIVITY
Ensure your training diet contains extra carbohydrate but avoid increasing your intake of fat and protein.

Ensuring that you have a balanced diet which features all the essential food groups is good health advice for everyone. However, if you are a regular exerciser you will need to consume more of some food groups than of others. To get the right balance of foods for regular exercise, your diet should comprise 65 per cent carbohydrate, 20 per cent fat (mainly from unsaturated forms such as vegetable and fish oils), and 15 per cent protein, such as lean meat, fish, soya, and legumes. While increasing your carbohydrate consumption is crucial for exercising effectively, you can also regulate the amount and types of other foods you eat – and when you eat them – to get the most benefit from your exercise sessions.

Eating for endurance
Training for endurance, or stamina, places the greatest demands on your body's energy supplies. It is important that you consume enough carbohydrate before, during and after exercising to fuel these energy needs. Organisation is the key. Start the day with a good breakfast and eat regular snacks throughout the day – carry some high carbohydrate snacks with you. Make use of low-fat products when possible. Ideally, avoid adding extra butter or margarine to meals, cut out fried foods and eat low-fat dairy products and lean meats. You can obtain carbohydrate in the form of fluids – drink a glass of low-fat milk, fruit juice or a commercial energy-replenishing drink.

Eating for strength
When exercising to improve your strength, you should still make energy your priority, not protein, and follow the basic principles of high carbohydrate intake. If you do

EATING FOR EXERCISE
The amount of carbohydrate you need depends upon factors such as weight and level of exercise. Most adults aged 25–40 who do moderate exercise each day should include 300–400 grams of carbohydrate in their daily diet. The menu below contains 340–400 grams of carbohydrate and has enough calories for a moderately active woman who weighs 57 kg (9 stone).

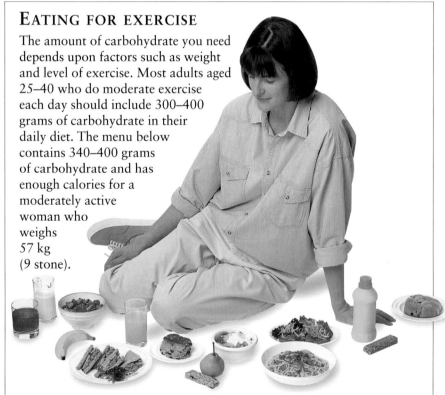

Breakfast (50–70 g)
1 bowl breakfast cereal with 180 ml low-fat milk and sliced strawberries; 200 ml glass fruit juice

Mid morning (15–25 g) 1 banana

Lunch (65–70 g)
Tuna and cucumber wholemeal sandwich made with 2 slices of bread; 1 bran scone; 200 ml orange juice

Mid afternoon (30–35 g)
1 pear; 1 muesli bar

Dinner (100–105 g)
250 g cooked spaghetti with Bolognese sauce, salad with oil-free dressing; 250 g fruit salad with 150 g low-fat natural yoghurt

Training (60–70 g)
500 ml fruit juice; 1 muesli bar

Late snack (20–25 g)
1 tea cake

not eat sufficient dietary carbohydrate to fuel your energy needs, you will end up using protein as a fuel rather than to build muscle. Some protein is essential in your diet, but select low-fat varieties. Cut visible fat from meat, choose white meat such as chicken and turkey more often than red meat, buy fish tinned in brine or spring water rather than oil, and choose low-fat or reduced-fat dairy products rather than full-fat versions. Pulses are also high in protein and low in fat. Eat a varied diet and combine foods to get the best protein quality, for instance, baked beans on toast, cereal and low-fat milk, lentils and rice.

Eating for quick energy access

Ensure that your daily diet contains sufficient carbohydrate for all your energy needs. One carbohydrate-loaded meal just prior to training will not compensate for a poor overall diet. If your muscle glycogen levels are likely to be low because of repeated or prolonged periods of exercise, then immediately prior to an exercise session it is better to eat foods that are low in fibre and have a high glycaemic index (see page 46), such as a jam sandwich, a banana, or an isotonic drink (see page 47). Sports drinks are the easiest energy supplement to take before, during or after exercise as they are not as bulky and filling as solid food and are thus more easily absorbed.

High energy recipes

The recipes below provide a good intake of carbohydrate to sustain you during exercise, especially if eaten 1–2 hours before the session.

TAGLIATELLE WITH PRAWNS, ROCKET AND TOMATOES

Pasta dishes can be the base for almost any number of quick, easy-to-make meals that are rich in energy-providing complex carbohydrates.

2 tsp olive oil
1 shallot, finely chopped
1 tbsp chopped parsley
450 g/1 lb plum tomatoes, peeled, seeded and chopped

300 ml/½ pint vegetable stock
225 g/8 oz raw tiger prawns, shelled and deveined
450 g/1 lb dried tagliatelle
50 g/2 oz rocket leaves
Salt and freshly ground black pepper

■ In a medium saucepan, gently heat the oil. Add the shallot and cook for 2–3 minutes until soft, but not coloured.
■ Add the parsley, tomatoes and stock. Bring to the boil, reduce the heat and simmer for 15 minutes until thickened. Add the prawns and cook for 5 minutes.
■ Cook the tagliatelle in salted boiling water for 10–12 minutes, until al dente. Drain.
■ In a large serving bowl toss the tagliatelle, sauce, and rocket leaves together. Add salt and pepper to taste.
Serves 4

HEARTY VEGETABLE HOTPOT

Root vegetables like potatoes, parsnips, turnips, swedes and carrots combine into a tasty, carbohydrate-rich casserole.

2 tbsp olive oil
1 large onion, thickly sliced
1 stick of celery, sliced
1 kg/2 lb mixed root vegetables, cut into chunks
1 green pepper, sliced
2 tbsp plain flour

600 ml/1 pint vegetable stock
450 g/1 lb tomatoes, skinned, seeded and chopped
1 tbsp tomato pureé
1 bay leaf
1 sprig of thyme
Salt and freshly ground black pepper

■ In a large heavy-base saucepan heat the oil. Add the onion and celery and cook for 5 minutes, until soft.
■ Add the mixed root vegetables, green pepper and flour. Cook stirring for 1 minute.
■ Add the remaining ingredients. Bring to the boil. Cover and simmer for 25–30 minutes, until cooked. Season with salt and pepper to taste. Remove the bay leaf and thyme sprig before serving.
Serves 4

HOMEMADE SPORTS DRINK
You can make your own sports drink to take to your exercise venue in order to replace the fluid and salt lost during exercise and supply carbohydrate, as sugar, to boost your body's energy stores. To make, add a level teaspoon of table salt and up to 8 level teaspoons of sugar to a litre (1¾ pints) of boiled water. Make it on the day you will need it, leave to cool and place in the fridge in a suitable container until you are ready to go. The sugar content slows the rate at which the water is absorbed. So when fluid replacement is the priority, for example on hot and humid days, you should reduce the level of sugar.

type of clothing worn. Exercise in hot and humid weather, for example, may result in the loss of up to 2 litres (3½ pints) of water per hour. All aerobic activity causes sweating. Even swimmers can lose enough fluid in their sweat for it to have a detrimental effect on performance, but because they are in water they are often unaware of this.

Water must be replaced at regular intervals or you will become dehydrated, leading to reduced strength, power and endurance. Even a small loss of fluid can affect performance, while losing more than 4 per cent of total body fluid can cause exhaustion and may be dangerous. You should drink a little fluid every 15–20 minutes while exercising, as well as drinking up to a litre of fluid before and after your exercise session.

Plain water is the ideal choice in events of less than 60 minutes, since fluid replacement is the main need. However, during periods of intense exertion, particularly in hot weather, the body also loses salt in the sweat which must be replaced. Adding a small amount of salt to drinks consumed during and after exercise can be beneficial.

DIET BEFORE EXERCISE
You can enhance your performance before exercise by eating low-fat carbohydrate-rich foods, such as bananas, cereal, low-fat milk, yoghurt, low-fat custard or rice pudding, bagel or toast with fruit preserve or jam.

It is sensible to leave two to three hours between eating a large meal and embarking on a heavy training session, but some exercisers find they can eat immediately prior to training without any problem. The interval is often dictated by the type of activity undertaken. It may be more difficult to eat immediately before sports involving running and jumping, as violent movement may cause feelings of nausea. Experiment with different foods prior to exercise to find out which ones you can eat without causing nausea, stomach pains or other problems.

By referring to the Glycaemic Index you can plan your carbohydrate intake to help ensure optimum performance. Research shows that low GI foods eaten before prolonged strenuous exercise such as an all-day hill walk, increase endurance. Low GI foods include apples, cherries, peaches, plums, and legumes such as baked beans, chick peas and lentils. So a good meal to have before a hill walk might be a chickpea

casserole, followed by fresh fruit and yoghurt. During the walk, when a more rapid energy intake is needed, sandwiches filled with sweetcorn and tuna, a banana and some raisins would be good choices.

REPLENISHING ENERGY AFTER EXERCISE
A good way to replenish energy stores is to eat within two hours of exercising as carbohydrates are converted to glycogen faster than usual during this period. Aim to eat 50 grams (1¾ oz) or more of carbohydrate. However, many people are not hungry after exercise and may find it easier to consume this initial carbohydrate in liquid form and replace lost fluid at the same time.

It is important to eat carbohydrate-rich meals, snacks or fluids at regular intervals throughout the 24 hours following exercise to replenish the glycogen in the muscles. The choice of carbohydrate will influence how quickly your body is refuelled. For optimal refuelling, eat foods with a relatively high GI during the two-hour post-exercise period. Ideal foods are bread, raisins, bananas, bagels, most breakfast cereals and sports drinks. After this period you should still eat high carbohydrate foods at regular intervals but they can be of a low GI, such as pasta and potatoes, as your body is no longer rushing to convert it to glucose ready for the next exercise session.

CARBOHYDRATE LOADING

In the days just before a major race, top athletes often follow a diet plan known as 'carbohydrate loading' to increase their glycogen reserves. Maximum glycogen storage is achieved in the 72 hours prior to an event by reducing training and consuming a high carbohydrate diet.

In the first 48 hours, athletes eat meals and snacks based on bread, pasta, cereals, potatoes and rice. They avoid fried food and keep both fat and protein to a minimum. They also drink plenty of water.

During the final 24 hours prior to the event, they consume only simple carbohydrates such as glucose drinks, fruit or fruit juices.

CHAPTER 4

TESTING AND MONITORING

Before you establish a suitable exercise programme you need to assess your current level of fitness by measuring your aerobic stamina, your strength, flexibility and fat composition. From this starting point, you can then monitor your progress towards a healthier body, and adapt your exercise routine to match your improved fitness levels.

EVALUATING YOUR FITNESS COMPONENTS

The key indicators of fitness that need to be assessed before starting an exercise regime are cardiorespiratory endurance (or stamina), muscular strength, flexibility and body composition.

UNDERWATER WEIGHTWATCHERS
Until the 1950s, body composition was assessed by densimetry, a method based on the subject's weight and the amount of water that is displaced when he or she is submerged in a water tank. Although accurate, this technique was very complicated and so was abandoned in favour of skinfold tests.

There are three indicators of general fitness: cardiorespiratory fitness or stamina, strength and flexibility. Each of these components needs to be evaluated separately to provide a general guide to fitness and to indicate areas of weakness. Many people find their fitness levels vary widely. Some people, for example, may have strong stamina and good muscular strength but poor flexibility.

In addition to these three components, most health clubs will assess your body composition – your height, weight and percentage of body fat – as part of an overall assessment of your fitness. As well as showing up any excess fat, body composition can indicate the amount of muscle present and provide markers for improvements that can be made in muscle tone and body shape, which are often the reasons many people take up exercise in the first place.

Cardiorespiratory fitness, which is also known as aerobic fitness or endurance, refers to the ability of the heart to pump blood around the body delivering vital oxygen and nutrients to the muscles. The harder the heart and lungs have to work to meet the body's needs during exercise, the lower the person's level of fitness. Good cardiorespiratory fitness is required to sustain low to moderate intensity exercise, such as brisk walking or swimming, over relatively long periods. The greater your stamina, the longer you can exercise without tiring.

Muscular strength is the total force that your muscles can exert – such as the maximum weight you can safely lift – in a single move; muscular endurance is how many times you can lift that weight. These are important fitness indicators as they reflect your ability to perform everyday tasks such as carrying shopping or lifting bulky items.

THE SKINFOLD TEST

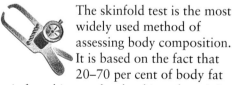

The skinfold test is the most widely used method of assessing body composition. It is based on the fact that 20–70 per cent of body fat is found just under the skin, where it is called subcutaneous fat. A device called a calliper (above) is used to measure the thickness of a fold of skin at one of several possible sites on the body and a mathematical formula is then used to estimate the total amount of body fat, taking into account the person's age and sex.

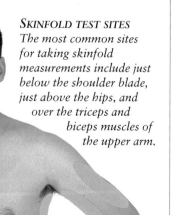

SKINFOLD TEST SITES
The most common sites for taking skinfold measurements include just below the shoulder blade, just above the hips, and over the triceps and biceps muscles of the upper arm.

ARE YOU READY FOR EXERCISE?

The following questionnaire can help you to decide whether you should seek medical advice before starting to exercise. If you answer yes to any of the questions below, see your doctor before increasing your activity levels. People aged 70 years or over should always consult their doctor before starting an exercise programme.

ASK YOURSELF. . .	YES	NO
Has a doctor ever said that you have heart trouble?		
Do you suffer frequently from chest pains?		
Do you often feel faint or have spells of severe dizziness?		
Has a doctor ever said you have high blood pressure?		
Has a doctor ever told you that you have a bone or joint problem, such as arthritis, that has been or could be aggravated by exercise?		
Are you aged over 69 and not accustomed to any exercise?		
Are you taking medication, such as that for heart problems or high blood pressure?		
Do you become very breathless when walking upstairs?		

Finally, many tasks require the body to turn, stretch or twist in various directions. Although this doesn't require large amounts of strength or stamina, it does demand a degree of all-round flexibility.

ASSESSING YOUR FITNESS

Testing your basic fitness level is important for several reasons. First, it indicates the intensity at which you should begin exercising. Measuring your heart rate is the easiest way to do this (see page 54), and will help you to avoid the risks of over-training. You will then be able to set yourself reasonable and attainable goals – these are crucial for maintaining motivation and helping you to achieve real improvements in fitness.

Secondly, identifying your strengths and weaknesses in the various components of fitness will help you to concentrate some of your exercise efforts on areas that are most in need of improvement. For example, if you have good strength but poor flexibility, you may focus on stretching exercises.

Finally, this initial testing will establish a baseline fitness level so that any degree of change can be monitored at subsequent testing. You will be able to highlight any improvements you have made, giving you a sense of achievement, but also make changes to the content of your programme if you are not making adequate progress.

ASSESSING YOUR HEALTH

Before starting an exercise programme, and when evaluating your fitness, you should assess your current state of health. Although most people only need to follow basic safety rules when exercising, there are some health conditions that require special care.

Generally, young and active people who have no symptoms and a low risk of heart disease can start an exercise programme without seeking medical advice. However, older people who have been inactive for a number of years should seek medical advice before beginning an exercise programme.

It is essential that people with symptoms of heart disease, whatever their age, have a medical examination before increasing their activity levels. You should avoid exercise if you are suffering the symptoms of an active infection, such as a chesty cough, or high temperature. Once you are fully recovered, begin with light exercise and build up your activity levels slowly.

Finally, if you have been advised to take up exercise for medical reasons, perhaps because you are overweight, your doctor should be involved in testing your current level of fitness and planning your training schedule. In this way he or she can measure any improvements in, for example, blood pressure or cholesterol levels, that you will not be able to measure yourself.

GET YOUR BLOOD PRESSURE CHECKED
If you suffer unexplained dizziness, breathlessness or headaches you may be suffering from high blood pressure, which is also called hypertension. Before starting a regular fitness programme, ask your doctor to give you a full physical check-up that includes blood pressure monitoring.

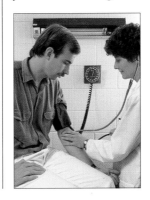

Cardiorespiratory Assessment

Use the tests featured on these pages to help you measure the efficiency of your cardiorespiratory system. The more oxygen your heart and lungs can transport to your muscles, the greater your capacity for endurance exercise.

The first step in measuring your cardiorespiratory fitness is to determine your resting heart rate by taking your pulse when you are inactive. The lower your heart rate at rest the more efficiently your heart is working. The next test is to take your pulse 30 seconds after a period of fairly energetic exercise such as the 3-minute step test (see right). This shows how quickly your heart recovers from physical exertion. Again, the lower the heart rate the fitter you are.

TWO WAYS TO TAKE YOUR PULSE

You can take your pulse at the wrist or neck. Take your resting pulse in the morning before getting up. It will probably be between 50 and 100 beats per minute (bpm). Take your recovery pulse rate 30 seconds after energetic exercise. Your pulse will be slowing down as you do this so, for accuracy, count the beats for 15 seconds and multiply this by 4.

WRIST PULSE
To take your wrist pulse, place two fingers just below the base of the thumb.

Make it accurate
Count the pulse beats for 15 seconds and multiply by 4 for an accurate pulse reading.

NECK PULSE
To take your neck pulse, place two fingers between the windpipe and the muscle at the side of the neck.

ASSESSING YOUR PULSE RATES

These charts provide guidelines to help you to assess your resting and recovery pulse rates based on your age and gender. If your resting pulse rate is in the poor category it is inadvisable to assess your own recovery pulse rate. Instead, ask your doctor to give you a full check-up and to devise a suitable fitness programme.

RESTING PULSE RATE				
AGE	POOR	FAIR	GOOD	EXCELLENT
MEN				
20–29	86+	70–84	62–68	60 or less
30–39	86+	72–84	64–70	62 or less
40–49	90+	74–88	66–72	64 or less
50+	90+	76–88	68–74	66 or less
WOMEN				
20–29	96+	78–94	72–76	70 or less
30–39	98+	80–96	72–78	70 or less
40–49	100+	80–98	74–78	72 or less
50+	104+	84–102	76–82	74 or less

RECOVERY PULSE RATE				
AGE	POOR	FAIR	GOOD	EXCELLENT
MEN				
20–29	102+	86–100	76–84	74 or less
30–39	102+	88–100	80–86	78 or less
40–49	106+	90–104	82–88	80 or less
50+	106+	92–104	84–90	82 or less
WOMEN				
20–29	112+	94–110	88–92	86 or less
30–39	114+	96–112	88–94	86 or less
40–49	116+	96–114	90–94	88 or less
50+	118+	100–116	92–98	90 or less

THE 3-MINUTE STEP TEST

In this test you step onto and off a step or sturdy box continuously for exactly 3 minutes, and then wait 30 seconds before taking your recovery pulse rate (see left). The lower your heart rate, the fitter you are.

In order to work to the correct pace during the 3-minute session it might help to use a metronome. Men should aim for 24 complete steps per minute, for which the metronome should be set to 96 beats per minute; women should aim for a rate of 22 complete steps per minute, which equals 88 metronome beats per minute. It is not essential to use a metronome, however, although you might need to do the test two or three times before you discover the correct pace to work at. In order to get an accurate assessment of your cardiorespiratory fitness, make sure you allow yourself plenty of time to recover between step tests.

1 *Step up fully onto the box with the left foot, ensuring that the heel touches first, and then follow with the right foot.*

2 *When both feet are flat on the box, transfer your weight to your right foot and step fully down to the ground with the left foot and then the right.*

ONE STEP AT A TIME
Full weight should be transferred to the leading foot before lifting the other foot onto the step. Keep looking straight ahead.

Keep to the beat
A metronome can help you keep to the rhythm. Set it to 96 bpm for men and 88 bpm for women. Each step has four beats – up/up/down/down.

THE 1-MILE WALK TEST

This test estimates your level of cardiorespiratory fitness based on the time it takes you to walk exactly 1 mile as fast as you can. It is recommended for people who have low fitness levels or who have been inactive for a long period of time. A reasonably fit person should be able to do it in under 15 minutes. If it takes more than 20 minutes you are unfit. By doing this test once a month you will be able to judge your improving fitness levels.

Up your pace
Cover the distance as fast as possible, without becoming too breathless. Aim to raise your heart rate above 120 beats per minute.

WALK TALL
Keep your head up. Don't carry anything, and wear light clothes and comfortable shoes. Avoid slouching.

Arms should remain relaxed and swing in time with the opposite leg

Steps should be the longest you can comfortably manage

PLANNING YOUR 1-MILE ROUTE

In order to do the walk test you will need to find a suitable route. You could choose a stretch of pavement near your home, ideally away from heavy traffic, or you could find an area of open land, a sports field, or a running track. Before you start, make sure that you have measured 1 mile (about 1600 metres). You can use a map or, if using a pavement, you could drive along the route beforehand and use the car's mileometer to measure out, say, half a mile. There and back will give you the correct distance. If using a club's sports field or track, the officials should be able to tell you its length.

Assessing Strength

Assessing strength is a way of gauging the ability of the muscles to repeat identical movements, or to hold a load or position for a period of time. Improving muscle strength will enable you to carry out physical activities for longer without tiring.

THE ABDOMINAL CURL TEST

When doing abdominal curls, your feet must not be held in position by anything because this would transfer the effort to the legs rather than the abdominal muscles. Similarly, keep your arms relaxed at your sides and avoid using them to provide extra leverage. Compare the total number of curls you complete in 1 minute with the tables below to gauge your standard, and keep a record so you can monitor your progress.

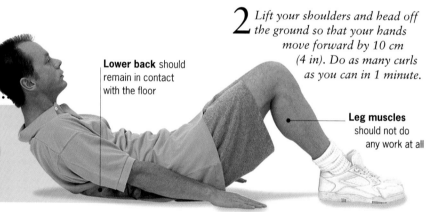

Shoulders should rest on the floor

Arms should be relaxed with palms facing down

Feet should be flat on the floor and unrestricted

1 *Lie on your back with your knees at 90 degrees and feet flat on the floor. Rest your shoulders on the floor and fully extend your arms by your sides with the palms of the hands facing down.*

2 *Lift your shoulders and head off the ground so that your hands move forward by 10 cm (4 in). Do as many curls as you can in 1 minute.*

Lower back should remain in contact with the floor

Leg muscles should not do any work at all

Make it controlled
Make sure you only move your upper back and arms throughout the manoeuvre. This will ensure that only your abdominal muscles are being used to lift the upper body.

ABDOMINAL CURL TEST – MUSCLE ENDURANCE RATING

The abdominal curl test is widely used as an index of muscle strength and endurance because the abdominal muscles play a crucial role in stabilising the body and in ensuring good posture. Compare your results with the tables below which show the average ratings for men and women according to age.

MEN					
AGE	VERY LOW	LOW	MODERATE	HIGH	VERY HIGH
29 or under	below 38	38–41	42–47	48–52	52+
30–39	below 30	30–33	34–39	40–44	44+
40–49	below 25	25–28	29–34	35–39	39+
50–59	below 20	20–23	24–29	30–34	34+
60–69	below 15	15–18	19–24	25–29	29+

WOMEN					
AGE	VERY LOW	LOW	MODERATE	HIGH	VERY HIGH
29 or under	below 34	34–37	38–43	44–48	48+
30–39	below 26	26–30	31–35	36–40	40+
40–49	below 21	21–23	24–30	31–35	35+
50–59	below 16	16–19	20–25	26–30	30+
60–69	below 11	11–14	15–20	21–25	25+

Measuring Flexibility

Flexibility is specific for every joint of the body. However, the test most commonly used as a measure of overall flexibility is known as the 'sit-and-reach test'. It indicates the suppleness in the lower back muscles and hamstrings.

THE MODIFIED SIT-AND-REACH TEST

For this test you will need a long ruler, a sturdy box and a partner to help you. Start by sitting on the floor with your back and head resting against a wall and your legs fully extended with both feet against the box.

Back should be kept straight

Do not bounce your muscles in order to reach further

Measure to your fingertips

1 *Place one hand on top of the other and reach towards the box without moving your head and back away from the wall. Your partner then rests one end of the ruler on the box and aligns the other end of it with your fingertips. This is your starting reference point.*

2 *While your partner holds the ruler firmly in place, slowly lean forward, moving your head and shoulders away from the wall, and slide your fingertips as far along the ruler as possible.*

Assess your progress
Take the furthest of three trials. Each time, record the distance from your starting point to the end of your range of motion.

MODIFIED SIT-AND-REACH SCORES (INCHES)

The figures below show average sit-and-reach scores for men and women according to age. It is important to remember that there is no single measure of flexibility.

These figures are intended as a general guide only. Anyone suffering from back or muscle disorders should seek medical advice before attempting this test.

MEN					
AGE	VERY LOW	LOW	MODERATE	HIGH	VERY HIGH
35 or under	below 9	9–13	13–15	15–18	18+
36–49	below 8	8–13	11–14	14–16	16+
50+	below 8	8–9	9–12	12–15	15+

WOMEN					
AGE	VERY LOW	LOW	MODERATE	HIGH	VERY HIGH
35 or under	below 10	10–15	15–16	16–18	18+
36–49	below 10	10–12	12–15	15–18	18+
50+	below 8	8–9	9–12	12–15	15+

Assessing Body Composition

Measuring your body composition will tell you how much fat you have relative to your level of muscle. The lower the ratio of fat you have, the fitter you are likely to be and the less risk you will have of contracting disorders such as heart disease.

In the past, changes in body composition were assessed using weight and height tables that gave a standard weight range for a given height. These tables were often misleading. For example, a man who has done a lot of weight-training will have put on muscle and gained weight. This does not mean that he is obese, but that he has a greater ratio of lean body weight to fat tissue. Now more accurate ways to assess changes in body composition are used, namely the waist-to-hip ratio and the body mass index (BMI).

BODY MASS INDEX

One way to assess the amount of body fat you have is the body mass index. To determine your BMI, weigh yourself – in kilogrammes – wearing minimal clothing. Then measure your height – in metres – from the top of your scalp, not your hair. Multiply your height by itself and divide this figure into your weight to find your BMI. For example, if you are 1.7 m tall and weigh 65 kg, multiply 1.7 by 1.7, which equals 2.89. Then divide 65 by 2.89 to give a BMI of 22.5. Being overweight is defined as having a BMI of over 25. A BMI of over 30 is associated with health risks such as heart disease, strokes and diabetes.

BMI scale
The table below shows the average range of BMI readings for the general population.

AGE GROUP (YEARS)	BMI
19–24	19–24
25–34	20–25
35–44	21–26
45–54	22–27
55–65	23–28
over 65	24–29

WAIST-TO-HIP RATIO

The waist-to-hip ratio is a way of comparing the amount of fat deposited in the upper body (waist) with that in the lower body (hips). To find your ratio, divide your hip measurement by your waist measurement. A healthy waist-to-hip ratio is believed to be 1.0 or below in men and 0.85 or below in women. The places where fat is most likely to be deposited tend to vary between men and women. Women are more likely to store fat in their breasts, arms and thighs, whereas men predominantly deposit fat on their waist and abdomen. Research indicates that the waist-to-hip ratio is a good predictor of future health as too much fat in the abdominal area is associated with medical problems such as heart disease, diabetes and certain forms of cancer.

Measuring waist and hips
Measure your waist just above the top of your pelvis, where your body naturally curves in. Measure your hips at their widest point.

ACHIEVING YOUR FITNESS GOALS

To ensure that you get the most from your exercise programme it is important to set yourself clear fitness goals, to understand the principles of exercise and to maintain your motivation.

Once you have assessed your current level of fitness you can use the information to identify the areas that most need attention. Your priority might be to raise your cardiorespiratory fitness, or to improve flexibility or strength.

It is important to continue to assess your fitness at regular intervals. Regular assessment will indicate whether or not your fitness levels are improving at an adequate rate as your exercise regime progresses. If not, you might decide to revise your exercise schedule – perhaps by increasing the amount or intensity of exercise, or by changing the type of activity – in order to progress nearer to your fitness goals.

Take some time to think about the reasons why you want to become more active. You may want or need to lose weight, or have a desire to feel generally healthier, or your goal might be something more concrete like getting fit to go on holiday or to take part in a half marathon. Even if your reasons are very general in nature, they will still help to keep you going. In addition, the results will form a basis from which you can set specific goals.

SETTING GOALS

To stay motivated it can help to set yourself short-term, easily attainable goals, as well as more demanding long-term ones. Each time you achieve one of these goals, your morale will be boosted, encouraging you in the drive towards a fitter, healthier body.

Your goals should be challenging, but realistic. They must also be easily achievable as the failure to reach them could lead to demotivation. For example, if it currently takes you 20 minutes to walk a mile (1.6 kilometres), it would be more realistic to set a starting target of 19 rather than 15 minutes. You should also try to be as specific as possible in your chosen targets, as this will give your programme more focus. For example, rather than setting yourself the global aim of increasing your overall muscle strength, you might set yourself the target of increasing the number of push-ups you can perform from 5 to 10, then to 15.

Your goals should also be short-term to enable you to reach them within a time frame that keeps you motivated. So, for example, rather than setting yourself the goal of losing 12.5 kilograms (2 stone) in total, it would be better to aim to lose 1.3 kilograms (3 pounds) per month. By setting yourself a series of such targets you're more likely to achieve success in the short term and go on to satisfy your ultimate aims.

EXERCISE ACHIEVERS

Some extraordinary exercise goals have been achieved by people determined to succeed. In 1993 a 60-year-old Venezuelan violin maker became the oldest person to climb Mount Everest. Another remarkable achievement was performed by Madge Sharples, who proved it is never too late to start a fitness regime. Mrs Sharples took no exercise at all until the age of 62 when she started doing yoga. She went on to include sessions of swimming, body building and weightlifting in her exercise routine. She ran her first marathon at the age of 64 and only gave up running in the London Marathon at the age of 73.

WHY DO YOU WANT TO EXERCISE?

Having a specific reason for starting an exercise regime can help you stay motivated. For example:

▶ *You want to improve your health and fitness.*

▶ *You're more breathless doing everyday tasks than you used to be.*

▶ *You always feel tired and lethargic.*

▶ *The doctor has advised you to get more exercise.*

HOLIDAY HOPES
Getting in trim to fit into holiday clothes is a good incentive to start an exercise programme.

as too much may do more harm than good by putting excess strain on muscles and joints before they have had time to adapt.

The amount of exercise that your body needs to perform in order to produce the desired effect depends on several factors. These include your current level of fitness, your specific exercise goals and the various components of fitness that you want to improve. It is also important to remember that you will need to continue to push yourself, so that once your strength or fitness has improved to the point that your current level of exercise is too easy, for example, you will need to increase your output in order to have an effect.

To help you decide how to raise your level of exercise at a steady rate you should bear in mind five principle factors – frequency, intensity, time, type and maintenance.

Frequency

Improving your fitness requires regular exercise, although the frequency required will depend on the fitness component being worked on and your current and desired levels of fitness. Generally speaking, you will need to exercise three to five times a week to promote any changes in your level

LOOKING FORWARD
An exercise programme that is geared towards a clearly definable goal, such as getting fit for a skiing holiday, will give you the incentive to keep going, even when you are feeling a little under par.

PRINCIPLES OF TRAINING

Your cardiorespiratory system and individual muscle groups will only improve in fitness if they have to work harder than they usually do. In other words, you have to push your body's physical limits in order to improve your fitness, otherwise you will just remain at the same level. This is called overload adaptation and it is important that you find the right balance. Too little overload will produce no training effect at all, where-

---

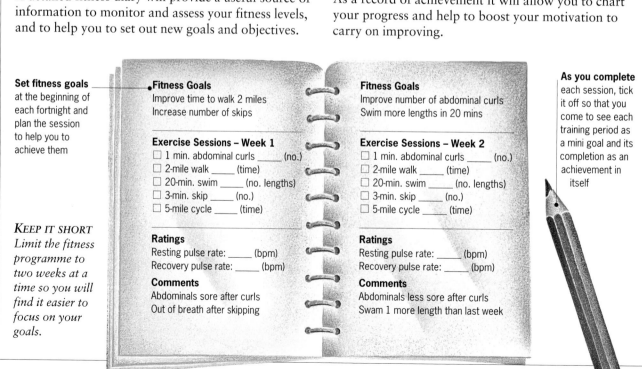

FITNESS DIARY

A detailed fitness diary will provide a useful source of information to monitor and assess your fitness levels, and to help you to set out new goals and objectives.

As a record of achievement it will allow you to chart your progress and help to boost your motivation to carry on improving.

Set fitness goals at the beginning of each fortnight and plan the session to help you to achieve them

KEEP IT SHORT Limit the fitness programme to two weeks at a time so you will find it easier to focus on your goals.

Fitness Goals
Improve time to walk 2 miles
Increase number of skips

Exercise Sessions – Week 1
☐ 1 min. abdominal curls _____ (no.)
☐ 2-mile walk _____ (time)
☐ 20-min. swim _____ (no. lengths)
☐ 3-min. skip _____ (no.)
☐ 5-mile cycle _____ (time)

Ratings
Resting pulse rate: _____ (bpm)
Recovery pulse rate: _____ (bpm)

Comments
Abdominals sore after curls
Out of breath after skipping

Fitness Goals
Improve number of abdominal curls
Swim more lengths in 20 mins

Exercise Sessions – Week 2
☐ 1 min. abdominal curls _____ (no.)
☐ 2-mile walk _____ (time)
☐ 20-min. swim _____ (no. lengths)
☐ 3-min. skip _____ (no.)
☐ 5-mile cycle _____ (time)

Ratings
Resting pulse rate: _____ (bpm)
Recovery pulse rate: _____ (bpm)

Comments
Abdominals less sore after curls
Swam 1 more length than last week

As you complete each session, tick it off so that you come to see each training period as a mini goal and its completion as an achievement in itself

A HEALTHY HEART

For safe exercise that achieves real aerobic fitness benefits you must make your heart work harder than it normally does while still keeping within safe limits. When you start your fitness regime you should aim to exercise at an intensity that pushes your heart rate to 65 per cent of its maximum capacity and increase the intensity as you improve. To avoid ill effects, however, never push your heart to more than 85 per cent of maximum output. Maximum heart rate is 220 minus your age, so for a healthy 30-year-old this would be 190 beats per minute. Therefore the target heart rate zone for training would be between 124 bpm (190×0.65) and 162 bpm (190×0.85).

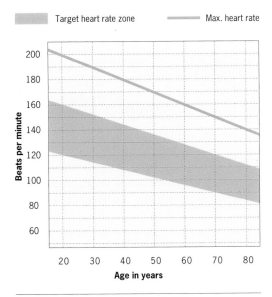

Target heart rate zone — *Max. heart rate*

Beats per minute (y-axis: 60, 80, 100, 120, 140, 160, 180, 200)

Age in years (x-axis: 20, 30, 40, 50, 60, 70, 80)

of fitness. Once fitness has been achieved, two or three sessions a week may be sufficient to maintain this new level.

Intensity

The intensity of exercise needs to be greater than that normally experienced to produce a fitness change. To improve cardiorespiratory fitness, most people exercise at between 65 and 85 per cent of maximum heart rate (see above). To check whether you are working at the correct intensity, take your pulse as you exercise. Start at the bottom of the range and work up.

Alternatively, you can use your body's response to exertion to gauge the intensity of the exercise (see page 36). As your fitness programme progresses you will be able to gauge the intensity. You should aim to do some exercise at around level three on our five-point scale ('somewhat breathless but can still talk'). As you get fitter, and your body adapts, you will find that you perceive the exercise as being easier, in which case you may grade the intensity as level two. When this happens it is time to increase the intensity, so that you once again perceive the effort as being around level three.

Time

To improve cardiorespiratory fitness it is usually necessary to exercise for a minimum of 20 minutes three times a week and to increase this as necessary as you become fitter. However, the duration of the activity is largely dependent upon the intensity of the exercise. The more intense a particular exercise session, the less time you will be able to spend doing it. For example, you can't sprint for as long as you can jog.

Type

When considering what form of exercise you are going to use to improve your fitness, you should first take into account any specific health needs. For example, if you suffer from osteoporosis you might consider including weight-bearing activities such as walking and running. However, always seek your doctor's advice first if you have a medical condition that might be affected by exercise. The other critical aspect is to choose an exercise that you enjoy. If you do not find it stimulating, you risk boredom or lack of motivation. Once you have chosen an exercise that will hold your interest, it is important to vary your programme regularly. Don't let the routine become boring. If you don't want to change the type of exercise then change the place you do it – try a different run or cycle route, or different people to exercise with. Changes like these will help to maintain your interest.

Maintenance

The final principle of exercise is that you must aim to maintain your level of fitness. This is because any gain is quickly lost if you return to a previously inactive lifestyle. This loss in fitness is very rapid, perhaps as much as half the gains that have been made overall can be lost in as little as two weeks. The simple message is 'use it or lose it'.

Maintaining your motivation

Exercising for its own sake can be a chore that becomes increasingly difficult to keep up. To stay motivated, look for ways to make exercise enjoyable and interesting. For example, choose activities that you really enjoy doing, encourage a friend to take up exercise so that you can give each other moral support, and vary the activities you do, or try to find attractive, new places to exercise so you do not get bored.

EXTRA EXERCISE
Incorporate more exercise into your everyday tasks, such as jogging to the shop for a morning newspaper.

TWO'S COMPANY
Exercise with a friend – you can provide support for each other and make the exercise sessions more fun.

CASE STUDY

The Misguided Exerciser

It is vital for physical and emotional health that your lifestyle includes regular aerobic exercise. Optimum health, however, comes from following a fitness regime that includes a variety of activities so that all the muscle groups get a thorough workout. You should also take care not to underestimate the importance of other lifestyle factors such as diet and stress.

Wendy is a 38-year-old marketing manager in a large firm. Her job involves long and often irregular hours and can be very stressful but is made worse by the fact that she finds it difficult to delegate. Her husband, Tony, is a maintenance engineer and often finds his job stressful at times, too.

Despite the fact that they both have demanding careers, Wendy finds that she is expected to cook a meal when she comes home in the evening and to fit washing and all the other household chores into the week without help from Tony.

Wendy also feels Tony doesn't spend as much time with her as she would like, preferring to be with his friends at the pub. He says it's his way of dealing with the stress of his job.

Wendy likes to go for long cycle rides in the countryside when she wants to unwind. She feels that these cycling sessions provide all the exercise she needs to stay fit.

She is conscious of her figure and limits the calories in her meals in order to keep her weight down. Unfortunately, she finds she gets very tired, especially when doing the housework, and her legs ache after

she has been on the go all day. She has also developed a nagging pain in her lower back which seems to be getting worse. She has had to stop cycling at the moment because it seems to aggravate the problem.

An extra worry is that her mother suffers badly from osteoporosis and Wendy is anxious to do everything she can to prevent the same thing from happening to her.

The combination of health concerns and work pressures is affecting Wendy's relationship with her husband and they are now starting to have rows.

EMOTIONAL HEALTH
Physical exercise is a good way of dealing with short-term stress, but unless underlying problems are addressed it cannot supply a long-term solution.

EXERCISE
Activities such as cycling that involve only a limited number of muscles in the body do not necessarily provide all-round fitness benefits.

DIET
Even if a diet is low in fat and contains plenty of fruit and vegetables, if it is not providing sufficient energy for your needs it cannot be said to be balanced.

WORK AND HOME
Combining a busy career with domestic chores can strain a relationship, especially if one partner believes the workload is not being shared evenly.

HEALTH
A lifestyle that does not include regular weight-bearing exercise can increase the risk of developing osteoporosis later on in your life.

WHAT SHOULD WENDY DO?

Wendy saw her doctor who gave her a complete physical examination. This showed that there was no underlying medical problem causing the tiredness and back pain. In many respects, Wendy was very healthy because her heart rate and her blood pressure were quite low.

The doctor recommended that Wendy continues to avoid cycling and suggested a programme of exercises that would relieve her back pain and strengthen her bones. The doctor thought that Wendy might consider joining a health club where she would get advice on planning a comprehensive exercise programme.

Wendy's doctor also suggested that she take a close look at her diet to ensure it was providing sufficient energy throughout the day as this might be contributing to her fatigue.

The doctor recommended that Wendy try to delegate more work both in the office and at home. She should also sit down with Tony and talk over her grievances. If they were still unable to resolve their difficulties, the doctor suggested that Wendy might consider seeking the advice of a relationship counsellor.

Wendy and her husband could consider employing a cleaner to do some of the household chores in order to lighten the load. She might even try to get Tony interested in joining her exercise programme.

Action Plan

EMOTIONAL HEALTH
Tackling stress involves a range of measures, not just exercise. Look at your routine to see if you can manage your time better or share the workload, and rethink your priorities so that you are not wasting time on unimportant matters.

EXERCISE
Seek advice on putting together a fitness programme that provides an all-over workout but has been specifically tailored to your individual needs and lifestyle.

DIET
Don't skip meals, especially breakfast, and make sure all your meals are high in complex carbohydrates but still low in fat. If necessary, include high-energy snacks before exercise sessions when you will be burning up extra calories.

WORK AND HOME
Ensure there is a fair division of labour at home and work and avoid letting resentments build up by failing to air your grievances. The first step towards dealing with a relationship problem is for both partners to talk it through.

HEALTH
Exercise such as walking, jogging or high-impact aerobics, when combined with a diet that includes plenty of calcium, can help build up bone mass and resist the effect of osteoporosis.

HOW THINGS TURNED OUT FOR WENDY

Wendy stopped cycling for a while and started going for long walks instead, which she found to be equally good at helping her to unwind. She forced herself to delegate more of her office work and this gave her time to go swimming at lunchtimes.

The fitness trainer at Wendy's health club devised a programme of aerobic step routines, plus muscle-toning and strengthening exercises to strengthen her bones and build up all-round fitness levels. The health club also gave Wendy a diet plan to follow that included recipes to get more complex carbohydrates into her diet, such as low-fat pasta meals, as well as some high-energy snacks that she could eat between meals.

Wendy had a heart-to-heart with Tony. Although he wasn't keen to take on much housework himself, he did think it was a good idea to employ a cleaner.

Wendy found that her back pain has been greatly eased and that all the exercise she was doing gave her a healthy appetite without leading to an increase in weight. Wendy now has much more energy and feels far less stressed.

Although Tony hasn't been persuaded to take part in Wendy's fitness sessions at the health club, he does join her on long country walks – which usually include a visit to an attractive village pub.

CHANGES YOU CAN EXPECT TO NOTICE

During the early weeks of an exercise programme, you will probably not detect much change in your appearance or notice any major physiological adaptation to the increased demands you are placing on your body. However, even after the first few sessions you should feel that the exercise is slightly easier than when you first started. This change in perception probably happens because the interaction between muscle and nervous system adapts quite quickly to exercise. In essence, the coordination between nerve and muscle becomes more efficient.

Four to six weeks

Between weeks four and six of your fitness programme (depending on the components of fitness that you are training) you should start to see some evidence of changes in the structure of your body. Your clothes, particularly around the waist, should be looser. In addition, the muscles that you are predominantly exercising should start to become more defined. These cosmetic changes will continue as you progress with your programme.

Eight to twelve weeks

After eight to twelve weeks of your fitness programme you should notice that you are performing much more intense exercise than at the beginning of the programme, but that subjectively it feels no harder than when you first started exercising. This is a result of cardiorespiratory and muscular changes. At this stage you should be able to detect the cardiorespiratory improvements by measuring your resting heart rate. When compared with the figure recorded before the start of the programme, this should have decreased, indicating that your heart is stronger and more efficient and so needs to beat less often. You should also notice that you sweat more during exercise than you used to. This is a normal adaptation as the thermostat of the body becomes more efficient and is able to disperse heat produced by the exercise more rapidly.

Twelve weeks and upwards

At this stage you should be noticing both physical and psychological benefits. You should feel less fatigued by everyday events and be better able to cope with stressful situations. The quality of your sleep should have improved and you will feel healthier. In addition, you will actually feel slightly depressed if you miss an exercise session, owing to the absence of the body's natural mood enhancers, endorphins, which are produced during exercise. Your body will have started anticipating the release of these factors and, if this does not occur, you may experience a slight withdrawal sensation.

Origins

The modern Olympic games were founded in 1892 by a Frenchman, Baron Pierre de Coubertin (1863–1937). De Coubertin was an expert in physical fitness, and it was during a study tour of Europe that he conceived the idea of reviving the Olympic games and recapturing the spirit of ancient Greece. He proposed the idea of the games during a lecture at the Sorbonne in Paris in 1892. The first modern Olympic games were held in Athens, Greece, in 1896, approximately 1500 years since they had last been held.

De Coubertin was an idealist who believed in the original ideals of the ancient Greek Olympics. His maxim was that the most important part of sport was not to win, but to take part. It was de Coubertin who declared that Olympic athletes should retain their amateur status in order to promote sportsmanship and excellence for its own sake.

OLYMPIC REBIRTH
In 1894 de Coubertin met representatives of twelve countries, and the International Olympic Committee (IOC) was inaugurated.

CHAPTER 5

EXERCISING SAFELY

*Most injuries suffered during exercise are
due to overexertion or inadequate preparation.
By warming up and cooling down before and after
exercise, wearing appropriate clothing and footwear,
training in moderation and using good technique, you
can exercise with confidence knowing that you are
working both safely and effectively.*

WHEN EXERCISE IS HARMFUL

Although most people can take part in a fitness programme quite safely at any time during their life, there are occasions when exercise should be moderated or avoided altogether.

KEEP ACTIVE
Many injuries do not stop you exercising completely. Wherever possible you should try to adapt your training programme to compensate for an injury so that you can remain active.

It is now accepted that the risks to health of being inactive far outweigh the risks of being active. But there are some risks associated with exercise and there are times when extra caution or even abstention from exercise may be necessary. Factors such as illness or pregnancy may require you to rest or make a change to your normal regime.

ILLNESS AND EXERCISE

Exercising when ill can be dangerous. In the case of minor infections such as a sore throat, tonsillitis or earache gentle exercise is possible when the infection or fever has passed. With active infections, however, especially if there is a raised temperature or muscular aches and pains, exercise should be avoided. Viral infections can cause inflammation of the lymph nodes ('glands'), lungs, muscles and heart. Myocarditis (inflammation of the heart muscle) is common to many viral illnesses including flu and glandular fever and can be fatal due to the added stress that exercise imposes.

When the body is fighting an infection, the extra demands of exercise may lower the body's resistance to disease and so increase the severity and complications of the illness. Exercise may also prolong convalescence and increase the risk of depression. After recovering from an illness, you should always return to exercise gradually.

Taking medication can cause additional problems. Exercise can actually alter the effect of some drugs, as well as increasing oxygen consumption and carbon dioxide production, and promote sweating, resulting in increased dehydration. As a consequence you may need to reduce the amount of exercise you do while taking medication. If in any doubt, seek medical advice.

AFTER SURGERY

Most people notice a decline in aerobic fitness, as well as increased feelings of fatigue, for at least the first month after surgery. The deterioration in fitness is similar for both sedentary people and regular exercisers and is proportional to the amount of time spent recovering in bed.

These post-operative changes may be due in part to hormonal responses to surgery, which can affect the metabolism and can cause temporary immobilisation. The extent of the surgery, the loss of muscle mass, body weight and strength, and reduced aerobic fitness all exacerbate the feelings of fatigue.

Gentle exercise after surgery can offset the damaging physiological effects and speed recovery, enabling you to return to everyday activities more quickly. Exercise rehabilitation is now incorporated into the standard care of patients with coronary heart disease and many doctors advise exercise as soon as possible after discharge from hospital. The exercise should be low intensity and build up slowly over a period of months. It should only be undertaken on doctor's advice after an adequate period of convalescence.

PREGNANCY

Keeping fit helps the body to cope with the physical and emotional strain of pregnancy. Regular exercise will strengthen the heart and lungs, help to alleviate back pain, aid weight control, relieve stress and regulate or prevent diabetes during pregnancy (gestational diabetes).

Check with your doctor before planning a fitness programme during pregnancy. The doctor will need to take your general health and current fitness level into account. Fatigue and nausea may necessitate a

WHEN EXERCISE IS HARMFUL

DID YOU KNOW?

Exercising while pregnant sends a rush of endorphins across the placenta to the baby so that unborn infants experience a similar adrenaline rush to the mother, making them calm and happy. The aftereffect of this hormone rush has a calming effect that can last up to eight hours.

change in routine, and lax ligaments (a consequence of pregnancy) may increase the risk of injury. Aerobic exercise sessions should be regular (three to five sessions per week) for a maximum of 30 minutes per session. The intensity should be geared towards health rather than performance.

For women who were not regular exercisers before their pregnancy, low intensity exercise such as walking, swimming and stationary cycling is the most suitable.

After pregnancy

Many of the changes in a woman's body last for weeks or months after the birth so aim for a gradual return to a full fitness regime. If the delivery was problem-free, exercise can be resumed four to six weeks after the birth or after the bleeding has stopped. If the birth involved complications or surgery you should consult your doctor before resuming exercise. In addition to aerobic exercise, some light strength work will help regain muscle tone and posture, and exercises to strengthen the pelvic floor muscles will help to prevent stress incontinence.

Many women suffer lower back or leg pain during pregnancy because of changes in weight and posture. This may continue for a while after the birth, partly due to the hormone relaxin, which continues to cause lax ligaments for several months afterwards. Retraining your posture and lifting correctly is vitally important. Flexibility exercises

RECORD-BREAKING RECOVERY
Many of the world's top women athletes have returned to their sport after pregnancy feeling stronger, fitter and more determined. Just a few months after giving birth, Liz McColgan set a new 10 000-metre world record.

PREGNANCY AND EXERCISE

Drink plenty of fluids before, during and after exercise to keep you and your baby fully hydrated. Keep to a moderate pace and avoid jarring or jumping motions as ligaments are more susceptible to injury during pregnancy. Wear properly fitting training shoes for good grip, and ensure stretches are slow and gentle.

HEAD AND NECK
To relieve tension in your head, neck and shoulders, gently tilt your head to the side and then straighten. Repeat from the other side. Perform twice on each side.

Keep your back straight and your arms relaxed

ARMS AND SHOULDERS
To ease aching arms, raise one arm above your head and bend it at the elbow. Grasp your elbow with your other hand and gently pull towards your head to feel the stretch.

Apply gentle pressure to the elbow

Feel the stretch through your spine

BACK
Sit cross-legged with your back straight. As you exhale, twist your upper body to the right and place your right hand on the floor behind you. Hold for 2 seconds, then return to the centre and repeat to the left.

LEGS AND FEET
Sit with your back straight and your legs straight in front of you. Place your hands on the floor beside your hips and slowly bend and straighten each knee in turn. Then draw small circles in the air with each foot. Repeat 3 times.

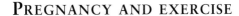

Iron discipline

Women need 5 mg of dietary iron a day more than men so it is vital that their training diet contains iron-rich foods such as fortified cereals, seafood, figs and spinach. The quantities shown below are for standard servings.

16 g of bran cereal contains 10 mg of iron

Six oysters contain 16.5 mg of iron

56 g of spinach contains 1.52 mg of iron

Five dried figs contain 2 mg of iron

should be continued but avoid stretching to the limits of your range of motion. After pregnancy it takes some time for the abdominal muscles to return to normal and overworking them can cause permanent damage. Standard abdominal curls and sit-ups from lying flat should be avoided during the first three months.

It is important to wear a well-fitting support bra when exercising, as the breasts are heavier both during pregnancy and after childbirth and supporting ligaments are easily stretched. Breastfeeding women should feed the baby before exercise and limit their weight loss to no more than 0.5 kilograms (1 lb) a week. If it is greater than this, they should ensure that, in addition to a well-balanced diet, they eat nutritious snacks between meals, and drink plenty of water.

OVEREXERCISING

Overexercising or overtraining are problems more commonly associated with competitive athletes rather than the average exerciser, but it is easy to push yourself beyond safe levels. Common signs of overexercising include reduced immunity, iron deficiency anaemia, susceptibility to injury, excessive weight loss and menstrual disorders.

Reduced immunity

While moderate exercise is believed to boost your immune system, there is evidence that strenuous exercise can harm it. For reasons not fully understood, the immune system appears to be suppressed by overtraining and people who regularly engage in very strenuous exercise may be more prone to illness and infection. Indeed, athletes seem to have an unusually high incidence of upper respiratory infections. A study of marathon runners in the United States has found a two-fold increase in respiratory infections among athletes who ran more than 100 kilometres (60 miles) a week.

Iron deficiency anaemia

Iron is a vital component of the pigment haemoglobin in red blood cells and is the principal means of transporting oxygen in the blood. Iron deficiency leads to reduced levels of haemoglobin, a condition known as anaemia, which causes general sluggishness, fatigue and loss of appetite. Excessive exercise is thought to promote a high degree of iron loss through the destruction of red

> **C A U T I O N**
> *In most cases iron supplements are sufficient to restore the body's iron stores, but exercisers should still try to ensure that their diet is sufficiently rich in iron and in the vitamins which are essential for iron absorption and synthesis.*

blood cells. Women are more susceptible owing to the further loss of iron through menstrual bleeding, and pregnant exercisers face an even greater drain on their iron stores because of the demands of the baby.

Susceptibility to injury

Continuous, excessive exercise can cause muscle pain and tissue damage which, in time, may progress to more serious problems, including muscle tears and stress fractures. To avoid injury, reduce your level of exercise as soon as you feel any discomfort.

Excessive weight loss

Intensive training can often lead to weight loss, partly because exercise can cause a loss of appetite, but mainly due to the simple fact that energy expenditure may exceed energy intake. If the weight loss is rapid, progressive muscle wasting, loss of body fat and a low blood-sugar level may result. Because productive muscle mass is lost, performance and the ability to sustain exercise is likely to be impaired. Extreme weight loss in women may lead to further complications such as menstrual disorders.

Menstrual disorders

Menstrual irregularities, such as irregular periods (oligomenorrhoea), and cessation of periods (amenorrhoea), are more common in women who do strenuous exercise. Intensive exercise can also lead to delayed menarche (onset of menstruation). The disruption to the menstrual cycle may be associated with low levels of body fat or extreme weight loss, hormonal fluctuations resulting from sustained intense exercise, or with the psychological stress associated with intensive training. While there appears to be no lasting or irreversible effects on the reproductive system, there is concern that athletes experiencing menstrual disorders may be at greater risk of developing osteoporosis.

PREPARING FOR EXERCISE

Good preparation will reduce the risk of injury during exercise. Choose suitable clothing and footwear and have a warm-up before each exercise session and a cool-down afterwards.

The correct clothing to wear during exercise depends on the activity you are undertaking and the conditions under which you are doing it. If you are in a gym, for example, doing a moderate to intense work-out, then loose-fitting cotton clothing will stop you overheating. If you are running outside in the cold, then several layers of warm clothing are preferable.

Similarly, it is crucial that you choose the correct footwear for different activities as many injuries result from wearing the wrong type of training shoes. Running shoes, for instance, should not be worn for an aerobics class as they provide little support for the ankles, which could result in a sprain or other joint damage.

CLOTHING

Cool cotton clothing is recommended for sportswear. Rubber or plastic exercise suits became fashionable a number of years ago as a means of losing weight but these are especially dangerous. Not only are they ineffective as a means of weight loss (no fat is lost, only water), but they raise body temperature, increase the tendency towards heat disorders, and cause excessive stress on the cardiovascular system.

Visibility is an important consideration for anyone who exercises on roads or pathways, such as cyclists, runners and joggers. If you exercise in the early morning or at night it is essential to be seen. Choose bright clothing, reflective bibs and/or arm bands.

VITAL SUPPORT
For women, a sports bra is essential when exercising, not only for comfort, but also for the long-term protection of the suspensory ligaments that support the breasts.

THE SPORTS WARDROBE

Clothing should be comfortable and cool and should not restrict movement. To avoid overheating, material that comes into contact with the skin should be porous to allow perspiration to evaporate and let air in to cool the body.

THE IMPORTANCE OF LAYERING
Wearing several layers makes it easier to control your temperature by removing or adding items of clothing.

Under layers

Outer layers

Mid layers

DRESSED TO JOG
A jogging suit helps to prevent injuries such as strains and sprains by keeping the muscles and joints warm as you exercise.

Warming Up and Cooling Down to

Prevent Injury

Warming up and cooling down are vital components of any exercise programme. Too often, however, they are either carried out inadequately or are overlooked altogether, and often the result is unnecessary pain and injury.

The extent to which you need to warm up and cool down depends on the intensity and duration of your fitness session, environmental factors such as temperature and humidity level, and your physical condition.

Follow these guidelines on how to warm up effectively before your exercise session and have a thorough cool down afterwards to ensure that you exercise at your optimum level and reduce the risk of injury.

WARM-UP ROUTINE

Your warm-up should last 8–10 minutes and include exercises to aid mobility and to raise your pulse. Mobility exercises include shoulder circles, arm circles, knee lifts and hip circles and involve free and easy movements designed to move your joints in a controlled manner, helping to warm and circulate the synovial fluid. Pulse-raising activities include brisk walking, gentle jogging and jumping jax to gradually raise your pulse and prepare the cardiovascular system. During this part of the warm-up you should feel warm and breathe more rapidly than normal.

JUMPING JAX
Warm-up exercises such as jumping jax (see page 74) help to prepare your cardiovascular system for the full aerobic work-out.

Static warm-up stretching

Warm-up stretches help to prepare the muscle fibres to be lengthened safely. Stretches should be static (held still), maintained for 6–10 seconds each and should only be performed when your muscles are warm – after the pulse-raising activities. Most exercises involve the major leg muscles such as the calf muscles, hamstrings and quads, so aim to stretch these in the routine.

COOLING-DOWN PROCEDURE

A cool-down should last for at least 5 minutes and should include both pulse-reducing exercises and stretches. As the name suggests, pulse-reducing exercises gradually return your cardiovascular system to its pre-exercise state. You can use the same exercises as in the pulse-raising section of the warm–up. For the cool-down, however, gradually reduce the speed and intensity of the exercise so that, for example, you slow from a jog to a walk, to let your muscles cool slowly.

Static cool-down stretching

Your cool-down is an ideal time to improve flexibility as the muscles are already thoroughly warmed. It is most effective to perform cool-down stretches in comfortable positions on the floor or on a mat. Hold the stretches longer than during your warm-up: 10–30 seconds or more. When stretching, try to relax, ease slowly into the stretches and hold them still. As you stretch you should feel mild tension in the bulky part of the muscle but no pain.

EASING THE ACHES
Stretching after exercise is important as it improves flexibility and helps to prevent or reduce post-exercise soreness.

FOOTWEAR

It is important to select the correct type of shoes for your chosen sport or exercise, and to replace them when they are worn. The three most common types of exercise shoe are cross trainers (multipurpose shoes), running shoes and aerobics shoes.

Cross-trainers are ideal if you work out in the gym, cycle, jog occasionally and play racquet sports like badminton, but they are not recommended for any frequent high-impact activities like aerobics.

Running shoes should be lightweight and have a wide, cushioned and elevated heel with good shock absorbency in the midsole to protect the ankle, knee and hip joints from jarring. Running shoes should not be used for racquet sports, as they do not give sufficient support for the feet and ankles when making sudden changes of direction.

Aerobic shoes should grip firmly, have extra cushioning and shock absorbency in the toe to protect the ball of the foot from repeated impact, and provide ankle support.

PREPARING YOUR BODY

A warm-up before exercise and a cool-down afterwards is vital in order to minimise the chance of injury and speed your body's recovery from the normal effects of the exercise session. Muscle fibres, tendons and ligaments are more pliable at higher temperatures and so by warming up before exercise you reduce the risk of strains and sprains occurring. A warm-up also helps to increase your flexibility.

This improvement is thought to be due to a number of physiological changes which take place within the body. For example, the lungs work more efficiently, and by raising blood and muscle temperature, a warm-up makes the delivery of oxygen to the muscles more effective and increases the speed and efficiency of muscle contraction. A warm-up can further aid performance by mentally preparing a person for exercise.

After exercise, it is important to follow a cooling down routine to get your heart and breathing rate back to normal gradually, and not stop exercising suddenly. This is because blood flow to the muscles increases during exercise, so if you stop too quickly the muscles continue to receive a rapid blood flow which they no longer need. This can result in the blood pooling in the legs, which may cause dizziness or fainting.

After exercise, therefore, it is important to ease the body down gradually by doing simple movements that slowly return the body to its pre-exercise state.

A GYM CHECKLIST

Make a checklist of what to take with you to the gym. Include:

▶ *Clothing such as shorts, T-shirt, leotard, training shoes, sports socks.*

▶ *Water bottle.*

▶ *A towel for drying perspiration off yourself and also from the equipment when you have finished, and another towel for the shower.*

▶ *Flip-flops to wear in the shower.*

THE SPORTS SHOE

A sports shoe should be comfortable, hard-wearing, flexible and, most importantly, suitable for the activity and the surface on which it is to be worn.

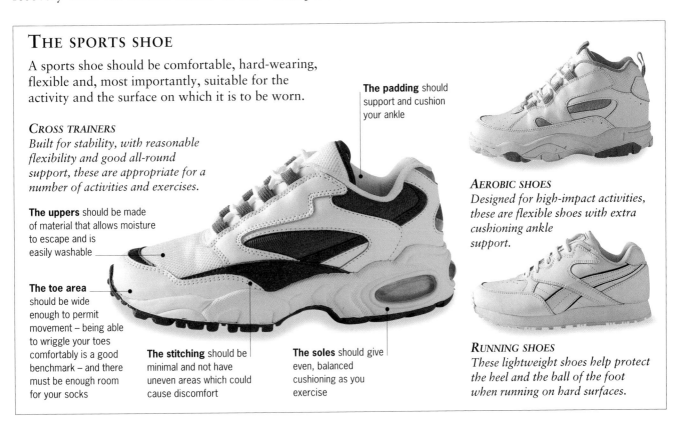

CROSS TRAINERS
Built for stability, with reasonable flexibility and good all-round support, these are appropriate for a number of activities and exercises.

The uppers should be made of material that allows moisture to escape and is easily washable

The toe area should be wide enough to permit movement – being able to wriggle your toes comfortably is a good benchmark – and there must be enough room for your socks

The stitching should be minimal and not have uneven areas which could cause discomfort

The soles should give even, balanced cushioning as you exercise

The padding should support and cushion your ankle

AEROBIC SHOES
Designed for high-impact activities, these are flexible shoes with extra cushioning ankle support.

RUNNING SHOES
These lightweight shoes help protect the heel and the ball of the foot when running on hard surfaces.

CASE STUDY

The Exercise Addict

Exercise addicts are compulsive, obsessive exercisers who work out not necessarily to improve their fitness, health or performance, but to experience the buzz and adrenaline rush which accompanies it. Conversely, exercising also provides relief from the negative feelings they experience when not working out. Exercise becomes the centre of their lives to the exclusion of all else.

Linda is a 34-year-old graphic designer who initially took up exercise to lose a few pounds. She joined a local gym and enrolled in an aerobics class. When Linda first started she exercised twice a week, but somewhat to her surprise found herself really enjoying working out and rapidly began to do more and more. She now goes to the gym every evening after work, does one or more aerobic classes a day, and has taken up running. The more exercise Linda does, the more she enjoys it and the better she feels. Exercising now takes up so much of her time that she has no other interests and is losing touch with her friends. She is often so exhausted after exercising that she finds it difficult to concentrate at work.

WHAT SHOULD LINDA DO?

Unless Linda slows down and reduces the amount of exercise she does, she is likely to injure herself or encounter other problems associated with overtraining. She needs to realise that while a moderate amount of exercise keeps her fit and healthy, her current exercise regime is actually putting her health and emotional well-being at risk. She should limit the amount of time she puts aside for exercise each day and give herself easy exercise days, as well as complete rest days. Her exercise programme should be flexible so that if she misses a day she does not feel guilty. She should then devote the additional free time she has to keeping in touch with her friends and resuming old interests.

Action Plan

LIFESTYLE
Set some time aside each day to rest and relax. Consider taking up a new interest or hobby, possibly with friends. Arrange to go out socially at least once a week.

EXERCISE
Draw up a new exercise programme which is flexible, less intense and time-consuming, and which has built-in rest days.

HEALTH
Follow and stick to the new exercise programme. Remember, a moderate amount of exercise is very beneficial to your health.

LIFESTYLE
The body needs time to recover from the demands that exercise places on it. Periods of rest and relaxation should be built into your daily lifestyle.

HEALTH
Too much exercise can result in increased vulnerability to illness and infection, and susceptibility to injury, depression and excessive weight loss.

HOW THINGS TURNED OUT FOR LINDA

Linda has modified her attitude to exercise. Although she still exercises regularly, because she values and enjoys it, she now restricts the amount she does. She has built rests days into her programme and reminds herself that she does not need to exercise every day. She now understands the importance of rest and feels much better for it. She has taken up French classes at night school and socialises with her friends regularly.

EXERCISE
An intense exercise regime which offers little flexibility can be physically and mentally damaging.

UNSAFE EXERCISES

When exercising you must be fully confident that what you are doing, and how you are doing it, is safe. Some surprisingly familiar exercises are potentially harmful to the body.

Certain exercises, such as touching the toes while keeping the legs straight and deep knee bends, can be harmful. Generally speaking, they cause damage because they place too much stress on certain anatomical structures of the body, such as the joints. It is important to realise that any exercise can lead to injury if it is performed incorrectly. Some exercises are problematic not because they are inherently damaging, but because they are often performed with poor technique.

Harmful or poorly executed exercises, if performed repeatedly on a regular basis, can cause immediate injury and/or long-term damage. The areas of your body that are particularly susceptible to harm are the neck, the knees and the lower back.

PROBLEM ISSUES

The exercises that are most likely to lead to injury are those in which the joints are subjected to extreme extension or arching, known as hyperextension, or extreme flexing or bending, which is called hyperflexion. In addition, ballistic – bouncing or flinging – movements and stretches, continuous high impact moves and isometric exercises can be problematic and are likely to be inappropriate for most exercisers.

Ballistic work

In ballistic actions, such as swinging the arms vigorously from side to side, muscles and other body structures are taken to the end of their range of movement at speed. This can strain the muscles and place excessive demands on the joints, ligaments and tendons. These movements are often seen in mobility work during warm-ups, or aerobic dance or circuit sessions, but they are not advisable and can lead to problems such as muscle tears as well as resulting in unnecessary muscular stiffness and pain.

Overstretching of the ligaments can lead to weakened joints and recurrent sprains. To avoid these problems, exercises should be performed at a controlled pace and stretches should be held static without bouncing.

Impact

Too much high-impact exercise places the joints under undue stress as they repeatedly absorb the body's weight on landing. This can be particularly problematic if the landings are poorly performed or are performed on hard surfaces such as concrete or unsprung wood. Where possible, intersperse high-impact activities with low-impact activities, in which one foot always remains in contact with the ground.

Isometric work

Isometric exercises or exercises such as weight training in which there is tension in the muscle but little visible movement have the potential to raise blood pressure and should be used with caution or, in some cases, avoided altogether. Isotonic exercises – in which the muscles can be seen to be working – are safer and more effective, because they work muscles through a wider range of movement (see page 130).

THE IMPORTANCE OF CORRECT TECHNIQUE Although many sports, such as hurdling, involve actions that look risky, if they are carried out with the correct technique, learned from qualified instructors, you should not experience any particular injury problems.

Exercising Safely

Any exercise can be harmful if done incorrectly. The correct ways to carry out some familiar and widely used exercises are shown here, together with some of the more common mistakes made by exercisers.

Keep your arms controlled and close to the body

Jumping jax (astride jumps)
Stand with your feet together and hands by your sides. Jump up and land with your feet 0.5 m (1½–2ft apart), raising your arms above your head at the same time. Make sure you jump with your knees facing outwards (over the toes) and bring your heels down to the ground on landing.

Do...keep the elbows loose.

Don't...stay on your toes as you land without bringing your heels down.

Don't...jump with the knees locked – this places excess pressure on the knee.

Leg lifts
Kneel down with your palms flat on the floor. Raise your leg slowly and in a controlled way until horizontal.

Do...make sure your arms are directly below your shoulders.

Don't...lift your head up.

Don't...rotate the leg at the hip or knee.

Don't...raise any part of the leg above horizontal.

Knee bends/squats
Stand with your feet 0.3 m (1 ft) apart and arms straight out in front of you. Bend your knees slowly to lower your body. Stop before your thighs are parallel with the ground.

Don't...lower your bottom down to or below knee level.

Don't...push your head back.

Tilt the head gently to the side until you feel slight resistance ✔

Lunges

Place your feet a shoulder-width apart. Step forward as far as you can comfortably manage. Lower the rear leg to around 15cm (6in) from the floor. Draw your leading leg back and straighten up. Repeat, leading with the other leg.

✔

✗

Don't...push the leading leg beyond the vertical as this can put the knee and back under stress.

Don't...lean forward. Keep your back straight and your upper body centred over your hips at all times.

Curl-ups

Lie on your back with knees bent, feet flat on the floor and hands lightly touching your head. Breathe out as you slowly lift your shoulders off the floor. Keep your lower back on the floor and avoid using your hands to assist.

✔

✗

Don't...keep your legs straight. This places the back under stress and causes ligament and spinal damage.

Don't...clasp your hands tightly behind your head. This causes the cervical spine to hyperflex, compressing the spinal discs and putting pressure on the nerves.

Push-ups

Lie face down on the floor with your hands directly under your shoulders, palms on the floor, and feet supported on your toes. Push your body up off the floor until your arms are straight, still supporting your lower body and legs on your toes. Then lower your body again. Keep your back straight at all times.

✔

Head tilts

Stand with your back straight and feet a comfortable distance apart. Tilt your head to one side, and then straighten. Repeat on the other side.

Don't...move the head in circles, as this overextends and overflexes the neck and can damage the cervical spine and compress the nerve endings.

✗

Don't...allow your hips and lower back to sag, which compresses the lower spine and can damage the spinal discs and back muscles.

Don't...tilt your head back or lock your elbows.

Don't...rest between press ups.

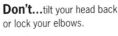

✗

SPORTS INJURIES AND REMEDIES

An understanding of the causes and effects of common sports injuries will help you learn both how to treat them yourself and how to prevent them occurring in the first place.

The most common physical disorders related to sport and exercise involve soft tissue damage, which accounts for approximately 80 per cent of all injuries sustained during active leisure pursuits. Soft tissue injuries involve the skin, muscles, tendons and ligaments and include blisters, bruises, strains, sprains, cuts and tears. More serious exercise injuries, such as fractured bones, dislocated joints, or head injuries, are relatively uncommon.

MUSCLE INJURIES

Soreness is the most common muscular complaint. There are two types: soreness felt during and immediately after exercise, and soreness or stiffness that usually does not appear until 24–48 hours later. The first type is associated with the accumulation of lactic acid following anaerobic exercise and usually passes quickly. The second is due to damaged muscle fibres and may last longer, depending on the extent of the damage.

In some injuries, large numbers of muscle fibres may be torn causing serious bleeding in the muscle. Painful swelling results and movement is severely restricted. This kind of injury occurs through sudden overstretching or overreaching, often because insufficient time was spent warming-up or stretching muscles beforehand. Lunging in racquet sports like tennis, for instance, or stopping abruptly and turning in sports such as football, are common causes of torn muscles. A pulled muscle occurs for similar reasons but is a less serious injury in which only a few muscle fibres are torn.

TENDON INJURIES

Overuse of a limb can cause inflammation in the soft tissue surrounding the tendon, the paratenon. This is known as peritendinitis and causes the area to swell and become very tender. Tendinitis is an injury in which the tendon itself becomes inflamed causing considerable pain. It most commonly affects the Achilles tendon, the groin or the wrist.

A partial or complete rupture of a tendon can occur very suddenly under severe stress. The Achilles tendon and biceps are most often affected. Following a rupture you are unable to move the limb and bleeding occurs in the gap between the split ends of

---

FOOT INJURIES

The foot is a complicated structure with ligaments, tendons, muscles and many small bones packed tightly together. Excess or repeated strain during exercise or sport can cause pain and injury and result in long-term weakening and instability, especially around the ankle joint.

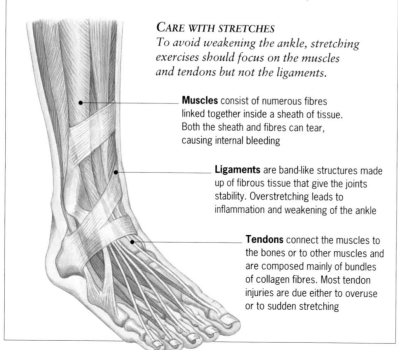

CARE WITH STRETCHES
To avoid weakening the ankle, stretching exercises should focus on the muscles and tendons but not the ligaments.

Muscles consist of numerous fibres linked together inside a sheath of tissue. Both the sheath and fibres can tear, causing internal bleeding

Ligaments are band-like structures made up of fibrous tissue that give the joints stability. Overstretching leads to inflammation and weakening of the ankle

Tendons connect the muscles to the bones or to other muscles and are composed mainly of bundles of collagen fibres. Most tendon injuries are due either to overuse or to sudden stretching

COMMON SPORTS INJURIES

This chart shows the 10 most common sports and exercise injuries revealed in a recent UK survey; sprains and strains accounted for the largest percentage.

TYPE OF INJURY	PERCENTAGE
Sprains and strains	45.3
Unspecified pain and injury	21.9
Bruising	12.2
Cuts and scrapes	7.7
Illness	5.7
Tenderness, swelling, blisters	2.3
Dislocations	1.8
Fractures	1.8
Burns	1.1
Concussion	0.3

the tendon, which fills with blood and clots. A ruptured tendon is treated by resting and immobilising the limb in a plaster cast.

LIGAMENT INJURIES

The most commonly injured ligaments are in the knee and ankle joints. Such injuries most often occur when the joint is twisted through an abnormal range of movement or excess sideways pressure is exerted on it. This may result in a sprain, in which a few fibres are torn, or a complete tear, and usually causes severe pain and swelling.

OTHER INJURIES

Many other injuries can be avoided if consideration is given in advance to potential problems. For instance, if you are going to be doing a lot of running consider the effect that the constant pounding on hard road surfaces will have on your limbs. Similarly, if you suffer from back problems you should ensure that training involving the back should be moderate or avoided.

Backache

Backache is common among exercisers and non-exercisers. However, where exercise involves excessive uncontrolled twisting, lifting or contact, lower back pain may

result. As well as muscle tears and spasms, or ligament tears, other common back complaints include prolapsed disc (slipped disc) and sciatica. A prolapsed disc occurs when an intervertebral disc ruptures and its gelatinous core seeps out putting pressure on a nerve emerging from the spinal canal. The pain which radiates down the leg as a result of a prolapsed disc is known as sciatica. Although it can occur suddenly, it is usually the result of years of incorrect technique or overuse and not a direct result of the exercise you were doing at the time. Any exercise that puts undue stress on the back, however, if carried out incorrectly, could be the catalyst for injury.

Shin splints

This is the term commonly used to refer to pain down the front of the lower leg within the tibia. Shin splints can be caused by inflammation of the tendons, swelling of the muscles attached to the shin, or by a stress fracture. If caused by muscle swelling, shin splints may give rise to poor circulation and sometimes a feeling of numbness in the foot. Too much high-impact exercise, such as high-impact aerobics, or repetitive pounding on hard surfaces, as in road running, are common causes of shin splints.

REMEDIES FOR INJURIES

You can treat many of these injuries yourself. You should, however, always consider the seriousness of the injury. If you feel it is something more than general aches or pains, pulled or strained muscles or bruising, you should seek professional help.

Basic first-aid for injuries

For most types of acute injuries the treatment is the same. To treat bruises, muscle, tendon and ligament injuries use the four-stage RICE technique: Rest the injured limb; apply Ice to the injury; apply Compression; and Elevate the injured limb.

Applying Rest, Ice, Compression and Elevation to an injured area will stop any bleeding and prevent swelling and inflammation which can cause further tissue damage. It will also ensure an early start to the healing process and promote a quicker recovery, while minimising the risk of developing scar tissue and adhesions that might otherwise result in restricted movement in the injured limb.

Minimising post-exercise soreness
The muscle soreness often experienced the day after strenuous exercise is sometimes referred to as DOMS (Delayed Onset Muscular Soreness). While no measures guarantee avoiding DOMS completely, it can be minimised by warming up thoroughly prior to exercise and cooling down afterwards. An adequate cool-down will help to dissipate lactic acid (a by-product of anaerobic work, see page 33) and maintain and develop flexibility in shortened muscles.

NECK SUPPORT
The correct support during exercise can often minimise the risk of injury. For example, some yoga practitioners suggest placing a folded blanket under the shoulders before trying to do the shoulder stand.

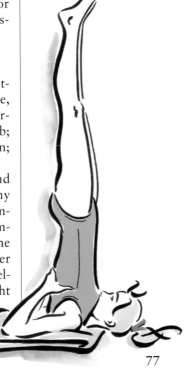

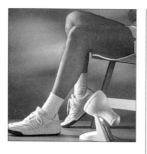

HOT STUFF
There are many varieties of home-treatment heat lamps available today. They are useful for easing tense muscles, relieving general aches and pains and speeding the repair of minor tissue damage. For more serious injuries, however, seek expert medical advice before using a heat lamp.

Rest

Rest is vital as continued use of an injured limb may increase inflammation, bleeding, or swelling and cause further damage.

Ice

Ice applied to an injury reduces pain by numbing the nerves and chilling the pain receptors. It also slows the blood circulation which stops bleeding and reduces inflammation and swelling. Ice should be applied for a maximum of 15 minutes at a time, but can be reapplied every hour or so once the limb warms up again. Ice treatment may be continued for one to two days following injury.

Compression

Compression in the form of a bandage is applied to the injury to stop bleeding and help prevent swelling. A hard pad can be used on the injured area and a bandage then wrapped around it so that the pressure is concentrated on the damaged area.

Elevation

The injured limb should be elevated whenever possible in order to prevent pressure from gravity causing the limb to swell and increasing bleeding and inflammation.

Heat treatment

After the RICE technique has been applied, administering heat treatment by means of infrared heat lamps or heat packs can help to speed the repair of soft tissue damage as well as relieving general aches and pains. Heat treatment can usually be applied two to three days after an injury but it should not be used in the initial treatment as heat increases blood circulation which could lead to more swelling and internal bleeding.

Heat increases blood flow to the affected area which helps to wash away waste products and substances released by the damaged tissue. As waste products are removed, the tense muscles relax and pain is reduced. Heat also increases metabolism which

NATURAL FIRST AID FOR SPORTS INJURIES

A well-stocked first-aid kit that combines natural remedies with conventional items can ease pain and speed recovery time. As well as bandages, sticking plasters and cotton wool, petroleum jelly is a useful addition and can be applied to prevent friction burns caused by clothing rubbing against the skin. You might include ibuprofen or aspirin to ease inflamed joints and paracetamol for general pain relief.

First-aid kit

Tea tree   **Calamine**   **Witch hazel**

Arnica   **Calendula**   **Wintergreen**

Lavender water   **Bach rescue remedy**   **Rhus tox**

Tea tree oil
as an antiseptic for minor cuts and grazes

Calamine lotion
to soothe bruises, grazes and friction burns

Witch hazel
to relieve blisters and friction burns

Arnica cream
to ease the pain of bruises and sprains

Calendula cream
relieves inflammation and minor injuries

Wintergreen oil
for muscle aches and to aid warm-up exercise, to relieve blisters and friction burns

Lavender water
to soothe minor burns, sunburn and headache

Bach rescue remedy
can alleviate shock following injury

Rhus tox
homeopathic remedy for cramps, sprains and strains

Treating a

Pulled Muscle

Strained muscles are one of the most common and easily sustained injuries, so it is worthwhile knowing how to deal with them. Although easy to treat, if you are at all unsure about the seriousness of the injury you should see a doctor.

ALTERNATIVE ICE PACKS
To improvise an ice pack use a packet of frozen peas wrapped in a tea towel, or a compress soaked in a bowl of iced water.

The leg muscles are susceptible to pulls and strains, especially when exercising. A pulled muscle is felt as a sharp pain and there is bleeding and discoloration visible under the skin. With appropriate treatment, the muscle will usually recover relatively quickly and heal within a couple of weeks. It is important to start light stretches as soon as possible to stop scar tissue forming, which may restrict movement in the muscle.

RICE – REST, ICE, COMPRESSION, ELEVATION

The immediate treatment for a pulled muscle is the application of RICE for at least 24 hours and preferably for longer, around two to three days.

After applying RICE to the injured leg, gentle movement and simple stretches can be started but keep within the limits of pain. Attempting to stretch or work the damaged muscle any sooner is likely to cause further pain and increase bleeding within the tissue, which will retard the healing process. It is usually possible to start gentle stretching exercises (see pages 126–7) when bruising appears on the surface of the skin. Over the next seven to ten days, gradually increase the amount of exercise you do. By this time a minor muscle tear should have repaired itself. If the muscle is still painful after a week or so, however, seek medical attention.

After recovery, continue to do stretches regularly in order to keep the muscle supple and prevent further injuries.

1 *While resting the leg, place as little weight on it as possible. You may find it helpful to use crutches to ensure that the limb is fully rested.*

2 *Apply an ice pack to the area. Leave the ice in place for between 5–15 minutes. Repeat the treatment every hour if necessary. To avoid ice burns, protect the skin by applying a layer of grease or petroleum jelly, or wrap a soft, damp cloth around the pack.*

A tea towel will prevent the ice from burning the skin

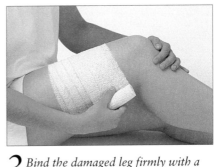

3 *Bind the damaged leg firmly with a bandage to compress it, but not so tight that it stops your circulation. This will reduce the swelling.*

4 *The leg should be elevated to a level higher than your heart as often as possible, resting the limb on anything that is comfortable. This will reduce the pressure within the damaged blood vessels and so reduce bleeding and inflammation.*

Seeking medical help for concussion

A blow to the head that causes unconsciousness is known as concussion and is potentially a very serious condition. A concussed person may feel sick, dizzy, or have a headache. Never allow a concussed casualty to continue playing sport until seen by a doctor. If the person was unconscious for more than 3 minutes, or if there is blood or clear fluid seeping from the ears or nose, call an ambulance. Otherwise get the person to rest, check him or her regularly, and seek medical help if the condition worsens.

stimulates the repair processes in the body. Heat should not be applied for more than half an hour at a time as tissue repair begins to suffer if a high temperature is maintained for too long. Treatment can be repeated, however, soon after the temperature of the tissues has returned to normal.

Stretching

Sometimes excess tension in the muscles can contribute to or even cause injury as well as slowing down the recovery process. Static stretching can reduce the tension in the muscle (see pages 126–7) and aid recovery. As with heat treatment, stretching should not be an initial treatment as it can lead to more swelling and internal bleeding. After a few days of rest, however, stretching will help to speed up the healing process. Only perform stretches when the muscles are warm. Ease into them slowly and then hold still. You should feel mild tension in the muscle while stretching but there should be no pain.

Self-massage

Self-massage may be useful in treating injuries and in reducing muscle tension. However, this technique is not recommended in the early days of injury. By practising self-massage it is possible to become aware of muscle tension in the area being treated and so give treatment whenever you feel tension building up. The benefits of self-massage are the same as for massage that is performed by others, although not all techniques can be performed in the same way.

You can make a soothing herbal massage cream with the infused oils from herbs and spices such as cayenne pepper or mustard, or try the soothing massage oil shown below. These oils warm the muscles and ease away tension, aches and pains.

Liniments and ointments

Liniments and ointments for the relief of sports injuries usually contain substances that act as an irritant to the skin and cause dilation of blood vessels near the surface. This in turn causes blood to be diverted to the skin from the deeper tissues, thus creating a sensation of warmth and relieving pain. Ingredients most often found in liniments and ointments include salicylic acid, nicotinic acid, Spanish pepper (capsaicin) and etheric oils such as turpentine or menthol. Some of these ingredients are allergenic, which means they may cause allergic reactions in some people. If you have sensitive or broken skin you should look for products labelled hypoallergenic.

MAKING YOUR OWN MASSAGE OIL FOR ACHING MUSCLES

Making a massage oil for the relief of muscle ache is very simple, requiring few ingredients and little time or effort. By combining the essential oils of herbs such as comfrey or camomile (available from herbal suppliers and some chemists) which stimulate cell repair; rosemary or eucalyptus to aid circulation; and the infused oil of St John's wort to reduce any minor swelling, you will create a relaxing muscle rub to soothe muscular aches and pains.

2 Before each massage shake the jar well. Warm the oil by rubbing a little between your hands, before applying it to the muscle. Reapply when the oil gets absorbed into the skin.

1 Slowly combine 250 ml (9 fl oz) of St John's wort infused oil with the essential oils of camomile (5 ml/100 drops), eucalyptus (2 ml/40 drops) and comfrey (1 ml/20 drops) into a glass jar.

Massage the oil into the muscles using gentle, smooth, sweeping movements to begin with, making the strokes firmer as the muscles warm up.

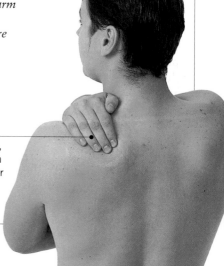

TREATING INJURIES PROFESSIONALLY

There may come a time when you sustain an injury during exercise that is too severe for self-treatment. If this happens, you should consider which type of professional help you require.

With an injury or exercise-induced illness, it is important to know when to consult your doctor or seek emergency aid, and when you can safely treat yourself. If you suspect a fractured limb, avoid movement to prevent further damage. When a limb is broken movement will be difficult and the limb may be badly swollen or hanging at an unusual angle. If in doubt treat the injury as a fracture.

Some kinds of pain arising during or immediately after exercise are warning signals that you require attention by a doctor. These signals include pain that gets worse over a matter of days or weeks, pain that is accompanied by other symptoms such as vomiting, dizziness, pins and needles, tingling and numbness, or other unusual long-term symptoms.

Once an acute injury is treated the doctor may refer you to other specialists for further treatment and rehabilitation.

Physiotherapy

Physiotherapy involves the use of progressive muscular exercise combined with various treatment methods in order to facilitate rapid tissue repair and the restoration of full mobility. The specific form of treatment selected will depend on the type, age and depth of the injury. Common treatments include cold, heat, ultrasound (a form of heat and massage treatment using high frequency sound waves), electrical stimulation, manipulations, massage and exercise.

Osteopathy and chiropractic

These involve the use of manipulative techniques to free mechanical blocks in the musculoskeletal system (such as freeing a locked joint), to break down adhesions that are preventing a full range of movement, or to reposition damaged spinal disc material. The manipulations are usually performed at the sites of joint injuries. The joint is taken to the end of its current range of motion and then the practitioner applies a quick thrust to free the blockage. These actions require a high level of skill and so should only be performed by qualified practitioners.

Massage

Massage can be used in both the prevention and treatment of injury. It can reduce muscle soreness and pain, break down scar tissue helping to restore muscle integrity and full range of movement, and promote overall relaxation. Gentle massage can usually be applied to muscle strains two to

continued on page 84

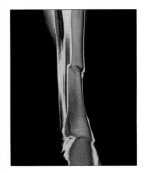

HAVE IT EXAMINED
If there is the possibility that an injury might involve a fracture, seek professional help. Minor fractures may join out of alignment if left to set by themselves.

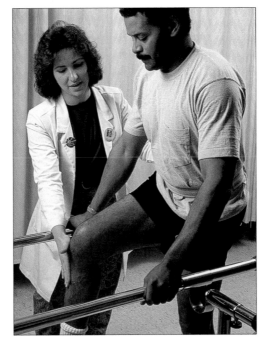

UNDERSTANDING NEEDS
A physiotherapist will try to encourage a patient with a damaged joint to exercise the limb as soon as possible after the injury to ensure that the healing process does not lead to restricted movement. The physiotherapist will usually need to monitor the injury for weeks, months or even years, depending on its severity, to check that there are no lasting flexibility problems.

Sports Physiotherapist

No matter how fit or experienced you are in your chosen discipline, all exercises and sports carry the risk of injury. If an injury is serious and cannot be treated by yourself or your doctor, you may need the services of a sports physiotherapist.

SPEEDY ASSISTANCE
Muscular injuries are extremely common for athletes and sportsmen. A sports physiotherapist understands the need for fast and effective action and is on hand throughout a game to act immediately.

Sports physiotherapy emerged from the general practise of physiotherapy. These therapists specialise in the treatment of sportsmen and women, although they can also treat members of the general public who may have sustained a sports related injury.

What does a sports physiotherapist do?

Primarily, they treat sports injuries, but they also supply training and exercise advice for patients until they are able to participate fully in their

sport again. Sports physiotherapists can also work as first-aiders when an injury occurs and be involved in every stage of the healing process until recovery. They have specialised knowledge in injury treatment and prevention, an awareness of exercise physiology, sports psychology and sports medicine. They liaise with the patient and with medical and surgical specialists as well as other paramedic practitioners.

Who else do sports physiotherapists consult?

This depends on the nature of your injury and your activities. A sports physiotherapist is likely to liaise with orthopaedic surgeons (who specialise in the treatment of disorders of the bones and joints), podiatrists (who are concerned with disorders of the feet and lower limbs, particularly those that affect normal walking), dieticians, sports psychologists, exercise physiologists, first-aiders, masseurs, coaches, trainers, physical education teachers, parents, managers and promoters, sometimes even the media. A cardiac specialist, for instance, might be called in to treat sports players who have developed a heart disorder, perhaps as a result of overtraining.

Origins

The roots of physiotherapy can be traced back to the medicinal massage techniques practised in ancient times, but it was not until 1894 when the Society of Trained Masseuses was formed that the discipline first gained public recognition in Britain.

The Society was founded by four young nurses and midwives, largely to distinguish medicinal massage from the illicit 'massage parlours' prevalent at the time. During its early years, men were ineligible to join the Society or to receive therapeutic massage. However, an influx of casualties from the First World War led to a change of heart and by 1920, when the society was granted a Royal Charter, men were being accepted both as patients and members. The Society is now

ROSALIND PAGET
Miss (later Dame) Rosalind Paget, a midwife, was the first chairperson of the Society of Trained Masseuses.

known as The Chartered Society of Physiotherapy and has proved the therapeutic worth of physiotherapy to generations of sick and injured people.

Where do they practise?

Sports physiotherapists may practise in general and private hospitals, GP surgeries, rehabilitation centres, physiotherapy clinics and health centres. They can also work for sporting clubs or health and fitness centres. In many cases, sports injury treatment takes place alongside other types of physical rehabilitation, such as that for road accident victims.

What sort of injuries do they treat?
Sports physiotherapists treat the whole range of musculoskeletal problems from bruises, strains and sprains to joint, spinal and head injuries. They also help with mobility problems from inflammation and repetitive strain injury. A significant proportion of their work, however, is injury prevention, which involves advising athletes and sports players on correct stretching and warm-up procedures and avoiding damaging or risky techniques.

What methods and equipment do they use?
Many techniques may be used as part of general physiotherapy practice, including massage and manipulation, electrotherapy, hydrotherapy, ultrasound, lasers, heat and cold therapies, traction, acupuncture, relaxation techniques and exercise therapy. Your therapist should be aware of your physical fitness needs

and therefore should know how to combine your fitness training schedules alongside remedial exercise treatment for your injury.

How long has sports physiotherapy been around?
The practice has been around since the 1950s, but formal accreditation of qualified physiotherapists in sports injuries began in Britain in the 1970s, when mass-televised international sporting events such as the Olympic Games produced an unprecedented rise in public interest in athletics and physical culture. Important breakthroughs in sports medicine, science and technology also encouraged this momentum, and by the fitness boom of the mid-80s, sports physiotherapy was well established.

How do I choose one?
In Britain, the term 'physiotherapist' is not a protected title so it is best to see a chartered sports physiotherapist who has been specifically accredited to treat sports injuries professionally. The Association of Chartered Physiotherapists in Sports Medicine

(ACPSM) retains a register of such practitioners, all of whom are governed by a code of professional conduct, covered by appropriate liability insurance, and are qualified for state registration.

What training is required?
Chartered sports physiotherapists complete a three or four year full-time degree training course, and the Association of Chartered Physiotherapists in Sports Medicine is making ongoing professional training mandatory for its members. Non-chartered physiotherapists, however, do not have the same qualification and have been known to practise after as little as two or three weeks of practical experience.

What can I expect from my first visit?
Your physiotherapist will examine the injury and provide some initial remedial treatment. He or she may also prescribe some exercises for you to perform on your own which will aid tissue repair and joint mobility and help to ensure the muscles do not weaken through inactivity.

WHAT YOU CAN DO AT HOME

While the physiotherapist's skills can do much to speed the healing process, measures that you take will play a vital part in ensuring a full recovery. For example, you should rest the injured limb at first but, as soon as the physiotherapist advises, you should begin a planned programme of exercises to regain flexibility in the joints and strengthen the muscles. In addition, by following a balanced diet you will ensure your body has the vitamins and minerals it needs to aid tissue repair. Foods such as oily fish, garlic, broccoli and cauliflower have been found to be particularly beneficial in reducing inflammation and strengthening the muscles and joints.

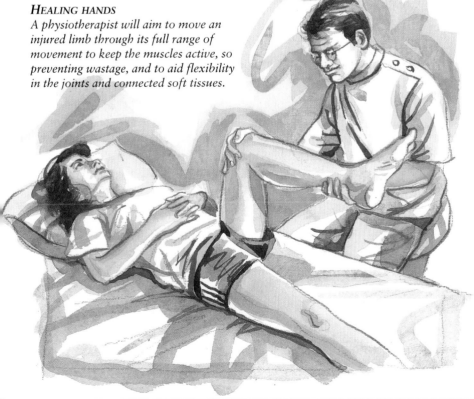

HEALING HANDS
A physiotherapist will aim to move an injured limb through its full range of movement to keep the muscles active, so preventing wastage, and to aid flexibility in the joints and connected soft tissues.

HOMEOPATHIC REMEDIES
Homeopaths recommend several remedies for exercise-related injuries. These include Rhus tox for muscular strains and cramps, Ruta grav for aching bones and muscles, and Arnica for bruising and shock.

three days after the injury, and with mild or moderate strains deep massage can usually begin after seven days. Massage improves the circulation, helping to reduce muscle tightness and improve tissue elasticity, tone, flexibility and overall muscle balance.

Aromatherapy
The use of essential oils as a preventative and curative treatment is now a very popular form of therapy. The oils are extracted from flowers, leaves, fruit, bark, roots and wood, and can be used for a variety of complaints. Each oil has its own unique medicinal properties. Aromatherapy oils are best applied through massage or compresses, or added to the bath water. When using aromatherapy oils for massage, always mix them with a base, such as almond oil, first.

Acupuncture/acupressure
These Eastern forms of healing involve locating channels and pressure points in the body, which are believed to contain and control the flows of energy that course through the body. Stimulating the points by

Pathway to health
As there is such a wide choice of complementary therapies to choose from, pick the one that is most appropriate to your injury or symptoms and convenient for you. This may mean combining one or two different treatments. Backache, for example, can be temporarily relieved by hydrotherapy or massage, but you might also need to see an osteopath to get to the root of the problem. Always follow all the instructions carefully when preparing any treatment for yourself or others and, if in any doubt, seek help from a specialist.

inserting needles (acupuncture) or by applying pressure (acupressure) influences the energy flow. Both can be used to relieve pain, alleviate exhaustion, fatigue and muscle tension, and treat bruising, concussion, cramp, fractures and sprains.

Hydrotherapy
Hydrotherapy involves the use of water as a means of treatment and rehabilitation. Whirlpool baths, water jets, hot and cold showers, massage and baths are the tools of hydrotherapy used to tackle a range of common injuries. It is particularly beneficial when there is limited movement, temporary muscle weakness, impaired coordination or decreased balance following injury. The buoyancy of the water relieves the stresses of weight bearing on joints, while the warmth of the water relieves muscle pain or spasm and helps to reduce bruising and swelling by increasing circulation. Swelling is also reduced by the pressure of the water on the affected area.

Homeopathy
Homeopathic treatment does not claim to supplant the different methods of manipulative therapy, but advocates homeopathic remedies in place of orthodox drugs because they produce no undesirable side effects. Homeopathy is believed to provide relief from shock and pain, and to be effective in healing sprains, fractures and other injuries. Various general remedies are available from pharmacies and health shops.

SHIATSU
Shiatsu is a form of soft tissue manipulation which can be used to induce muscular and general relaxation, speed up recovery after injury and treat specific injuries and illnesses. Its origins lie in ancient Eastern therapeutic techniques but it was not developed into a comprehensive therapy until early in the 20th century. As in acupressure, the fingers and thumbs are used to manipulate acupuncture points. However, a shiatsu therapist may also use the knee, shin and foot to apply stronger pressure.

HEALING TOUCH
Shiatsu can be used to enhance relaxation and concentration before an exercise session and to aid muscle recovery and tissue repair afterwards.

CHAPTER 6

SPORTS FOR FUN AND FITNESS

*There is a vast range of sports and other leisure
pursuits to choose from, so you should be able
to find an activity that suits you. Before selecting
your exercise pursuit, however, it is important to
think about your fitness goals, the demands your
lifestyle places on you, and whether you need
to take account of any health problems*

SPORT CHOICES FOR ALL AGES

Many factors may play a part in determining your choice of physical activity. You need to take account of your health, age, skills, lifestyle and fitness goals – and what you enjoy doing.

AGELESS EXERCISE
Some sports, such as fencing, are accessible to people of all ages. They make more demands on suppleness and mobility than on strength and stamina.

Age doesn't have to dictate the choice of sports activities for you or your family, but every age group has particular needs which present factors to consider when making up your mind. As a general principle think about ways in which you can involve your whole family. For example, if you have a young family, playing with the children is good exercise for all of you. In the same way, think about involving your own parents in your exercise plan, or planning activities between grandchildren and grandparents.

Family exercise also helps to strengthen relationships as well as improving everybody's fitness and general health.

Children

For younger children, the focus should always be on fun. Try not to confuse or intimidate young children with the complexities of organised sport too soon. Playing simple ball games, or playing in a swimming pool are great exercises for younger children, while cycling or hill walking are fine for children over the age of seven. As children grow older, team games help them to develop social skills and learn to interact with others and also to accept and respect the need for rules.

Encouraging children to play physically, rather than watch television or play computer games, often requires the help of a

---

A HEALTHY LIFESTYLE

Whatever sport you choose, the most important point to remember is that it should be part of a healthy lifestyle.

Make sure that your body has adequate rest and nutrition to cope with the increased demands being placed on it.

ADEQUATE SLEEP
Ensure that you get as much rest as your body needs and keep to regular sleep and waking times.

BALANCED DIET
Have at least three meals a day and never skip a meal. Make sure your diet includes plenty of fresh fruit and vegetables and starchy carbohydrates.

HEALTHY EXERCISE
As well as attending fitness classes, incorporate additional exercise into your day whenever you can. For example, walk to the shops instead of using the car or bus, go swimming during your lunch breaks, and go for a brisk walk or jog if you have any free time in the evening.

DEVELOPMENT OF SPORTING SKILLS

Children enjoy games from an early age but their approach changes over time as their coordination and skill levels improve. It is important to bear this in mind when encouraging children to play physical games so they stay motivated.

UNDER 8
Small children enjoy simple bat and ball games that they can play on their own and can improve on with regular practice.

AGES 8 TO 11
Games that can be played with friends can help keep older children interested.

AGES 12 TO 14
Young teenagers are best motivated by games that require high skill levels.

AGES 15 TO 18
Older teenagers often need a strong element of competition in their sport.

professional. Clubs and sports centres offer a variety of activities for children to explore, but remember that children subjected to intensive training often suffer injuries and disappointments. Being pushed too hard can actually lower their self-esteem and discourage them from taking part in sport rather than encouraging them in an active, healthy lifestyle. Try to ensure that exercise is always fun and don't place undue pressure on children to exceed their capabilities.

Teenagers

During puberty boys tend to become more physically adept and more capable at sport, while girls often find that their changing body adds new challenges. Girls who take up sports such as gymnastics, where a small physique to facilitate quick, dainty movements is an advantage, may find that particular sport no longer possible after puberty. These teenagers need to be encouraged into other sports where they can continue to use and enjoy the skills they have learned. For example, aerobic dance can be a good choice, utilising the coordination skills already learnt in gymnastics.

Some teenagers give up a particular sport because of pressure to excel from parents, teachers or coaches. In such cases, encourage teenagers to try different sports and to enjoy sport either in a non-competitive environment or at a level that challenges without overwhelming them. Activity holidays and summer camps provide multiple activities for teenagers, and may help them to discover a new type of activity that they can enjoy. Encouraging teenagers to walk or cycle rather than driving them in the car can also increase their exercise levels considerably – although considerations of safety obviously come first.

Young adulthood

Many people find that the opportunity and desire to play sports and have regular exercise dissipates on leaving school, especially when sports facilities become less easily accessible. Many jobs force people into more sedentary lifestyles than they knew at school and starting a family can leave little time for exercise and sporting pursuits.

Although you may want to return to a sport you once enjoyed in your teens you may find that you are no longer fit enough to launch straight in. Follow the adage: 'Get fit to play sport, don't play sport to get fit'. For those who have been inactive for some years, a gradual reintroduction to exercise followed by a steady build-up is important.

Bear in mind lifestyle factors as well: if stress, anxiety or depression are factors in your life, it may be helpful to think about forms of activity that could target your particular problems. For example, if you feel under constant pressure at work, choosing a relaxing form of exercise such as yoga may meet your needs. Houseparents may need to choose an activity that they can do while the children are at nursery school.

The Disappointed Dancer

Rapid physical change during puberty can mean that activities that were once suitable for a girl are no longer appropriate for a fuller-figured teenager. Many girls attend classical ballet classes, only to find that once they gain their adult height and build they no longer meet ballet's requirements. But with family encouragement and support this needn't mean girls cease to be active altogether.

Sylvie is a 15-year-old student living at home with her parents and younger sister, Jane. Up until the age of 13 Sylvie was a keen ballet dancer, but with puberty it became obvious that she was going to be too tall and well-built to be a classical ballet dancer. Sylvie loved dancing and was very upset to give up her girlhood ambitions. To make matters worse her younger sister is still studying ballet and teases Sylvie about the fact that she no longer dances and about her new fuller figure. Thinking that if she's going to be big and fat she may as well eat what she likes, Sylvie takes comfort in high fat foods. This, combined with her lack of exercise, is contributing to her weight problem.

WHAT SHOULD SYLVIE DO?

Sylvie needs to find a form of exercise that can be adapted to her former interests and skills. There are plenty of other activities that involve music and movement and aren't so restrictive in terms of body shape. She needs support from her family rather than teasing. Her parents should help her to find alternative forms of exercise and encourage her to change her diet, reducing her consumption of high fat snacks, and reorientating her towards healthier options. Her mother also needs to help Sylvie feel comfortable with the rapid physical changes that have taken place: shopping together for clothes that flatter Sylvie's new shape could be a confidence booster.

Action Plan

DIET
Make sure that your diet is well-balanced with lots of fruit and vegetables rather than increased fatty or snack foods.

EMOTIONAL HEALTH
Talk through any worries you have about your lifestyle or appearance. You may find a great deal of support and understanding from family and friends.

EXERCISE
Find alternatives to pastimes you have outgrown. Most skills learned in one sport can be applied to others.

DIET
High-fat 'comfort' foods offer only short-term relief and can exacerbate a weight or body shape related problem.

EMOTIONAL HEALTH
Feelings of inadequacy and embarrassment at adolescent changes in body shape can cause sadness and fear in young men and women.

EXERCISE
The sudden stoppage of regular exercise can have an immediate effect on fitness and body shape.

HOW THINGS TURNED OUT FOR SYLVIE

Sylvie's mother encouraged her to take up flamenco dancing as an alternative to ballet. Initially sceptical, Sylvie soon found that the dramatic style of flamenco reawakened her interest in performing. She began paying closer attention to her diet and substituted high-fat snacks with low-fat energy-foods, such as bananas. Sylvie found that her return to dancing improved her self-confidence and she's now content with her new figure.

Middle age

This is an age when many people decide to take up exercise for the first time. Often an increase in weight or a medical check-up prompts this change in attitude. Regular exercise is recommended to help to combat the stresses of work and home-life, control weight gain, and ensure that the physical decline that is often thought inevitable in old age is minimal. For example, the risk of osteoporosis can be lessened by undertaking weight-bearing exercises such as walking or aerobics which help to increase bone mass.

Choose an activity that fits in with your lifestyle, rather than rearranging your lifestyle to fit around your choice of exercise. A busy executive may only be able to fit exercise in before work, for instance, and the programme will need to be as time efficient as possible.

Start with a gentle form of exercise such as walking to build up your aerobic fitness. Measure improvements in your heart rate, and as your basic level of fitness improves think next about any special fitness requirements of your favourite sport. For example, a degree of suppleness is required for racquet sports, so specific flexibility training will help to make a return to these sports much easier. You could also investigate clubs that run masters and veterans sections both for training and competition.

Old age

Some physical decline in old age is inevitable. However, severe disability can be as much a result of inactivity as of natural ageing. Research shows that strength can not only be maintained but can actually be improved in old age, and that this is associated with an increase in bone density, so helping to avoid osteoporosis.

Stamina and flexibility can also be improved, allowing older people more freedom of movement and a greater vitality and ability to enjoy life. Further studies have shown that the slowing in reaction times that often occurs in sedentary older people is not so marked in those who take steps to remain physically active.

Walking, swimming, moderate weight training, exercise to music and dancing are all appropriate forms of exercise for the older adult. For those who have remained actively involved in sports, continued participation in that sport is possible providing

there are no precluding health problems. For the frail elderly, improvements in strength, stamina and flexibility will enhance their quality of life, but exercise should always be supervised by qualified instructors or specialists.

For many old people, a lack of independence is linked to a loss of ability to cope with everyday tasks such as washing your own hair, walking upstairs or getting in and out of the bath unaided. Much of this loss of ability is related to a reduction in strength and power, which in itself is associated with a decrease in muscle mass, bone density and balance. Therefore, for older adults muscular strength work is the keystone to an active and independent retirement.

Remember, though, that if you have a particular health problem it is very important to discuss exercise options with a doctor or other health professional. This is because various forms of exercise tax different parts of the body, so you need to be sure you are choosing a form of exercise that will be of most benefit without over-stressing weak areas. For example, if you suffer from asthma, activities such as swimming, which control breathing and strengthen lung capacity, are of particular benefit. If you suffer from loneliness or boredom, a team or social sport where there are more opportunities for interaction with other people may be just what you need.

CHOOSING A SPORT

Understanding what level of fitness you need for a particular sport, the equipment necessary, and how it is likely to benefit your health will help you to choose the right sport for you.

ADVENTURE SPORTS
Adventure sports are outdoor leisure activities that combine a high degree of skill and physical effort with an element of risk. They appeal to people who enjoy the challenge of pushing themselves to the limit, both physically and mentally. Adventure sports have strict safety rules that should be adhered to at all times, and all require strict training under expert supervision to keep risks within acceptable limits.

Although you may not think of yourself as the traditional 'sporty' type, the wide range of sports and physical activities on offer means that you are almost bound to find one that meets your particular needs, whether you are looking for non-pressured socialising, outdoor fun, a physical and mental challenge, or something that allows your creativity full reign.

When choosing a sport, it is important to take into account personal factors such as temperament, commitment and individual skills. For example, some people are happiest when playing as part of a team, while others prefer sports that require self reliance and individual skill and flare.

Similarly, some sports may require a greater commitment in terms of financial outlay, practice sessions or training than you are prepared to give. By choosing an activity that you will enjoy and that fits into your lifestyle you will make it easier to maintain your motivation and thereby achieve your fitness goals. Whichever sport appeals to you, age need not be a barrier. With the increase in youth, masters and veterans categories in many sports, opportunities to take part abound for all age groups.

MAKING YOUR CHOICE

To help you to choose a sporting activity that best suits your abilities, interests and personal aspirations, the following pages feature a broad range of sporting activities and describe the demands that each one makes in terms of costs, skills, time, fitness and equipment.

Some activities featured, such as walking, running and swimming, will suit the solitary exerciser who wants to be able to fit the activity into a busy life. Other sports are for those who prefer the camaraderie of team

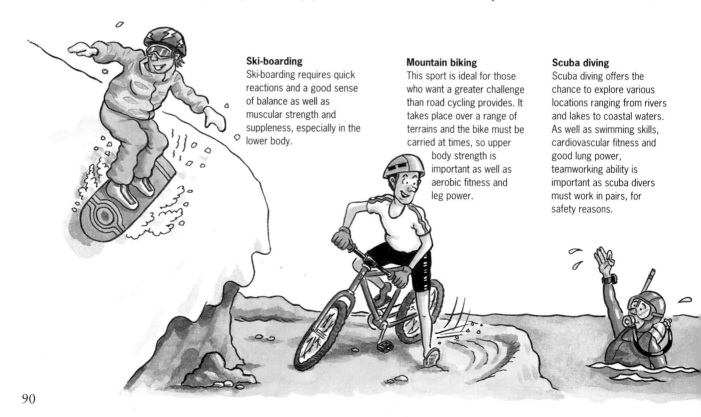

Ski-boarding
Ski-boarding requires quick reactions and a good sense of balance as well as muscular strength and suppleness, especially in the lower body.

Mountain biking
This sport is ideal for those who want a greater challenge than road cycling provides. It takes place over a range of terrains and the bike must be carried at times, so upper body strength is important as well as aerobic fitness and leg power.

Scuba diving
Scuba diving offers the chance to explore various locations ranging from rivers and lakes to coastal waters. As well as swimming skills, cardiovascular fitness and good lung power, teamworking ability is important as scuba divers must work in pairs, for safety reasons.

play, or the hand and eye coordination of racquet sports. This chapter also focuses on particular skills that you will need in order to get the most from the sport, and other exercise you can undertake specifically to improve fitness and the muscles required for your chosen sport.

If you are interested in any of these sports the best way to get started is to check to see if they are featured in the sports pages or classified advertisement sections of your local newspaper – many teams advertise locally for new players – or check out work-based sports and social clubs. You could also ask at your local library, church hall or sports or community centre. Don't be put off by the need for specialist equipment. Most sports clubs will lend or hire equipment to beginners or occasional players.

FIT TO PLAY

In all sports, getting fit before you play ensures better performance, a lower risk of injury and more enjoyment. Fatigue, in particular, is the enemy of good performance. Once fatigued you will lose strength, speed and skill, and become injury prone.

For multiple sprint sports, football and rugby, for example, basic aerobic fitness is important, and this can be achieved through regular walking and/or running. Many sports require a combination of different types of fitness such as flexibility, muscular strength and endurance. This can be achieved by combining resistance or circuit training with aerobic activities.

Different sports, however, place their own unique demands on the body. The physical effect of a fast and furious game of ice hockey is completely different from that of a tennis match or a day hill walking. It follows that each sport needs its own type of fitness training, coupled with the right mental outlook, to get the most benefit from the game.

Contact sports such as rugby or judo need overall muscular strength to withstand tackles and throws. Horse riding requires balance and muscular endurance to remain in the saddle and in control as the horse moves, gallops, or jumps. Swimming and gymnastics require flexibility, combined with strength and stamina.

As with all exercise, sports players should prepare with a good stretch and warm-up routine. At the end of a game they should stretch thoroughly, paying particular attention to the hamstrings and hip flexors.

You can take up any sport you wish so long as you are in good shape, reasonably fit and have no medical conditions which may impair your performance or result in danger to yourself. If you have a history of diabetes, chest pain or angina, asthma, epilepsy, high blood pressure, have had recent surgery, or you are pregnant, then always consult your doctor before deciding.

MOST POPULAR ACTIVE LEISURE PURSUITS*
The following figures show the most popular exercise activities carried out in the UK by people aged over 16 during a typical 12-month period.

ACTIVITY	%
Walking	65
Swimming	42
Aerobic dance and keep fit	18
Cycling	14
Running and jogging	10

*General Household Survey 1990

Windsurfing
For individuals who enjoy the elemental forces of wind and water, windsurfing may be just the thing. Good swimming ability and muscular endurance is needed, particularly when acquiring the basic skills, to avoid becoming fatigued too quickly.

Rock climbing
Climbers normally work in close-knit groups of two or more people, so teamwork skills and a high degree of trust are important aspects. Climbing also requires suppleness, muscular endurance and strength, a strong sense of balance plus good hand-eye coordination.

White-water kayaking
Paddling on fast-flowing rivers, or 'white water', is exhilarating and physically demanding. It requires aerobic fitness and suppleness, as well as good upper body strength.

Sports for Fitness

Walking, running, swimming and cycling all provide a solid grounding in basic fitness, and are probably the best activities to choose if you have been inactive for some time. The level of intensity can be increased as fitness improves.

WALKING

Walking is a low-impact weight-bearing activity that places less stress on the joints than many other forms of exercise. There are more forms of walking than many people imagine but they will all improve aerobic fitness and tone the muscles of the lower body (and upper body to an extent). If you have been inactive for a while, walking is an excellent way to regain fitness, but start slowly and build up gradually.

Walking faster, further, uphill or on rough terrain increases the intensity of a walk and is therefore

> Walking needs little equipment and can be tailored to suit the fitness levels and needs of anyone. It improves stamina and – if a gradient is included – also builds strength.

more demanding. When starting a walking programme, assess the activity you do on a regular basis and begin your walking programme just above this level of activity. For example, if you only walk for 10 minutes to and from the bus stop every day you would need to improve your general fitness level before attempting a full day's ramble or a steep hill climb.

Getting started

Plan your route before you start. Where possible, avoid roads with fast or congested traffic and keep to pavements and clearly marked footpaths. If you feel up to it, include at least one gradient in the route, such as a low hill, depending on your level of fitness.

Start out gently with your shoulders relaxed and your head up. As you begin to warm up, gradually increase speed until you reach a comfortably steady pace. Develop a relaxed walking style with broad strides and swing your arms in time with your legs. Your breathing will become a little deeper and you will become warmer.

As you reach the end of your walk gradually slow your pace down until your breathing returns to normal. Spread your walking sessions out across the week with rest days in

Preparation and safety

Trainers or ordinary shoes are fine for walking on dry, flat surfaces, but on hilly or rough ground choose boots or shoes that provide support and grip. Wear thick socks for warmth and to

avoid blisters. To provide extra insulation in cold weather, wear several thin layers of clothing rather than just a thick garment.

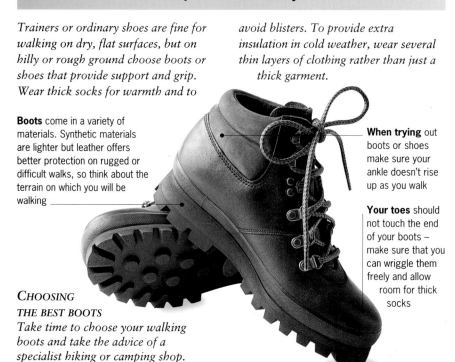

Boots come in a variety of materials. Synthetic materials are lighter but leather offers better protection on rugged or difficult walks, so think about the terrain on which you will be walking

When trying out boots or shoes make sure your ankle doesn't rise up as you walk

Your toes should not touch the end of your boots – make sure that you can wriggle them freely and allow room for thick socks

CHOOSING THE BEST BOOTS
Take time to choose your walking boots and take the advice of a specialist hiking or camping shop.

between. You will steadily get faster and find that you need more demanding walks as you progress.

Rambling, backpacking, hill and fell walking

The countryside is covered with a network of trails, walks and footpaths. They all have their own rewards in the form of picturesque scenery, peace and tranquillity. Many of these paths are not easy, so if you do intend to tackle them check the degree of difficulty first, perhaps with a local walking club or tourist office. If you want to tackle very ambitious routes, get expert advice on how to kit yourself out and training in mountain craft skills and map reading. Prepare for a long ramble with a series of shorter walks of increasing length.

Whether walking up or down a hill, you considerably increase your work load and energy cost compared to walking on the flat. Walking downhill uses the opposing muscles in your legs to those involved when walking uphill. Unaccustomed downhill walking may make you sore as it uses the muscles as shock absorbers. If you are planning a hill walking holiday take rest days to allow your muscles to recover.

On fell walks wear a wind and waterproof jacket and carry a small rucksack packed with items such as a warm drink, energy-boosting food, a woollen hat and scarf, extra warm clothing, a survival blanket, a first-aid kit, a compass and the relevant Ordnance Survey map. Carry your backpack as high as possible to avoid back strain.

When walking, always respect the laws of the countryside. Keep to the path or right of way, close gates behind you, and keep dogs on a lead near farm animals. It is important to check the weather forecast before venturing out and seek the advice of experienced local walkers about problem areas on your route. Always inform a responsible person about the route you are taking and your expected time of arrival.

PLANNING YOUR WALKING ROUTE

You can make walks more interesting or relaxing and gain maximum fitness benefits from them for all the family by planning your route in advance. A town walk could take in historic features, a park or a river towpath to vary the physical demands and maintain interest in your route. In most towns and cities, blue plaques draw attention to the former homes of famous people.

Country walks could be planned to take in hills and stiles for a good work-out. Woodland and river banks offer varied terrain with interesting sights and sounds, particularly for younger children. Make sure that you follow the country code when walking.

COUNTRY WALK
Climbing over rocky or difficult terrain, gates and stiles gives the muscles of the upper body a work-out. Walking up and down hills helps to strengthen muscles and bones, particularly of the legs and back.

Indoor treadmill walking

If it is dark, cold and icy outside, foggy or extremely windy, treadmill walking is a useful substitute for outdoor walking. It is also a good way of plotting your fitness progress as many modern treadmills can be programmed to emulate various terrains. This will help you to achieve the best possible workout without braving the weather.

Walking tips

▶ *Wear loose comfortable clothing appropriate to the weather, including headgear – 40 per cent of body heat is lost from the head and neck.*

▶ *Always check the weather forecast before you set out.*

Fact file
The greatest distance walked in a 24-hour period is 228.93 kilometres (142 miles 440 yards) a record set by the American Jose Castenada at Albuquerque, New Mexico in 1976.

RUNNING

Running and jogging are excellent ways of strengthening the heart and lungs. In reality the only difference between them is one of pace: running can be done at a moderate pace (jogging) or at speeds up to an all-out sprint. Running can be a sociable activity or a personal one. It can be easy or hard, competitive or friendly. You can run at any time of the day or night, anywhere you happen to be and for however long you want. Sprinting is an anaerobic activity that requires a great deal of power output from the muscles; in contrast, jogging and other forms of long-distance running are aerobic activities and require muscular endurance. Running is a high-impact activity and so can help to maintain or increase bone density, helping to offset osteoporosis. However, because it is high-impact, it does place a lot of stress on the joints.

Preparation and safety

When running on hard surfaces such as tarmac wear shoes with cushioned soles which reduce the impact on the knee and ankle joints. When running at night it is safer to run in groups and to stick to lighted streets, keeping away from dark alleys and subways. It is a good idea to leave your route details and expected time of return with someone. Don't run while listening to a personal stereo – you will not be able to hear approaching cars. Never run when suffering from a viral illness or fever. Once you are completely recovered, start gently, and build up your speed and distance very gradually.

Reflective clothes and a flashing light will help with night safety

NIGHT-TIME SAFETY
On busy roads, make sure you can be clearly seen by wearing light-coloured or reflective clothing and run facing traffic.

Getting started

To start running, all you need is a little enthusiasm and a comfortable pair of running shoes. Petroleum jelly is useful to lubricate parts of the body that rub against clothing, such as the top of the legs and arms or the nipples. For women a well-fitting sports bra is essential. Wear loose, non-restrictive clothing – in summer, shorts and a T-shirt are sufficient; in winter, a tracksuit or a pair of thermal tights, a long-sleeved thermal top and windproof jacket are ideal. In very cold weather you should wear a hooded jacket or hat and gloves as a lot of body heat is lost through the head and hands.

Running tips

▶ *Keep your body straight, not leaning back or swaying from side to side.*

▶ *Swing your arms in a relaxed way, keeping them close to the body.*

▶ *Steps should be light and springy so that the ankles, and the calf and thigh muscles share the work equally.*

▶ *Avoid overstriding or high back kicks.*

Fact file
The world's fastest runners – 100 m sprinters – can achieve speeds of over 43 km/h (nearly 27 mph). But such speeds are not sustainable for long. The average speed of mile runners is around 26 km/h (16 mph).

Running needs no special equipment, apart from well-cushioned trainers. It provides good stamina and bone-building exercise but can place excess stress on the joints.

As with all exercise you must start by warming up. Set off walking briskly and swinging your arms vigorously, then gradually break into a slow jog. Your level of fitness will determine when you are ready to step up the pace. Listen to your body. Remember, although your breathing will be heavier than normal, you should not be so out of breath that you can't talk. Run at a pace at which you can hold a conversation. If you are getting too

DIFFERENT FORMS OF RUNNING

Whether you choose fun runs, marathons or the athletics track, your technique will be of utmost importance. Fun runs allow each runner to complete the course at his or her own pace and tend to require stamina rather than speed. Events on the athletics track, particularly sprints and field events, require the muscle power to produce short bursts of high speed. Events such as middle and long-distance running demand a mixture of speed and the stamina required to run for long periods at a more moderate pace.

FUN RUNS
Designed to allow everyone to enjoy the pleasure of running, fun runs are highly sociable and mainly non-competitive. A broad range of ages can run together at a pace suitable to all.

FIELD EVENTS
Many field athletics events, such as the long jump, triple jump and pole vault, require sprinting power. Athletes must develop strong leg and gluteal muscles in order to generate rapid acceleration.

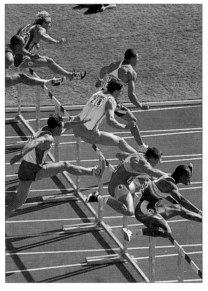

HURDLES
A hurdler requires several forms of fitness. Hurdling incorporates sprinting speed with jumping ability, and stretches the athlete to maintain timing and speed with accuracy and agility.

breathless to talk, slow down or walk until you have recovered, then set off again.

As you run put your heel down first and roll through to your toes. Stay relaxed and avoid using more effort than needed. Sprinters need to lift their knees high to gain extra power, but joggers and distance runners should aim for lower and smaller steps. Try to keep your shoulders relaxed. At the end of each session you must cool down. Slow down gradually, finishing with a slow jog or brisk walk until your heart rate and breathing return to more normal levels. While your muscles are still warm, stretch well, concentrating in particular on your calves, quadriceps, hamstrings, abductors and hip flexors.

Cross-country running

For those who feel that jogging is not taxing enough, cross-country running may be the answer. You can make the course as difficult as you want, and can also set the speed to suit your current level of fitness and exercise goals. Cross-country demands great stamina and strength because the various forms of terrain place different demands on the body.

Plan your cross-country route to take in different terrains. Try to include woodland, grass, pavement and, if possible, sand. A one-mile run on a firm, level surface may be easier than a mile run over hills and dunes, so don't overdo it at first. Aim to vary the gradients you run on to include both hills and level surfaces. Gradually extend the distance you

cover and/or the speed you are running at, until you feel you are getting a full work-out.

To make cross-country running a mental challenge as well as a test of stamina and strength, many people take up orienteering, in which runners use maps to find their way between fixed control points. As well as needing aerobic fitness and muscular strength, orienteering requires good navigational and tactical skills in finding the quickest route between the control points.

Orienteering courses range from 1 km (just over half a mile) to about 16 km (10 miles) and vary in difficulty depending on the age and experience of those taking part. There are courses for all ages from children to the elderly.

SWIMMING

Swimming is extremely popular with all age groups and provides an all-round fitness workout. Swimming improves the condition of the heart and lungs and works both upper and lower body muscles. Regular

Preparation and safety

Take great care when swimming in open water. Sudden changes in temperature in lakes and rivers, particularly below the surface or in the shadow of trees, can cause debilitating and potentially fatal muscle cramps. Tides and currents can cause problems for the most experienced swimmers. Even seemingly calm stretches of water can have dangerously strong currents beneath the surface. Don't swim alone in unfamiliar water and never swim after drinking alcohol or within 2 hours of eating a big meal.

Adjustable straps will ensure a watertight fit

GOGGLES
These will help to protect your eyes from the irritation of chlorine or salt water and allow you to see more clearly when swimming. They should be watertight and fit snugly around your eyes and nose.

swimming will help to maintain strength, stamina and flexibility, especially in the shoulders. Good swimming ability is also an important safety requirement of other water sports. Swimming can be extremely informal or can involve serious training and competition in galas. Swimming clubs generally cater for all age groups, often with opportunities for the senior swimmers to become involved in the coaching or running of the club.

Getting started

The most important equipment is a snug-fitting swimming costume or swimming trunks. Learners may find buoyancy aids, such as arm bands and floats, useful until they feel confident in the water. No other equipment is necessary, but a hat is advisable if you have long hair; goggles and a nose clip are useful if you are sensitive to chlorinated water or when swimming in the sea; and ear plugs are advisable for those who are prone to ear infections.

Most swimming pools offer lessons for improving technique and set aside times during the week for those who wish to swim in earnest. There

Swimming requires little equipment and so involves minimal expense. It boosts strength, suppleness and stamina, and the water's buoyancy aids the disabled and those with joint disorders.

SYNCHRONISED SWIMMING
Advanced swimmers who prefer a different challenge from speed or distance swimming may enjoy synchronised swimming. Somewhat like dancing, synchronised swimming demands a great deal of strength, stamina and flexibility, coupled with control and a sense of timing.

are also many advantages in training with a swimming club in addition to the fun of competition. The session is set for you by the coach who will help to improve your stroke and breathing techniques. Strong swimmers can enrol on lifesaving

Swimming tips

▶ *Keep your body as streamlined as possible to reduce water resistance.*

▶ *Try to breathe regularly while swimming and tailor your swimming stroke to make breathing easier.*

▶ *If you feel tired, turn on to your back and float in the water until you feel ready to continue swimming. The body is naturally buoyant.*

▶ *Swim with a partner so that you can encourage one another.*

Fact file
Swimming was recorded as far back as 36 BC in Japan, yet three of the four strokes, front and back crawl and butterfly, are 20th-century inventions. The fourth, breast stroke, dates from the 16th century.

courses which, as well as showing how to carry out water rescues and teaching first aid, can help you to improve your swimming skills.

Pool-based sports

Many of the techniques you learn while swimming can be used to play pool-based sports such as octopush and water polo.

Octopush is a form of underwater hockey and provides particularly good stamina and muscle-building exercise as well as being great fun. Water polo was developed in the mid 1800s and has grown in popularity so much that it is now an Olympic event. It is described as being a cross between swimming and football. Each team tries to score goals in the opposition's net, one at either end of the pool, by passing the ball and dribbling it – pushing the ball ahead while swimming.

Swimming skills and speed and agility are necessary to play at most levels, but simpler versions of the game can be played in shallow water with the water acting as a cushion against dives for the ball.

WATER POLO
A physically demanding sport, water polo requires constant activity – treading water, swimming and throwing the ball.

ROWING AND PADDLING

Rowing includes 'sweep rowing', where each rower handles one oar, and 'sculling', where the rower uses two smaller oars. Paddling involves the use of a special kind of 'oar' called a paddle. This has a blade at both ends, for kayaking, or at one end only, for canoeing. Kayaks and canoes can be for one person, and so require individual skill and effort, or built for two or more people, demanding teamwork.

Rowing is regarded by many as the complete exercise. It utilises most of the major muscles of the body and can tax them at varying intensities, offering both aerobic and anaerobic work. Paddling requires good upper body strength, while rowing makes demands on the leg muscles as well as the upper body.

Getting started

Paddling and rowing are taught at specialist clubs and outdoor leisure centres. As with all water sports, it is important that you are a competent swimmer and have good knowledge of water safety before you go out in a boat. The instructor will teach you the rules and dangers specific to the waterways you will be using.

A kayak is a mostly enclosed craft which can overturn and trap the inexperienced paddler, so you will be taught the Eskimo roll – an intentional overturning and righting

of the kayak – so that you can right your craft in the event of capsize. You will then be able to practise the basics. Never row or paddle alone on unfamiliar water and ensure that you can control your craft at all times, even when you capsize – by righting the craft or swimming it to the shore.

Rowing machines

Although normally thought of as a water sport, the introduction of rowing machines that mimic the feel

Rowing and paddling require some financial outlay for club fees and hire of equipment. They are good for building stamina and upper body strength and endurance.

of rowing on water has made it far more accessible to many people. Indoor rowing is a non-weight-bearing exercise with an easily adaptable intensity level, so it is suitable for people of all ages and fitness levels, provided they do not suffer from a back disorder.

Preparation and safety

Bad rowing technique can result in chronic lower back disorders. Correct technique involves keeping a straight back. When you pull back on the oars *the effort should come from your legs and arms, not your back. When paddling, keep a smooth steady stroke and twist your upper body from the hips.*

LIFE SAVERS
Safety is very important in water sports. Always wear a good-quality life jacket and helmet, especially when rowing or paddling at sea or in fast-flowing water.

Check there is no sign of wear or damage

Ensure the life jacket has adjustable straps

CYCLING

Cycling is an excellent activity for strengthening your heart and lungs, relieving stress, and increasing muscular strength and endurance. It is good for building anaerobic fitness and tolerance to lactic acid (see page 33) as the large muscles of the leg produce excess amounts of this waste product during cycling.

Cycling is also a cheap and pollution-free means of transport. Cycling to and from work or the shops integrates exercise into everyday activities, while cycling for fun is a great way of exploring the countryside. With the growing interest in cycling in recent years, cycling clubs and competitive events have increased and cater for everyone from the serious rider to the occasional cyclist.

The Cyclist Touring Club and Audax, the long-distance cycling club, are international and have local branches throughout Britain and Europe. They are aimed at cyclists who want to ride with a group and set themselves challenges but who do not want to race. Other cycling clubs cater for competitive road-race, track and time-trial cyclists. Mountain bike clubs are for those who want to explore the countryside, or orienteer on a bike, or who like to race off-road. They welcome all age groups and experience levels, and many mountain bike clubs also have a children's group.

Getting started

The most important part of starting to cycle is to ensure the bike is the right size for you. If a bike is the wrong size, or is incorrectly adjusted you will have an uncomfortable ride and risk injury. It is especially dangerous for children to ride a bike that is too large for them as they will not be able to control it properly. As a guide, the 'standover' height of the bicycle (the distance between the cross-bar and the top of the rider's inside leg when straddling the cycle) should be at least 7–8 cm (3 in). Seat, pedals and handlebars must also be adjusted to the individual.

Most bike shops adjust the bicycle when it is purchased and advise on suitable clothing and the correct helmet. Padded cycle shorts improve

Cycling provides good aerobic and muscle-building exercise but requires an initial financial outlay and commitment to training to ensure safe and problem-free riding.

FAMILY OUTINGS
Cycling can be a great way to enjoy family outings. Children should always be taught road safety and cycling proficiency before riding on the roads.

comfort and a close fitting cycle jersey reduces wind resistance and prevents a build-up of moisture.

A common mistake that beginner cyclists make is incorrect use of gears. Using too high a gear causes leg fatigue very quickly. Choose a gear which allows the pedals to turn smoothly without straining too much – a low gear when cycling uphill and a higher gear for downhill.

A warm-up is necessary and the cyclist should start out gently then gradually increase the workload by pedalling faster or using a higher gear. Incorporate a gradual cool-down at the end of the session.

On-road cycling

A tourer or racing bike is a good investment for someone who wishes to use cycling to explore the countryside or to commute to work. These bicycles are generally light and have several gears in order to cope with hills and changing traffic speeds. They also have mudguards, lights and usually a luggage carrier. Touring cycles also have good

---

Preparation and safety

It is important to maintain your equipment. Carrying a small tool kit is recommended because punctures and minor wheel damage are common, especially on poorly maintained roads and rough countryside terrain. Make sure you can be clearly seen by other road users at all times. It is an offence to cycle at night without showing a white light in front and a red light at the rear.

Streamlined shape reduces wind resistance

CYCLING HELMET
A specialised safety helmet is vital for cyclists, particularly those cycling in traffic or over rough ground.

Cushioned inner helps absorb the shock of impact

Adjustable chin strap ensures a tight fit

brakes, which are essential for safety in traffic. Some racing bicycles have curved handlebars but it is important to hold the top of these when cycling on busy roads, or to choose a bicycle with straight handlebars. Bending to hold the curved bars can produce excessive tension in the neck and shoulders, cramp the abdomen, and impair breathing. Crouching over the bicycle can also be dangerous on the road as it impairs your field of vision, so curved handlebars should be used only for racing or off-road cycling where there is little danger of traffic accidents.

Before you cycle on the road, make sure you know the highway code and that you have reached a good degree of cycling proficiency. Wear bright-coloured, reflective or fluorescent strips or clothing and ensure your lights are in good working order.

Off-road cycling

For more adventurous cycling, off-road and exploring hard-to-get-to places, a mountain bike is the better option. These have wide tyres to grip both soft and hard surfaces, and the frames are light but also very strong to withstand the excessive stress and strain put on them. Mountain bikes are designed with sport in mind, so they do not usually have luggage carriers or mudguards like touring cycles, as these would make them heavier and slower. They have very low gears so that the cyclist can climb steep inclines, and high gears to make it easier to descend.

Off-road cycling requires more upper body strength and greater balance than road cycling, but the rewards are a traffic-free environment and access to places that are unattainable by car.

A good way to start off-road riding is to put the bike in the car and take it to a place with some fairly level off-road trails. Always check beforehand that you are not cycling on private or restricted land. When you start cycling off-road do not plan to cover the same distance that you would on roads as you will be travelling much slower for the same amount of effort.

Cycling tips

▶ *Always carry a basic tool kit, comprising tyre levers, puncture repair kit (adhesive, sandpaper and patches) and a spare inner tube, if possible.*

▶ *Make sure that your lights and reflectors are clean and working.*

▶ *Wear a good-quality smog mask in heavy traffic.*

Fact file
The modern pedal bicycle was invented in Scotland in 1840 and has developed over 150 years into the many specialist varieties of racing, mountain and touring bikes popular today.

TYPES OF CYCLE

When choosing a bicycle, bear in mind the type of cycling you will want to do and the road conditions or terrain you will be facing. For example, a racing bicycle may not be suitable for riding along pot-holed country roads. Specialist bicycle shops offer information on choosing the most suitable bicycle.

ALL-PURPOSE TOURER
A sturdy bicycle, the traditional tourer is favoured for its versatility and reliability.

MOUNTAIN BIKE
Cycling over rugged terrain demands a strong, durable frame and sturdy tyres.

RACING BIKE
The light frame and drop handlebars make the racing bike ideal for speed. The position of the handlebars curves your body into a streamlined shape.

Dancing

Dancing is an enjoyable and sociable way of improving heart and lung fitness and of toning the body. There are hundreds of dance styles to choose from and many professional sports people include some form of dance in their training.

JAZZ AND TAP

Jazz and tap dancing are more energetic than many other forms of dance and are excellent for toning and strengthening the legs and feet. Once the basics are learned they can be combined in any way the dancer wishes. This means that you can tailor your physical and aerobic work-out to suit your needs.

Getting started

It is almost impossible to learn these dances without joining a class. Once you have mastered the basics, you

> Jazz and tap dancing aid all-round fitness although some may find them physically very demanding. Many of the steps take time to learn and can require natural ability.

can choose whether to remain in the class environment or not. Jazz and tap are not overly social forms of dance, however, and it may be difficult to find fellow dancers outside a class. Many classes will enter competitions and put on special performances to allow their members to show off their skills.

LINE DANCING

Line dancing originated in the mid-western and southern states of the USA and has quickly become one of the most popular forms of contemporary dancing. You don't need a partner for line dancing because, as its name suggests, the dances are performed in grid lines of equal rows, or lines, of dancers.

Line dancing is a very sociable activity because you are dancing the same dance at the same time with dozens of people rather than alone or in a couple. Most line dances have simple step patterns that are easy to learn and are not too physically taxing. Once you have mastered the basic steps you will soon be able to line dance to almost any country song you hear.

Physically, line dancing has a similar effect to performing a low-impact aerobics class, making it a

good form of cardiovascular exercise. It consists mostly of step work – indeed, the hands are often secured by keeping the thumbs in the

LINE DANCING
Fun and highly sociable, line dancing has become an extremely popular dance form with all age groups.

> Line dancing is inexpensive, easy to learn and highly sociable. It offers gentle aerobic exercise without being too demanding, but it will not provide all-round physical fitness.

pockets – so line dancing is likely to be of most benefit to the lower body. Therefore, for all-round fitness you may need to find an additional activity that works the upper body.

Getting started

It is easiest to begin line dancing by enrolling in a class or by joining in at a country and western venue. Because of the growing popularity of line dancing, most towns will have a venue that offers lessons or holds dancing evenings and will welcome newcomers. You can practise the dances alone or with a partner, but the real enjoyment comes from dancing in step with a large group.

BALLROOM

Ballroom dancing is a thorough way to exercise and helps to develop muscle coordination and good posture. In the main, ballroom is made up of two disciplines, Modern and Latin, and can range from fast, energetic dancing, to slower, graceful styles. The basics are fairly easy to learn as all dances are based on simple walking steps set to rhythm.

An evening spent ballroom dancing, particularly at a class, provides a complete exercise session with warm-up and cool-down routines and, as the dance progresses, a full aerobic work-out.

Dancing greatly improves suppleness and stamina, especially in the faster dances such as the jive or foxtrot. For a beginner, however, the exercise can be mostly anaerobic, as the emphasis is placed on position and posture. As you become more familiar with the dances you can concentrate more on the fitness elements of dance. Sports involving fluid movements such as cycling and swimming combine well with dance.

Getting started

Ballroom dance classes are held in village and community halls, and private dance studios, and there are social events such as tea dances that include some tuition. You can learn as one of a group or opt for one-to-one instruction. Most classes welcome new dancers of every level, but it may be worthwhile checking that the class will be of benefit to you, depending on your level of experience. Individual instruction is more expensive but enables you to learn the basics more quickly.

Many people enjoy the chance to dress up that ballroom dancing affords but casual clothes are acceptable at most dance schools. The most suitable are loose trousers for men and a flowing skirt for women. Ballroom dancing provides an exercise routine for people of all ages and fitness levels.

> Ballroom dancing requires commitment to learn the steps and may take many years to master. It provides all-round exercise, relaxation, and a strong social element.

Preparation and safety

Dance shoes are lighter and more flexible than ordinary shoes, with brushed suede soles and non-skid heels for a good grip. You can adapt ordinary shoes by fitting special stick-on soles.

DANCING FEET
When dancing, it is important to wear shoes that are well-fitting, comfortable and will not slip or slide beneath you.

Dancing tips

► *Wear loose, comfortable clothing that does not restrict your movements.*

► *Warm up beforehand and cool down and stretch thoroughly afterwards.*

► *Move your legs freely from the hips and keep a fluid action in the knees.*

► *Don't forget to use your arms, hands, body and head too.*

Fact file
Ballroom dancing requires special 'strict tempo' music only played by dance bands. For example, the tango and samba are danced in 2/4 time, the waltz is in 3/4 time and the foxtrot, jive and quickstep are in 4/4 time.

OTHER DANCE

There are many types of popular dance on offer. Classes for specialised forms of dance, from salsa, flamenco and lambada to disco dancing, ceroc and even morris dancing can be found in most areas. These are all excellent ways of improving coordination and strength and for building up cardiovascular fitness. Most classes cater for dancers at all levels but don't underestimate the demands of dance; make sure you warm up well before a dance session and stretch before and after. Some more advanced dance classes incorporate ballet training to improve suppleness, posture and muscular strength.

Team Sports

Team sports are best for those who enjoy the camaraderie of a closely knit group of like-minded sports people. They are also good for people who feel they need the encouragement and support of other team members to motivate them to keep fit.

RUGBY

There are two main forms of rugby, rugby union and rugby league. Both involve running, passing the ball and tackling. Rugby union includes more set-piece moves, such as scrums, rucks, mauls and lineouts, which make the game more tactical and less flowing in nature. Rugby league has simpler rules with fewer set pieces so that running and passing represent a larger proportion of the game and there are fewer stoppages.

Getting started
Many people play rugby at school or college and then lose touch with the game when they leave. Getting back into the sport can be difficult because you will have to prepare yourself physically for the game and practise the skills required. For these reasons it is necessary to start by joining an established rugby club. Rugby was traditionally a male-only sport, but today there are many women's rugby teams. Rugby is intensely physical, demanding a high degree of upper body strength. It requires speed and agility for sprinting and quick directional changes, coupled with strength in the legs, arms, and shoulders for tackling and scrums.

> Rugby is ideal for those who like competition and camaraderie and don't mind rough physical contact. For optimum enjoyment, and safety, you need good stamina and strength.

Touch football
This was developed to avoid the extreme physical contact of traditional rugby and is growing in popularity, particularly with children and women's teams. Instead of tackling, as in traditional rugby, players catch and touch the opposition in order to win the ball.

Rugby tips

▶ *Resistance training either with weights or utilising body weight is very important to build both strength and muscle bulk.*

▶ *A running-based aerobic training programme will help to facilitate recovery and delay fatigue.*

Fact file
Rugby was invented at Rugby school in 1823 during a football match when pupil William Webb Ellis picked up the ball and ran with it.

THE DEMANDS OF TEAM BALL GAMES

Team ball games are mainly multiple sprint sports, where the individual is alternately sprinting, jogging, walking or standing still. The muscular demands of these actions are interspersed with the power and coordination required to catch, strike, throw or kick the ball. Depending on which game is being played, your position on the field and the level to which the game is played, varying degrees of fitness and different combinations of the components of fitness (see page 52) are needed. Most clubs cater for a range of skill and fitness levels by having several teams of different standards.

FOOTBALL

Soccer can be played outdoors on a football pitch with 11 players per team, on a smaller indoor court with five or six players on each side, or as an informal kick-around in the local park. The fitness demands depend on the level of playing and the position of the player within the team.

Getting started

Soccer can be enjoyed by people of all levels of skill, but it is best to play with footballers of similar ability. One way is to encourage friends to join you for sessions at the local sports ground or any suitable open area. You can also set up a company team and play other firms in your area. The basic skills of football are relatively easy to learn and quickly improve with practice.

Eleven-a-side soccer played on a full-sized pitch involves intermittent bouts of activity, with plenty of rest

breaks between sprints. Five-a-side and six-a-side games are much more energetic and afford few opportunities to rest and so players need good stamina and muscular endurance if they are to last the full game.

A lack of stamina will reduce your playing ability as fatigue will set in earlier and affect your ball control and speed. The sudden changes in speed and direction involved in the game also put players at increased risk of joint or muscular strains and injury.

You can help to guard against this by doing regular strength and flexibility training. A good way to prepare for the physical stress of the game is to do regular circuit training sessions incorporating exercises that concentrate particularly on the running, jumping, twisting and turning elements of the game.

Football is an inexpensive game that can be enjoyed at all skill levels. It offers all-round exercise but, for safety, you should aim to get reasonably fit before playing.

Football tips

▶ *To reduce the risk of injury, especially when playing after a long break, players need to develop cardiovascular fitness with regular aerobic activities, and build muscle strength.*

▶ *Whether passing, shooting, heading or tackling, keep your eye on the ball until the moment you play it.*

Fact file
Modern football was organised in England in the early 19th century but a form of the game was played by the ancient Greeks, Chinese, Egyptians and Romans.

Preparation and safety

Football or rugby boots are best for playing on grass, while trainers are more suitable for playing indoors or on asphalt. Football is not usually considered a dangerous sport, although knee and ankle injuries are common. Regular fitness training can help reduce this risk. Rugby, however, is a potentially dangerous contact sport demanding high levels of strength, fitness and flexibility at all levels of the game. Before you start to play, train well to meet the physical demands of the sport.

PLAYING SAFE
Most players recommend some protective equipment, such as gum shields in rugby and shinpads in football.

FOOTBALL OPTIONS

If you would like to get involved in playing football but do not feel you have the particular skills needed to be a striker, midfield player or defender, all is not lost. There are two other important roles you could play. First, one of the most important positions in a team is that of goalkeeper and it demands the ability to catch, throw and kick the ball, as well as tackle. Second, joining in as referee can give you a full work-out as you run to keep track of the game, but will not demand the football skills of a team player.

GOAL!
The position of goalkeeper requires agility and hand to eye coordination but does not make the cardiovascular demands of the other positions.

BASKETBALL AND NETBALL

Basketball and netball are team games played on outdoor or indoor courts. Both are relatively simple and can be enjoyed by beginners with little initial training. The games involve frequent changes of speed and direction, bending and jumping. They require a good level of aerobic fitness as well as coordination, suppleness, balance and ball skills.

Each team defends a hoop, or basket, at one end of the court and scores by shooting the ball through the opposing team's hoop or basket at the other end. A basket is slightly lower than a hoop and has a backboard that you can bounce the ball off to score. One main difference between the two games lies in the way the ball is moved around the court. In netball, the ball is thrown from one player to another, with the person holding the ball staying stationary. In basketball, the players can throw or pass the ball to each other, but a player can also decide to run with the ball – so long as the ball is constantly bounced, or dribbled, as the player runs.

Getting started

Netball and basketball are played at most colleges and sports centres. There are few rules and so they are simple and quick to learn. You can join an existing team or it is easy to set up your own. You need relatively strong, supple joints to cope with the frequent changes of direction, jumping and twisting during a game.

A degree of strength in the arms and hands is also necessary for catching and throwing the ball. It is helpful to strengthen the muscles through regular resistance and stretching exercises, and to warm up well before playing a match.

Netball and basketball are cheap to play and, apart from the baskets, require only basic kit of sport shorts or skirt, a top and good trainers. Both are skilful games that aid all-round fitness.

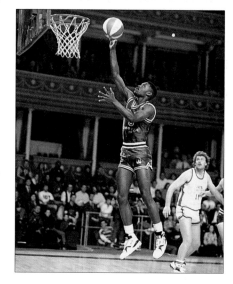

SPRING POWER
Scoring a basket or netball hoop requires leg strength to gain extra height and supple wrists and fingers for shooting.

It is also useful to spend time practising the techniques of the game, such as passing, shooting, and dribbling, as this will enhance both your skills and your physical fitness.

To get the most out of basketball and netball, you should build up a basic level of fitness before you begin to play. It is important to train for strength and stamina in order to play competitively. During either game, a player can run up to 5 kilometres (3 miles), usually in short, fast bursts of sprinting. Basketball demands more consistent running, but both sports require stamina and agility.

Netball and basketball tips

► *Keep your steps loose and springy and your knees slightly flexed and feet apart, especially as you land after jumping.*

► *In netball, only designated players can 'shoot' for the net, but in basketball any player can score.*

► *The main skill in basketball is dribbling, which can be practised alone.*

Fact file

Modern basketball was invented by James Naismith in 1891 in the USA but the Olmecs of Mexico played a similar game over 1200 years ago. Netball is one of the few women-only sports; it was developed from basketball, also in 1891 in the USA, as the women's version of the game.

VOLLEYBALL

Volleyball was developed in 1895 by William Morgan, an American physical education director, as a simple sport that people of all fitness levels could play. Originally it consisted of an inflated bladder that was 'batted' over a piece of rope. Today it is a popular six-a-side sport played indoors and out.

Getting started

Simple to set up, volleyball requires minimal equipment and can be played almost anywhere and with as few as two players. There are few rules to learn so beginners quickly pick up the basics. It is best to join a club in order to learn the correct skills, and to develop the teamwork and tactical play necessary.

BEACH VOLLEYBALL
Volleyball played on a sand court or on a beach has become extremely popular as dives are cushioned by the sand.

Volleyball is a simple and enjoyable game for all skill levels. It does little to enhance stamina, however, and needs a degree of suppleness and strength to avoid injury.

Preparation and safety

It is a common mistake to think that volleyball requires little preparation, but the stop-start nature of the game means there is a risk of joint and muscle injuries unless players do a thorough warm-up first. Learning the correct arm position to play the ball will help to protect against injury. It is important to use the right type of ball; avoid moulded rubber balls which can be painful on the arms and discourage beginners.

HOCKEY

Hockey can be played indoors or out with teams of five or 11 players. It is a fast game involving steady running interspersed with sudden bursts of speed and rapid changes of direction which strengthen the lower body muscles. The upper body muscles are strengthened by the constant use of the stick when dribbling, passing, tackling and shooting while the constant steady running provides a good cardiovascular work-out.

Getting started

Hockey is played by men's and women's teams. It needs agility, stamina and good hand-eye coordination. It is necessary to join a club and, like all team sports, hockey requires a high degree of commitment to attend regular training sessions as well as the matches. The first requirement is to develop stick skills and team playing, but proficiency soon comes with practice.

Hockey requires only a minimum level of equipment but regular training sessions are necessary to maintain fitness and skills if players are to get the most from the game.

Preparation and safety

Hockey is a fast game and, with the sticks and the small hard ball, it can be a dangerous one. Players recommend wearing shin guards and knuckle and hand protectors. Because the ball is not always at ground level many players wear gum shields. Goalkeepers are well padded with large leg pads, kickers – metal foot protection – gloves, body padding, headgear, a face mask and arm protectors. The stick should be free of splinters and rough edges, which might make play dangerous, and must never be lifted above shoulder height during play. Players are advised not to wear jewellery.

Fact file
A game like hockey was played in Greece around 2500 BC. Modern hockey dates from 1875 when the English Hockey Association was founded.

Hockey tips

▶ *To push the ball, hold your hands well apart along the stick and move the head of the stick in a steady sweeping movement.*

▶ *Never kick the ball – it is a foul in hockey except when the goalie does it. The only permissible way to move the ball is with the stick.*

CRICKET

Cricket differs from other games in the range of skills that players bring to a team. Spin and fast bowling, fielding and batting all require different forms of hand and eye coordination. The various positions also demand different types of fitness. When fielding, quick reactions and flexibility are important. Medium and fast bowlers are constantly walking, running and bowling the ball. As they tire their bowling will become less accurate so all-round muscular strength and endurance are required. Batsmen need upper body power to hit the ball with force and accuracy, interspersed with short spells of sprinting between the wickets, so they need strength and flexibility.

Getting started

Cricket is unusual in the potential length of matches lasting many hours and – at top class level – several days. Most amateur cricketers play 'limited over' matches in which a limit is set on the number of balls that each side faces. Games such as pairs and eight-a-side cricket,

which are designed to hone cricketing skills, can be shorter and also make exciting competitions for all ages. Versions of the game are played indoors at sports centres, mainly to provide off-season training. Cricket involves skills that are mainly acquired and honed through pre-match training. As cricket can involve long periods of inactivity interspersed with sudden bursts of high activity the chances of injury are great. The muscles and joints can quickly become cold – especially at the start and end of the season when the weather can be chilly – and so when a player has to burst into action the chances of sprains and strains increase.

To avoid injury and enjoy the sport to the full, players need to develop a degree of

Cricket is a skilled game that requires a major commitment if played competitively. To avoid injury and gain most benefit it is important to get fit before you play.

FAMILY CRICKET
The basic rules of cricket can be modified to create a variety of simple games that are suitable for all the family to play.

cardiovascular fitness, flexibility and stamina beforehand. Players should aim to maintain and improve their fitness in the off-season and between matches to reduce the risk of injury. In particular, cricketers should work on muscular strength and endurance by doing resistance training, and on cardiovascular endurance with aerobic activities such as jogging. They should also work on general flexibility and mobility of the lower back and shoulders.

As the playing season approaches, cricketers could include sprint drills in their programme. A specially tailored system of circuit training that includes exercises to strengthen the muscles and joints most at risk in cricket can be particularly beneficial.

Preparation and safety

Cricket involves a hard ball that is propelled at high speed, leading to a risk of serious injury, especially when batting or keeping wicket. Gloves, leg pads and, for men, a cricket box to protect the genitals, are vital; for serious players a helmet with temple guards is also advisable.

Regular players usually prefer to use their own bat and gloves

Cricket tips

▶ *When batting, stand with your feet a bat's width apart and your weight evenly distributed on both feet.*

▶ *Keep your eyes level and head fully turned towards the bowler; your shoulders should be in line and pointing down the wicket.*

▶ *Make use of the time between overs and any other delays in play to stretch your arm and leg muscles.*

Fact file

The first county cricket match was played in England in 1719, but a similar game was known as far back as the 16th century. Early batsmen defended either a tree stump or a wicket gate.

BASEBALL AND SOFTBALL

Baseball and softball are similar games that originated in the United States. The teams are made up of nine players, one side batting and the other fielding. The aim is to hit the ball, thrown by the pitcher, and run around a square made up of three bases and the home plate.

A run is scored when the batter reaches the home plate. This can be done in stages, but if the batter gets round in one hit, it is called a 'home run'.

Baseball is the official national game of the United States. It can be very fast, requiring physical stamina and fitness. It is best to build up fitness levels before taking up the sport. It is important to stretch and warm up the muscles before starting in order to reduce the risk of injury.

Softball originated as the indoor version of baseball. The field of play is smaller and the ball is larger and lighter, thus reducing the risk of injury. Softball is not as fast as baseball; the pitching action is underarm, rather than overarm, which reduces the speed of the ball.

Getting started

Baseball is expanding in the UK and there are leagues for all age groups. Softball is a very social sport; teams are often mixed, with both men and women taking part in the same game. Perhaps because of this softball is becoming increasingly popular in sports clubs and leisure centres around the country. To prepare for the game it will help to work on your upper body strength, to aid batting and throwing, and to do aerobic exercise and leg strengthening to aid running round the bases.

Baseball, softball and rounders are fast and highly sociable games that can aid strength and suppleness when combined with a regular all-round exercise regime.

STRIKE RATE
In baseball the batter has three chances, or 'strikes', to hit the ball, which is approaching at up to 90 mph.

Baseball tips

▶ *Hold the bat at shoulder height and keep your eye on the approaching ball. Shoulders should be level and in line with the ball.*

▶ *As you prepare for the strike, swing the upper body and transfer your weight to the front foot to add force to the stroke.*

Fact file
Baseball dates back at least to 1839 and has been played in the UK since 1874, following a tour by a US team.

ROUNDERS

Rounders is a similar game to softball, although played with a small hard ball and smaller bat, and is very popular in the UK, particularly among children. The game allows for both individual skills and teamwork. Rounders predates baseball by almost a century – the first reference to the game in England is in 1744.

Preparation and safety

The baseball is small and heavy and can cause injuries, so serious baseball players need protective clothing. All batters must wear helmets. The catcher stands behind the batter and catches missed balls, so must be protected with helmet, mask, chest and throat protectors, and leg guards.

The catcher's mit protects the catcher's hands from injury through impact with the ball, particularly at close quarters

Racquet Sports

Racquet sports are enjoyable and, if played at a reasonable skill level against an opponent of equal ability, provide excellent exercise. They tax all of the body's energy systems, requiring a combination of skill, stamina, strength and coordination.

TENNIS

Tennis is a physically active sport that is as versatile as it is fascinating. It can be played indoors or outdoors on grass, concrete, clay or artificial turf courts. The game is played as either singles or doubles but some may find doubles less taxing than singles. Tennis has always included a strong social element which attracts players who want to meet new friends and socialise with old ones.

Getting started
Many health clubs and sports clubs have both indoor and outdoor tennis courts and most clubs also run 'short tennis', played with softer balls and on a smaller court with a lower net. This is a good way for children to acquire the skills of the game. If you have never played before, just take it easy and concentrate on returning the ball over the net. Do not try too hard to place powerful volleys or smashes as these skills will only come through practice and experience. Start off playing for only half an hour and gradually build up to playing for longer and then, when you feel match-fit, you can play full games and sets. Tennis involves all the muscles and joints in the body so warming up beforehand is crucial as your body will be stretched vigorously during the game. Tennis rarely provides aerobic exercise, however, except at the highest levels as only skilled and evenly matched players can sustain rallies long enough to test their cardiovascular systems. So, for all-round fitness, do aerobic activities, such as brisk walking as well.

> An enjoyable and highly sociable game requiring minimal financial outlay. Optimum health benefits are experienced by evenly matched players with reasonable skills.

Preparation and safety

Suitable clothing for tennis, and all racquet sports, should allow unrestricted movement, particularly of the arms. Sweat-absorbent wristbands are recommended in warm weather to stop perspiration running into the palm.

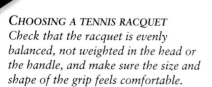

CHOOSING A TENNIS RACQUET
Check that the racquet is evenly balanced, not weighted in the head or the handle, and make sure the size and shape of the grip feels comfortable.

Tennis tips

▶ *Keep your wrist firm when striking the ball.*
▶ *Put your weight behind the racquet as you play the ball.*

Fact file
Real tennis, an early form of the game, dates back to the 16th century, but lawn tennis is credited to Major Walter Clopton Wingfield who introduced it at a party in Wales in 1873.

SQUASH AND RACQUETBALL

Squash was developed at Harrow school around 1850 and was originally played with a softer ball. It was derived from rackets, an earlier sport from the Middle Ages that is thought to be the precursor of most racquet-and-ball games. Squash is played in four-walled courts with sprung floors. When struck, the ball must first hit the front wall, but can then bounce off the four walls, which means that it is kept in play longer than is possible in most racquet sports. Because of this, squash usually provides a thorough cardiovascular work-out. The smallness of the court and the speed of the returns means that the game can be extremely fast.

Racquetball – another descendant of rackets – is similar to squash but is a more modern sport, having been developed in America in the 1950s from a combination of court handball and 'paddleball'. In racquetball, the ball can also be played off the ceiling as well as the walls. Racquetball can be played by two players, four players, or three players (cut-throat).

Getting started
Both games are played in specially designed courts that can be found at most leisure centres and health clubs. It is advisable to play a little to see if the game is for you before buying equipment – many courts have racquets for hire if you can't borrow one. The different coloured spots on squash balls denote their speed and so determine the degree of difficulty – the slower the ball the harder the game. Both sports are very demanding and should only be played by people with good stamina.

Squash and racquetball are sociable games requiring minimal financial outlay. They are physically demanding games and so are only suitable for the very fit.

THE COURT
The lines around the walls of a squash court denote the areas into which the ball can be hit and remain in play.

BADMINTON

Badminton is played indoors on a court with a high net. The players use a racquet to hit a shuttlecock, traditionally made of cork and feathers, which must not touch the ground during play. The design of a shuttlecock keeps it in the air longer than would be the case with a ball. This ensures that, while the most skilled players are extremely fast, it is possible for less skilled players and those just taking up the sport to have an enjoyable and energetic game.

Getting started
Badminton is a very versatile game that can be played in school and church halls as well as sports centres and health clubs. It can even be played in the garden on a calm day. Badminton is usually played with two or four players on the court, although it is possible to play with three. It can be played at virtually any pace from a leisurely knockabout to a fiercely competitive and frenetic speed. For this reason badminton is an ideal game for those who have been inactive for a long time and are now planning to build up their fitness levels, as well as those looking for more energetic exercise.

Badminton is an enjoyable and sociable game suitable for all ages, abilities and fitness levels. It offers an all-round work-out – even for beginners to the game.

Badminton tips

▶ *Stand on the balls of the feet with knees slightly bent to create a 'springy' stance.*

▶ *To avoid leaving large gaps, always return to a central position on the court between strokes.*

Fact file
Modern badminton was developed at Badminton House in the 1800s, but a similar game was played in China 2000 years ago.

Eastern Exercise

As well as enhancing your physical capabilities, Eastern exercises have an important spiritual dimension which, for those who wholeheartedly embrace the underlying philosophy, may alter the way they live their lives.

YOGA

Yoga was developed by the ancient sages of India and is the oldest system of personal development encompassing body, mind and spirit, with origins that can be traced back more than 5000 years. Today yoga is mainly practised for general health benefits, both preventative and curative. There are many types of yoga, but Hatha yoga is the most common form practised in the West. It includes exercises involving special body positions, or *asanas*, controlled breathing techniques and meditation.

Eastern yogis, or teachers, consider Hatha yoga to be only one aspect of attaining enlightenment. According to their teachings, care of the body is less important than spiritual awareness, as the body is mortal whereas the soul is immortal. It is not essential, however, to accept the philosophy of yoga to experience many of its benefits. Devotees believe the integrated approach of mind-and-body control can enhance physical and mental health and help practitioners to achieve mental peace and tranquillity.

> Yoga is suitable for people of all ages and fitness levels and has many therapeutic benefits as well as aiding suppleness, muscular endurance and relaxation.

Getting started

Yoga develops flexibility and muscular endurance and includes techniques to relieve mental states such as anxiety, depression and stress, and some physical disorders.

Technique is very important and so it is advisable to find a qualified teacher – perhaps by personal recommendation. For a yoga class, wear loose, comfortable clothing, and bare feet. A mat, or folded blanket is useful for some exercises.

Yoga tips

▶ *Never force your limbs or muscles into any position. The flexibility required for the more advanced poses will come with practice.*

▶ *Try to consider yoga a complete exercise and concentrate on breathing and relaxation as you practise the positions.*

Fact file

The word yoga comes from the Sanskrit Yug meaning union (with the Divine). It refers to the union of mind, body and breath.

Preparation and safety

There are some terms used in yoga to describe aspects of Eastern philosophy that it may be useful to know before you begin. Asanas are body positions in which one remains steady and comfortable, both physically and mentally, and which help the muscles to relax and also improve the circulation. Pranayama is the control and direction of vital energy by steady breathing. This increases the energy (prana) in the body, leading to good health. Meditation is a way of achieving inner peace by focusing the mind on an object such as a candle or photograph, or on a mental image of a favourite location. Some people also play a tape of music or natural sounds to help them, or chant a mantra – a phrase or sound that is constantly repeated.

T'AI CHI

T'ai chi chuan, more often referred to as t'ai chi, was developed from the Taoist study known as *chi kung* meaning 'Excellence of Energy'. Chi kung was dedicated to physical health and spiritual growth and evolved from a self-defence fighting system, and a healing art used by ancient Chinese monks. In Taoism, all things are a mix of two forces: *yin*, representing gentle, submissive, feminine qualities, and *yang*, denoting firm, active masculine aspects. T'ai chi exercises embody the two forces.

T'ai chi is now practised in China and elsewhere in the world for its numerous health and psychological benefits. In China, and increasingly in the West, the physical side of t'ai chi is demonstrated by the slow, graceful movements of practitioners in public parks, often early in the morning. This is the *taji* or 'form'. It is a series of coordinated exercises, derived from the actions of animals, flowing together so as to become one continuous movement. They are said to increase the body's range of movement, correct balance and posture, aid relaxation and reduce stress. The exercises are coordinated with the breathing to encourage *chi*, the body's energy, to flow freely through the energy pathways or 'meridians' in the body.

Initially, t'ai chi will lead to purely physical changes, but in time it is thought to aid mental, emotional and spiritual development as well.

Getting started

T'ai chi cannot be self taught so the first step must be to find a fully qualified teacher and enrol in a series of classes. Most libraries and sports centres will have details of t'ai chi classes held in their area. It is not necessary to prepare yourself physically before enrolling in t'ai chi classes as the basic exercises are slow, graceful and undemanding. Many people take up t'ai chi to help alleviate a long-standing health

GROUP EXERCISE
Practising t'ai chi in large groups in open parks and spaces is a regular morning ritual for many Chinese people.

problem such as back pain, and it is a good idea to tell the teacher in advance if you have a particular physical condition that needs to be taken into account. The teacher can then suggest an exercise programme that may benefit you.

T'ai chi tips

▶ *Correct posture is vital in t'ai chi – the stance should be relaxed and not static or stiff so that movements are free flowing.*

▶ *Ensure your weight is evenly balanced over your feet and keep your knees slightly flexed.*

T'ai chi aids suppleness and muscular strength and is believed to have many therapeutic benefits. It is particularly beneficial for those who have been inactive for a long period.

THE T'AI CHI HAND

T'ai chi focuses on finding a midpoint where balance and harmony are reached. As such the position of the hands during movements is very important.

HARSH HAND
If the hand is too stiff and tense it will make movements awkward and limit the flow.

WEAK HAND
If the hand is too lifeless and limp it will drag and detract from the movements.

CORRECT POSITION
The ideal t'ai chi hand is relaxed and open and moves through the air easily and gracefully.

Fact file

T'ai chi was devised by a Taoist monk, Chang San Feng, who based his first exercise on a fight he observed between a snake and a crane.

JUDO

Judo has its roots in the fighting system of feudal Japan. It developed from the art of ju-jitsu, the original form of hand-to-hand combat practised by the Samurai, which enabled them to carry on fighting even when deprived of their weapon. Judo is a wrestling sport which attempts to turn an attacker's force to one's own advantage. Skill, technique and timing, rather than brute strength, are the essential ingredients for success in judo.

Judo teaches flexibility, balance and the efficient use of leverage and movement in the performance and execution of its throws, grappling techniques and submission holds.

As a competitive sport judo offers the opportunity to compete at all skill levels, from club to national tournaments, right up to the Olympic Games, where it was first

included in 1964. The competitors are separated into weight divisions for men and women, boys and girls. Many people over 60 years of age enjoy the sport, as well as young children and some disabled people.

Getting started

To learn judo you must find a recognised instructor and join a reputable club or class. Most libraries and sports centres will have details of clubs in their area. During your first lesson you will probably be instructed on some of the history of judo and given an explanation of the modern-day grading system. You will then be shown some stretching exercises before you begin. Next, your instructor will introduce you to the throwing, grappling and strangleholds that make up the sport.

Judo helps to boost confidence and enhances a sense of self-reliance, as well as aiding strength and flexibility. For all-round fitness it must be combined with other exercises.

BREAKFALL
The first element of judo you will be taught is the breakfall – how to land safely after being thrown. It is the most important aspect of judo and ensures that you will not be injured in a bout.

Preparation and safety

When you begin judo you must expect to rank at the bottom of the group. How well and quickly you progress is up to you. Judo created the system of ranks, now used in most other martial arts, that recognise a person's degree of knowledge, ability, and leadership. There are separate ranks for juniors (under 17 years of age) and seniors. Judo ranks are identified by seven coloured belts, and then a further ten degrees of advanced grades for black belts.

White belt indicates a novice

Yellow belt denotes end of initial training

Green and **red** belts show advanced skills

Blue and **brown** belts are highly accomplished

Black belts are masters of the art of judo

Judo tips

▶ *As you learn judo you will also learn to respect your teachers and your opponents.*

▶ *It is important to remember that clubs teach judo solely as a sport, not as a means for aggression.*

Fact file

Translated from the Japanese, judo means 'gentle way'. Judo students learn how to give way, rather than use force, to overcome an opponent.

KARATE

The word *karate* is from the Japanese meaning 'empty hand'. It is a martial art dating back more than 1000 years and was first used by oriental monks and Chinese peasants as a defence method against armed bandits. Today karate is still chiefly associated with Japan, but it was introduced to the West via the United States after World War II.

Karate involves focusing blows from the feet and hands in coordination with special breathing techniques. The blows can be directed against an opponent or inanimate objects, such as wooden blocks. Taught as a self-defence skill, a competitive sport and a free-style exercise, it is said to emphasise self-discipline, a positive attitude and high moral purpose as students of karate are taught to respect both the fighting art and its participants, who may be any age or gender. Unlike judo, karate stresses techniques for striking, with kicks and punches that can be fatal, rather than wrestling or throwing an opponent. Karate trains the body and the mind together. Speed, strength and technique, along with concentration and awareness, are vital to skilful karate.

Getting started

Joining a club can be difficult for beginners with no prior knowledge of what to look out for. As a first step, get a list of all the recognised clubs in your area which have fully qualified instructors who are members of the national governing body for karate. This is so that any grading you are awarded by the club is accepted by other national bodies.

Decide which style of karate you wish to undertake (see left) as some styles may be unsuitable for you. Visit the clubs and watch the instructors to see whether the teaching method and style being practised will suit you.

Once you have decided on a club, go along and try it out for a couple of sessions before handing over any membership fees or splashing out on a karate suit, just to make sure it is the right sport and style for you.

KARATE STYLES

Karate evolved in Japan from a Chinese martial art called kempo. As it spread throughout Japan it began to split into distinct styles, mainly owing to cultural differences. There is now a wide variety of karate styles to choose from. Some styles incorporate elements of Eastern philosophy, while others concentrate on the physical aspects. Some are also more aggressive than others. Kyokushinkai, for example, allows punches and kicks to be landed on the upper body during competition and even permits kicks to the head. This style also puts great store by the ability of exponents to break blocks of wood or stone. Goju, on the other hand, is a more gentle flowing style in which practitioners counter a hard blow with a soft deflection.

Karate enhances muscular endurance and strength and helps to develop self-discipline. However, training is rigorous and demanding and requires commitment and motivation.

What you will need

The most important piece of equipment will be your suit. Loose enough to move freely in, yet never baggy or misshapen, there is much ritual and history in the dressing and wearing of the suit.

Karate tips

▶ *To gain the most benefit from karate and to reduce the risk of injury, regular strength, endurance and flexibility exercises are necessary.*

▶ *The sudden, rapid and focused actions of karate depend on holding an easy, relaxed stance with knees flexed and the weight of body evenly balanced over the feet.*

Fact file

Traditionally, karate is taught using a series of techniques performed in sequence called katas. There are more than 50 katas to learn, all of which have been preserved from the ancient masters.

Other Sports

Many sports require special equipment to be hired or purchased and a special facility, such as a club, centre or open water. Your choice of sport, therefore, may be decided on grounds of cost and the availability of a suitable facility in your area.

BOWLS

Bowls is an ancient game that has been played in some form since at least 5000 BC. It is an easy game to pick up, but gets more rewarding as your skill level grows. If you are currently inactive, taking up lawn bowls will greatly increase your activity levels and will improve your strength, balance and coordination.

Getting started

Bowls is mainly played outdoors, although there are some indoor bowling greens as well. As there are many council-run greens in local parks, it is not necessary to join a bowling club straight away. If you enjoy the game you can go on to join a club and play competitively as well as socially.

Bowls tips

▶ *Hold the bowl with the fingers underneath and avoid gripping too tightly.*

▶ *Use your body to supply the impetus while your arm mainly guides the direction.*

▶ *Develop an easy, relaxed swing and follow through smoothly with the arm.*

Bowls is a sociable and undemanding sport that is enjoyed at all skill levels. It offers gentle, all-round exercise in the open air and is ideal for less active people.

TEN-PIN BOWLING
The indoor sport of ten-pin bowling has enjoyed widespread popularity since the 1960s. The aim is to knock down ten pins, or skittles, by bowling a ball along a wooden 'alley'.

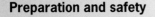

Preparation and safety

Before you begin a game, always have a thorough warm-up and include stretches for the hamstrings, thighs and lower back, as there is a lot of bending and controlled lunging involved.

Bowl – also known as a 'wood'

Target ball – called the 'jack'

USING THE BIAS
A bowl is designed to veer to one side near the end of a run so it can approach the jack from the left or right. Skilful players use this 'bias' to great effect.

GOLF

The growing popularity of golf may be due to the fact that it combines many different elements. It provides all-round exercise in the open air in pleasant surroundings, and there is a strong element of skill to the game. It affords social opportunities and can be played competitively, but can also be played as a solo sport.

Getting started

Even at a basic level golf requires quite a high financial commitment. For example, to get the most benefit from golf you will need lessons with a professional instructor in order to develop the basic skills – especially the grip and the swing.

You do not need to be a member of a private club to play as there are many municipal courses available. Even so, fees for use of the green and hire of golf clubs add to the expense. If you decide to join a private club and buy your own set of golf clubs, the sport can become very expensive. A moderate level of aerobic fitness is

ON THE RANGE
One of the best ways to develop the fitness and skills necessary for golf is to go out on a driving range and practise.

necessary to delay fatigue and to 'walk the course' at a pace that does not obstruct following players. To play golf proficiently, a player must develop the power and expertise to

> Golf provides all-round fitness benefits but demands commitment in terms of finance, time, training, practise and motivation in order to reach a reasonable standard.

drive a ball accurately and repeatedly over varied distances during a game. Power in the upper body, especially the trunk and shoulders, is necessary to drive the ball a reasonable distance, and muscular endurance is needed to keep repeating the shot.

As well as dynamic strength and power with which to hit the ball, the golfer needs to develop isometric (static) strength in order to fix a correct body position. At the end of a golf swing the club head is travelling at a great speed, so sufficient strength to slow the club down before damaging the shoulder joint is crucial, especially when a player is becoming tired.

A balanced programme of specific strength and flexibility will help with the development of power, and an aerobic endurance programme will help delay fatigue during a day's play and speed recovery after a game.

Walking is an appropriate activity for golf fitness; running, cycling, swimming and rowing would also be useful. Swimming may aid in the development of flexibility. A general strength training programme with free weights or fixed resistance machines, or circuit training of a general nature, may aid the golfer initially. A weight-training programme specific to golf may be useful in the longer term.

Preparation and safety

Golf can be played with just a few basic clubs. The steeper the angle of the club's head, the farther the ball will travel.

Wood – for long drives

Iron – for shorter drives

Sand wedge – for bunker shots

Putter – for shots on the green

Golf tips

▶ *To develop a good swing keep the arms, shoulders, back and hands relaxed and loose, and the legs, knees and feet flexed and springy.*

▶ *You will need flexibility and strength in the shoulders and trunk to create a smooth twisting action in the swing.*

Fact file
The birthplace of the modern game is St Andrews, Scotland, which has a course dating from 1754. However, it is thought that the Dutch played a game similar to golf, called kolf, around 1300.

ICE SKATING

Ice skating is popular both as a sport and as a recreational pastime. Each individual can make the sport as exciting and challenging as he or she wishes, either by enjoying gentle exercise, or by practising speed skating, or learning the more advanced jumps and dances.

Getting started

Although ice rinks are not as plentiful as sports centres, most people will find they have a rink within a reasonable distance, and that most rinks have coaches who are able to help with the first steps in learning to skate.

The techniques and training necessary for ice skating are good for developing strength in the leg and gluteal muscles. The sport also develops a keen sense of balance and improves posture. Cycling, running or rowing combined with resistance

SKATING LESSONS
You can often find professional coaches who are affiliated with a particular ice rink and will offer individual or small group tuition.

training are excellent methods of preparing for skating as they strengthen the muscles and increase stamina, which is required for all forms of skating. Sprinting practice is useful for ice dance and figure skating, while endurance training is

> Ice skating is an enjoyable and sociable sport that requires little financial outlay. It provides good cardiovascular exercise and is ideal for strengthening the leg muscles.

more useful for speed skating. Ice dancing and figure skating would also benefit from dance training, which enhances suppleness and ease of movement. The only specialised equipment required is well-fitting skates. Most rinks hire out skates so you can decide if you like the sport before splashing out on your own. You don't have to accept the first pair of skates the rink offers you. If they are at all uncomfortable or otherwise unacceptable, exchange them. Ice skates should fit very snugly, so the foot has very little room to move within the boot.

Skating on an ice rink

There are certain rules to follow when rink skating. Always skate anticlockwise around the edge of the rink – unless otherwise directed by a steward or coach – and be aware of other skaters. It is advisable to wear gloves at all times and for children under five years to wear some form of head protection – either a woollen hat or an ice hockey helmet are ideal.

Fact file
There have been some recent changes in the world of skating, one of which was the introduction of a new discipline that originated in Canada called precision skating. This involves groups of 12 to 24 people skating in formation to music – like synchronised swimming on ice.

Skating tips

▶ *If you have difficulty getting started, begin by simply walking on the ice in your skates then gradually begin to glide with each step.*

▶ *Keep your arms still and out to the sides. This may feel unusual but moving your arms will cause you to lose balance.*

▶ *When your weight is on one foot only, make sure the knee of that leg is bent.*

▶ *Get up from a fall by turning onto hands and knees before standing.*

Preparation and safety

The essential piece of equipment is a snug-fitting pair of ice skates. The skates should support your ankle and instep and should neither slip around your foot nor pinch it. The blades should be clean and the edges sharp. Bear in mind that an ice skate blade can be very sharp, so protect your fingers when learning to skate and wear thick warm clothing – the beginner tends to spend quite some time sitting on the ice! To test your blades for sharpness run your fingernail along each edge. If the blades scrape a little of your nail away they have an edge; if not they need sharpening.

You should not take loose articles of clothing, such as scarves, or other droppable items, such as drinks or personal stereos onto the ice. Anything you drop may become a hazard to other skaters.

Skating on open ice

In the British Isles it is very dangerous to skate on areas of natural ice, such as frozen lakes or rivers, because the ice is rarely solid enough to support a skater's weight and can give way without warning. Abroad, never skate on ice when you are uncertain of its thickness or what lies beneath it. Static ice often covers fast-flowing currents.

ICE HOCKEY

Ice hockey is a highly skilful and extremely popular game that combines the strength and balance of the skater with the hand-eye coordination of the hockey player. The techniques and training necessary for ice skating require powerful lower body muscles plus good upper body strength for stick work. There is a high initial financial outlay required because of the cost of the special ice hockey boots, stick and protective gear.

ICE HOCKEY
The protective clothing worn by ice hockey players gives an indication of the physical nature of the sport.

ROLLER SKATING

Roller skating is an adaptation of ice skating that has become popular worldwide and is an all-year-round, accessible and fun way to exercise. Roller skating really can be a sport for all the family and the majority of skates are reasonably priced. Most people take up roller skating informally, often as children who then 'grow out' of the sport.

Roller skating can be carried out virtually anywhere that is away from traffic and does not put pedestrians at risk. The skills necessary to take the first steps are easy to master and

with confidence and practice skating ability increases quickly. Just as in ice skating, however, there is scope for serious devotees to get involved in competitive events.

Roller skating is an excellent sport for developing balance, stamina, and strength in the leg and gluteal muscles. Dancing, cycling and weight training in a gym can help to build up the fitness and strength you will need to get the most out of the sport.

Roller blades, the latest innovation in roller skating, were invented as a summer training device for ice hockey players. They are more difficult to master because the wheels are in a line, mimicking the blades of ice skates, rather than positioned at the four corners of the skate. They were originally designed with men's feet in mind, but it is now possible to buy skates or inserts that are designed for women's feet.

Getting started

The four main types of competition in roller skating are artistic skating, speed skating, roller-skate hockey, and roller derby – a speed-skating event staged on a banked track – but most people take up roller skating informally as a fun and accessible way of exercising.

Apart from the purchase of roller skates and a modicum of protective gear there is little expense involved and the sport offers good all-round cardiovascular and strength exercise.

Roller skates should not be as tight-fitting as ice skates, but they should be snug. It is strongly recommended that you wear protective padding on your knees and elbows when roller skating and also wear a protective helmet – especially if you are skating on concrete or other hard surfaces.

Preparation and safety

Roller blades should support your ankle and instep, just like ice skates, and should neither slip nor pinch.

IN LINE SKATES
Your wheels should be clean and free of anything that may affect their movement.

ROLLER BLADING
The popularity of roller blading as a sport in its own right has grown immensely in recent years and the skaters' skills and trick manoeuvres are growing ever more incredible.

SKIING

Skiing is an exhilarating sport but also physically very demanding – it requires a high level of aerobic fitness and plenty of strength in the legs and upper body. Skiing is also very expensive so to make the most of your time on the slopes it is sensible to prepare yourself physically in advance.

Getting started

Before going on a skiing holiday – or even taking skiing lessons at a dry ski slope – it is advisable to work on strength, endurance and flexibility. The best physical preparation for skiing is to use an indoor ski simulator machine, which is designed to strengthen all the muscles you use when skiing. Alternatively, you can plan your own tailor-made work-out to achieve a similar effect. The crouched stance that is used in skiing can be very demanding on the thigh muscles so you should ensure your work-out pays particular attention to this area of the body. Step training, cycling or jogging will improve your strength and endurance, particularly in the large muscles of the legs.

As a beginner, you will also need to develop your upper body strength – first-time skiers tend to fall over a lot so they are constantly pushing themselves back up to a standing position.

Skiing on holiday

Skiing is the most popular winter holiday activity but people often set off without adequate preparation. There are many aspects of skiing that can prove far more demanding than you might expect. Being unprepared means you will quickly become exhausted and increase your risk of injury. Most resorts cater for novices, and instructors will ensure that you learn all you need to enjoy the sport in safety. Follow your instructor's advice precisely and don't take unnecessary risks. In particular, avoid pistes (ski slopes) that are beyond your level of skiing ability.

For most UK citizens, skiing can only be an occasional holiday activity. However, skiing is enjoyable and highly sociable and offers a good incentive to get fit beforehand.

DRY SKI SLOPES
Practising on dry ski slopes before you venture onto snow-covered ones can help you to master the basics without having to devote the first part of your holiday to learning how to stand and fall safely.

Skiing tips

▶ *Keep your feet hip-width apart and press your weight down on the whole length of both feet to help you keep balanced.*

  ▶ *Keep your knees slightly bent and steer with your feet, not with your shoulders.*

Preparation and safety

Ski equipment is expensive, so most people hire their equipment. Make sure the ski boots you use fit well and give good ankle support while still allowing normal bending and straightening. At mountain altitudes, more ultraviolet rays from the sun reach you than at sea level so always use a good quality sun block – factor 15 is the minimum, or a higher number if you are sensitive to sunlight.

SUN PROTECTION
In addition to protecting yourself from the cold you must also shield your eyes and skin from the sun. Wear protective goggles and apply sun block to exposed skin. A mixture of the sun and wind may chap your lips so lip salve is also recommended.

Fact file
The word 'ski' comes from the Norwegian for snow shoe. Earliest references to skiing date back to 2500 BC.

CHAPTER 7

EXERCISE AT HOME AND IN THE OFFICE

A major problem that many people face when trying to become more active is how to incorporate regular exercise sessions into a daily life that is already too busy. With a little planning and change in habits, however, you can turn your home and even your office into a highly effective fitness centre.

SETTING UP A HOME GYM

Although budget and available space are major considerations, the most important factor to consider when setting up a home gym is assessing exactly what it is you want and need from it.

If you want to see positive results from a physical exercise programme, it is essential to keep it going. The convenience of having your own gym at home may mean you are more likely to keep to your fitness regime and not become demotivated. Setting up your own home gym can be great fun and very rewarding.

Once the initial investment has been made there are no further costs, unlike attending a health club which requires membership fees and travel expenses. A home gym needn't break the bank, however – it is possible to utilise many household items (see opposite).

Lack of time is often used as an excuse not to exercise. With a home gym no time is wasted travelling and its use is not restricted to certain hours of the day. Exercising at home also has the advantage of privacy and you can listen to your own choice of music.

A home gym also offers an ideal way to encourage your family to take more exercise. As well as improving the health and fitness of the whole family, by creating the opportunity to exercise together you help to strengthen the family bond. Exercise equipment that is designed to improve aerobic, or cardiovascular, fitness is particularly beneficial for older people. Ensure that it is on the least strenuous setting when used for the first time and increase the difficulty level only very gradually once fitness levels have clearly improved. Equipment such as weights that are mainly designed to improve strength may be unsuitable for those with high blood pressure who should use them only after seeking their doctor's advice.

Children should not attempt to use weights before their early teens because their bones are soft and easily damaged. Most exercise machines will be unsuitable for young children to use but they can enjoy using simple pieces of gym equipment, such as skipping ropes and trampets, or mini trampolines. Aim to keep the exercise sessions short as a small child's attention span is limited. The focus needs to be on physical play so that the exercise is fun for the child, for example, by playing chase in the garden or by including simple aerobic actions in a game such as 'Simon Says' that the child can try to mimic.

Older children can be encouraged to use more sophisticated pieces of gym equipment, if you have them, but you must make sure that they know how to use them properly and are supervised at all times.

FACTORS TO CONSIDER
A home gym does not have to involve the purchase of complicated and expensive machinery. For some people clearing a space on the living room floor, putting on an aerobic workout video and exercising will be enough to increase their levels of

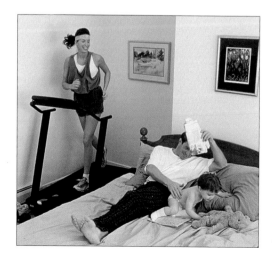

FAMILY FITNESS
Holding regular exercise sessions in your own home will encourage the whole family to get the fitness habit.

A Simple Home Gym Kit

You don't need to spend a fortune on exercise machines in order to keep fit in the comfort of your own home. Some simple items that can be bought quite cheaply make excellent fitness aids and there are everyday household objects that can also be used as pieces of home exercise equipment.

Tins of food
Standard sized food tins can double as dumbbells for exercises such as curls, lateral raises and dumbbell presses.

Do...develop a smooth rhythmical movement

Do...stand straight with your feet a shoulder-width apart

Skipping rope
Skipping provides excellent aerobic exercise. You can buy a skipping rope, or use a length of old washing line. Start with sets of 20–30 skips at a time and rest for a minute between sets. As you progress, build up to 60–100 skips a minute for up to 20 minutes.

Do...wear cushioned trainers

Don't...skip on hard surfaces

Do...ensure your ceiling is high enough to use the trampet safely

Do...make sure the trampet legs are locked in place before you start

Do...use a sturdy table

Do...keep your back straight

Don't...lock your knees

Trampet
A trampet can enhance aerobic fitness and also provide low-impact weight-bearing exercise to strengthen muscles and bones.

Shopping bag
A bag weighted with a standard bag of sugar can be used to tone and strengthen the leg muscles.

Stairs
Using your own stairs regularly provides good aerobic and weight-bearing exercise. Use the bottom stair for aerobic step programmes. Alternatively, use a sturdy wooden box or bench.

HERBY CHEESE & ONION POTATO BREAD

This delicious cheese, onion and potato-filled loaf is full of complex carbohydrates for energy. Enjoy a piece before your next exercise session to keep you fuelled.

425 ml (¾ pint) vegetable stock, lukewarm
25 g (1 oz) parmesan, grated
2 tbsp olive oil
2 tbsp honey
1 tbsp chopped parsley
1 tbsp chopped chives
2 tbsp active dry yeast
300 g (11 oz) mashed potato
400 g (14 oz) strong plain white flour
400 g (14 oz) strong wholemeal flour
½ tsp salt
½ onion, grated

■ In a large bowl, mix the stock, parmesan, oil, honey, parsley and chives, then gently stir in the yeast. Stir in the mashed potato. Set aside for 10 minutes until the mixture foams.

■ In another large bowl, mix the flours and salt. Gradually stir 550 g (20 oz) of the flours and the grated onion into the potato mixture to form a dough.

■ Turn the dough onto a floured surface and knead in remaining flour. Knead for 10 minutes or until elastic in consistency.

■ Lightly grease the bowl with olive oil. Add the dough, coating it with oil on all sides. Allow to rise in a warm, draught-free place for 30–40 minutes, or until doubled in size.

■ Punch the dough back down into the bowl and knead for 1 minute. Separate the dough into halves and shape into two loaves.

■ Lightly grease two 21 × 11 cm (8½ × 4½ in) loaf tins. Add the dough, cover and allow to rise in a warm place for 30 minutes or until twice the size.

■ Bake at 180°C/350°F/gas mark 4 for 30 minutes, or until the loaves sound hollow when tapped. Leave to cool on wire racks for 30 minutes.

Makes 2 loaves

fitness. However, you may feel the need for a more sophisticated home gym, either because you want a more comprehensive work-out, or to alleviate the monotony of doing the same exercise over and over again. Before you start buying equipment for your home gym it is important to consider what it is you want to achieve, how much you can afford to spend, and the amount of space you have available.

Deciding your fitness objectives

You should decide whether you just want to get aerobically fit, build up your strength, increase your flexibility, or do a mixture of all three. These factors will determine what kind of equipment you will need to buy. For example, if you want a machine that will give you a cardiovascular workout but do not want to do any resistance training, then a simple exercise bike or treadmill would meet your needs. If, however, you want to build your strength as well as get aerobically fit, then you will also need a set of weights or some resistance machinery.

Whatever your objectives, the most basic requirement of any home gym is a good quality exercise mat on which you can stretch-off and carry out floor exercises. A mat will cushion and reduce the stress of impact on your joints and it makes floor-work more comfortable.

Cost

Decide how much money you have at your disposal – there is no point planning a huge multigym if you only have a limited budget. Remember that your gym can start small and grow as your finances do. Obviously the more money you have the more comprehensive a gym you can have, but you can still pick up the necessary equipment cheaply to begin with by seeking the advice of professionals and shopping around.

It is important to know what type of equipment you are going to need to meet your exercise goals. Buying inappropriate equipment is costly and frustrating. To make the correct choice, start by reading up on what is available. If possible, test the various pieces of equipment and machinery at your local health club to see what suits you and will keep you motivated to exercise in the long term. Go into a sports shops and speak to trained sales assistants about your needs, and keep a look out for any special offers. Remember, if you don't like a piece of equipment at your health club, then you won't like it in your own home either.

Available space

Think about the space you have available – the inconvenience of elaborate setting-up procedures, such as moving heavy furniture, may tempt you to skip sessions. Make sure you have ample room to exercise in and that your space is well ventilated and free of electrical cables or any other appliances that might lead to injury while exercising. A full-length mirror can be useful for monitoring your technique and for motivation. Also, when planning your gym, take into account the height of your ceilings: some pieces of equipment, such as multigyms, can be quite tall. If the equipment is heavy, check that the floor or supporting walls are strong enough to take the weight.

Finally, check whether you have room to expand your gym as you become more proficient with the machinery you have and look to purchase new equipment. You could keep various pieces of gym equipment in different rooms, or in a cellar, garage or shed. Make sure any room you use can be kept warm and draught free, as a cold environment is likely to put you off exercising and increases the risk of injuries, such as strains and sprains.

STRENGTH TRAINING MACHINERY

If you want to increase your strength, power and endurance or build up your muscles, then you will benefit from devices such as an exercise bench, free weights (barbells and dumbbells) and/or fixed weight machinery, such as a multigym.

Exercise bench

An exercise bench is an invaluable addition to a home exercise set-up, particularly if it is adjustable. It is useful for weight training and can also be used for supporting abdominal exercises, tricep dips and push-ups.

Free weights

A basic set of free weights including a barbell and a pair of dumbbells is all you need for a resistance workout (see page 130).

A barbell is a hollow or solid steel bar about 1–2 metres (around 3-6 feet) in length. Pairs of weights, known as plates, weighing from as little as you like to as heavy as you can safely manage to lift, are then attached to the ends of the bar and held in place with collars.

Dumbbells are like short barbells, about 25–40 centimetres (10–16 inches) long. They can be one-piece and solid and come in sets of varying weights, or adjustable like

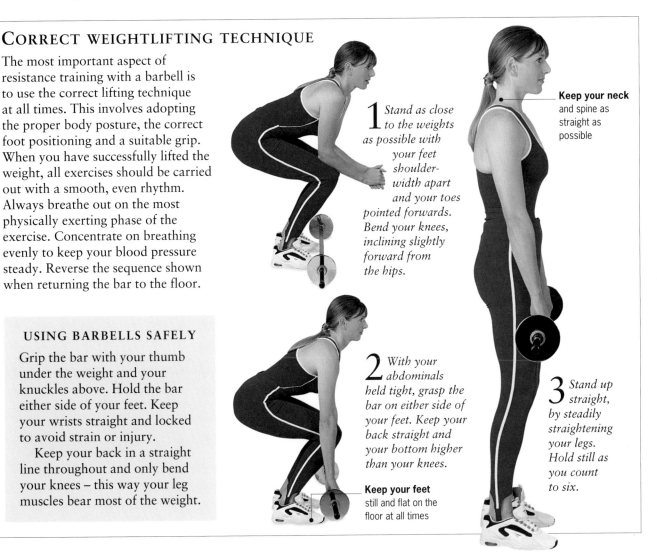

CORRECT WEIGHTLIFTING TECHNIQUE

The most important aspect of resistance training with a barbell is to use the correct lifting technique at all times. This involves adopting the proper body posture, the correct foot positioning and a suitable grip. When you have successfully lifted the weight, all exercises should be carried out with a smooth, even rhythm. Always breathe out on the most physically exerting phase of the exercise. Concentrate on breathing evenly to keep your blood pressure steady. Reverse the sequence shown when returning the bar to the floor.

USING BARBELLS SAFELY

Grip the bar with your thumb under the weight and your knuckles above. Hold the bar either side of your feet. Keep your wrists straight and locked to avoid strain or injury.

Keep your back in a straight line throughout and only bend your knees – this way your leg muscles bear most of the weight.

1 Stand as close to the weights as possible with your feet shoulder-width apart and your toes pointed forwards. Bend your knees, inclining slightly forward from the hips.

2 With your abdominals held tight, grasp the bar on either side of your feet. Keep your back straight and your bottom higher than your knees.

Keep your feet still and flat on the floor at all times

Keep your neck and spine as straight as possible

3 Stand up straight, by steadily straightening your legs. Hold still as you count to six.

WEIGHT SAFETY

Before you begin each weight-training session, follow these few tips for a safer work-out.

▶ *Make sure children and pets are out of the room while training. Always keep weights out of the reach of children.*

▶ *Remove fragile objects from your training area.*

▶ *Don't exercise on days when you are injured or feel unwell.*

▶ *Ensure that all collars or clips holding the weight plates in place are secure before lifting.*

▶ *Begin every training session with a thorough warm-up and finish with a cool-down and stretches (see page 70).*

CAUTION

People who suffer from high blood pressure or from back or joint problems should always consult their doctor before doing any weightlifting exercises. If your doctor deems it unsuitable, there are still many other toning exercises that you can do to stay fit and increase your strength.

barbells so that you can add plates to them to increase the weight. Start with weights that enable you to do the repetitions easily.

Free weights offer the best way of isolating individual muscles or muscle groups and working them in a controlled manner in order to increase muscle growth. Alternatively, by using lighter weights but more frequent repetitions, free weights can aid suppleness and improve muscle tone.

The disadvantage of free weights is that they require some degree of training to learn to control their movement safely and to make the target muscle perform the dominant share of the work. Without good control, the weight cannot be moved along the correct and safe path, and this can result in injury if excessive stress is placed on a joint or muscle too weak to cope.

Always seek expert tuition before using free weights for the first time to reduce the risk of accidental injuries and to avoid developing poor exercising techniques that can lead to long-term physical damage.

Fixed weight machinery

Machines with fixed weights, such as multi-gyms, perform the same job as free weights but allow you to lift heavier weights without the aid of a training partner and without having to change the plates for each exercise. They also combine lots of different exercises into a single piece of machinery which is safe and easy to use.

A good multigym will allow you to work all the major muscle groups via a system of pulleys attached to a central weight stack. By connecting various attachments and positioning the body in different ways you can effectively strengthen the muscles of the legs, arms and torso. When choosing a multigym, shop around for one that feels solid and fits your available space. Don't forget the height of your ceiling and the strength of your floor when calculating this.

BENEFITS OF DUMBBELLS

Dumbbells make ideal home fitness devices because of their great versatility, convenience and relatively low cost.

Their greatest asset is that they can easily accommodate each individual's physical strength and range of movement. They will need some initial training to use them safely and effectively, however.

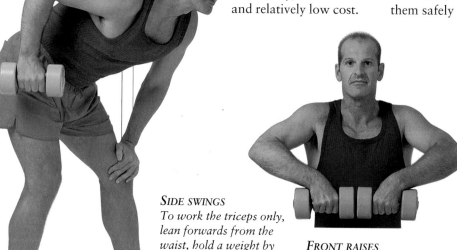

SIDE SWINGS
To work the triceps only, lean forwards from the waist, hold a weight by your side and swing the lower arm forwards and backwards.

FRONT RAISES
Slowly raise both weights to chest height to work the shoulder muscles.

CURLS
To strengthen your biceps and forearms, slowly raise one weight to your shoulder.

YOUR OWN HOME WORK-OUT

If you do not have the time or the inclination to attend an exercise course at a health club you can plan your own fitness programme and have a complete work-out at home.

The routines over the following pages are designed to be carried out in the home with inexpensive or little equipment necessary. Before you begin a home work-out, look carefully at the room in which you've chosen to exercise, making quite sure that it is safe and free of obstructions. Remove any loose rugs and mats and pull back the furniture. Take care to remove any electrical cables or flexes or telephone leads from the exercise area. Also check that you have plenty of room above and around you to move your arms – low-hanging ceiling lamps can be a particular problem.

If your floor is made of concrete overlaid with a single layer of carpet it is advisable to do all high impact exercises, such as jogging on the spot, on your exercise mat.

To balance your weekly exercise regime, and give the different muscle groups time to rest, do cardiovascular exercise and toning exercises on alternate days. Every exercise session must include a warm-up before and a cool-down after. For most people, short, regular work-outs are easier to maintain than lengthier but less frequent sessions. A full-length mirror can be very useful for checking your technique.

YOUR HOME CIRCUIT

Exercising on a circuit, known as circuit training, provides a varied work-out for the major muscle groups and the cardiovascular system. A circuit is a series of stations where different exercises are performed in succession. Each station may focus on cardiovascular and/or resistance exercises, sometimes using various pieces of equipment. It is easy to plan your own circuit at home, just make sure there is nothing to get in your way, such as furniture or trailing electrical flexes. Plan and set out everything beforehand and be sure to warm-up and stretch off properly before you begin (see page 70).

Station 1 ▶ *Stairs: Walk briskly up and down your stairs six times. If you don't have access to stairs, consider buying or making an aerobic step or perform knee raises (see page 128).*

Station 2 ▶ *Push ups: Find a clear space on your floor and perform 20 push-ups (see page 131).*

Station 3 ▶ *Curl-ups: Lie on an exercise mat or thick towel and do 20 curl-ups, taking care not to clasp your hands behind your head (see page 75).*

Station 4 ▶ *Lunges: Do ten dumbbell lunges on each leg (see page 130). If you do not have dumbbells use household objects such as filled plastic water bottles or tins of soup.*

Station 5 ▶ *Running: Run up and down your garden, or around the block, or run on the spot for 2 minutes.*

Station 6 ▶ *Sways: Find a clear space and do 16 sways (see page 128). Alternatively, do 16 half stars (see page 129).*

Station 7 ▶ *Skipping: Skip with a rope for 1 minute. Make sure you have ample room all around and above your head so that the rope can move freely.*

Station 8 ▶ *Chair squats: Squat down onto the edge of a chair slowly, feeling the contraction in your thighs, and then stand up again. Repeat this 20 times.*

▶ *Repeat the circuit at least once more, but to ensure a thorough work-out, aim to repeat it as many times as you can for up to 30 minutes.*

Stretching Exercises

You should always stretch before and after any type of exercise, but daily stretching is also beneficial for its own sake as it helps to maintain your full range of movement, reduce tension, improve posture and prevent injuries.

Remember...
Keep knees bent over toes. Tilt your hips forwards. Avoid locking your elbows.

Remember...
Keep your knees flexed. Tilt your hips forwards and look straight ahead.

Remember...
Keep your knees flexed. Tilt your pelvis forwards. Keep elbows slightly bent.

Upper back
Stand with your back straight and feet shoulder-width apart. Clasp your hands together in front of your chest, stretching your arms as far as they will go.

Back of upper arm
Stand with your feet shoulder-width apart. Bend one arm behind your head and touch your shoulder blade. With the other arm gently push the elbow back.

Front of chest
Stand with your feet shoulder-width apart. Clasp your hands together behind your back and pull them away from your body as far as you can comfortably manage.

Remember...
Keep your back straight and avoid leaning over too far

Sides of torso
Stand with your feet well apart and knees slightly bent. Rest one hand on your hip and stretch up with the other arm. Lean your torso over to the other side until you feel a slight tension.

Lower back
Lie on your back and raise your knees. Place your hands on your knees and slowly pull them towards your middle to feel the stretch. Hold for 2 seconds.

Remember...
Pull in your stomach muscles tightly. Make sure you lower your legs slowly. Keep your upper back and shoulders on the mat.

Mid back
Start in 'all fours' position with hands under shoulders and arms slightly bent. Breathe in as you slowly arch your back. Hold for 2 seconds. Breathe out as you reverse movement.

Remember...
Hold your abdominal muscles in and tilt your pelvis forward. Avoid locking the elbows and don't over-arch your back.

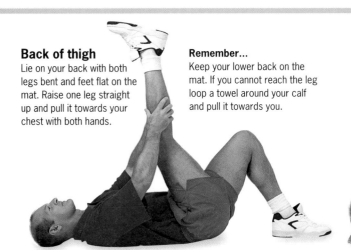

Back of thigh

Lie on your back with both legs bent and feet flat on the mat. Raise one leg straight up and pull it towards your chest with both hands.

Remember...
Keep your lower back on the mat. If you cannot reach the leg loop a towel around your calf and pull it towards you.

Front of thigh

Lie face down on the mat with your forehead resting on a forearm. Bend one leg behind you and grasp your ankle. Pull it towards your bottom and hold for 4 seconds.

Remember...
Keep your hips on the mat and your knees together. Hold your abdominal muscles in.

Hip flexor

Kneel on the mat and raise your left leg until you can place your foot flat on the mat. Move the right leg back as far as it will comfortably go. Place your hands on your left leg for support. Hold the stretch when you feel mild tension in the upper calf.

Remember...
Keep your head, neck and spine in line. Avoid twisting the knee.

Upper calf

Stand with your back straight. Stretch one leg back, keeping the other leg slightly bent. Push against the mat with the ball of the back foot until the stretch is felt in the groin.

Remember...
Hold your abdominal muscles in. Keep your knees flexed and feet facing forwards. Push your hips forwards.

Lower calf

Stand with feet facing forwards and move one leg back slightly, keeping both knees bent. Push against the back foot until the stretch is felt in your lower calf.

Remember...
Keep both knees bent. Place both feet flat on the mat and facing forwards.

Inner thigh

Sit on the mat with your legs as wide apart as you find comfortable and your hands flat on the mat. Keeping your back straight and abdominal muscles pulled in, reach forwards until you feel a slight tension in the inner thighs.

Remember...
Point your feet to the ceiling. Keep your legs and back straight.

BE SAFE AND EFFECTIVE

When stretching, make sure of the following:

► *Muscles must be warm – before stretching march gently on the spot for a couple of minutes or until your body has warmed up*

► *Move into the stretches slowly and gently – and avoid bouncing*

► *Hold stretches for a minimum of 8–10 seconds (except where shorter times are given)*

► *Stretch to a point of slight tension but not pain*

► *Always do the stretches on both sides of the body for equal lengths of time*

Aerobic Routine

This routine improves your cardiovascular fitness. If this is your first time, aim to exercise for 10 minutes at an intensity that makes you breathe harder than usual, yet still allows you to talk. If it feels too hard, slow down and stop.

Remember...
Keep your supporting knee in line with your toes. Pull in your abdominal muscles.

Remember...
Pull in your abdominal muscles. Keep knees in line with your toes. Don't squat below chair height.

Remember...
Lift the top of your head towards the ceiling. Tread lightly. Pull in your abdominal muscles.

Knee raises
Lift alternate knees up in front reaching towards them with the opposite hand for eight counts each knee.

Back lunges
Bend your left knee and extend your right leg straight behind you, touching the ground with the toes only. Lean slightly forward and extend your arms out in front of you. Repeat with the other leg. Alternate legs for 16 counts.

Squats
Stand with your hands on your hips and your feet slightly more than shoulder-width apart. Squat down for a count of eight, keeping your weight over your feet, and then stand up,

Sways
With a wide stance and knees slightly bent, transfer weight from side to side, swinging the arms across in front of you as you go. Continue this for 16 counts.

Remember...
Keep shoulders and hips square to the front. Look straight ahead.

Marching
March on the spot with the arms swinging naturally for 16 counts.

Remember...
Tread lightly. Pull in your stomach muscles. Keep your back tall and straight. Lift your knees as high as is comfortable.

BE SAFE AND EFFECTIVE

During your aerobic workout, graduate the intensity of your movements as follows:

▶ *1st time: gentle movements*

▶ *2nd time: bend and straighten the knees slightly more*

▶ *3rd time: bigger movements*

▶ *4th and 5th times: concentrate your efforts*

▶ *6th time: slightly smaller movements*

▶ *7th time: shallower knee bends*

▶ *8th time: slow down movements and do them gently*

Remember...
Keep your back straight. Push the bending knee out over the toes. Look straight ahead. Avoid tipping forwards.

Remember...
Keep your back straight. Look straight ahead. Tread lightly. If skipping, be sure to bring your heels all the way down to the floor.

Remember...
Look straight ahead to avoid tipping forwards. Hold your abdominal muscles in.

Half stars
Extend one leg out to the side along the floor while bending the supporting leg. Lift your arms out to the side and then down as you perform the movement eight times on each side.

Skipping
Skip on the spot for 16 counts (if you prefer, march vigorously).

Hamstring curls
Stand with your feet shoulder-width apart and knees slightly bent. Bring alternate heels up to your bottom, reaching in front of you as your heel lifts. Repeat for 16 counts.

Remember...
Keep the knee of the supporting leg flexed. If springing, ensure you bring your heels all the way down to the floor as you land.

Front kicks
Kick your left leg out in front of you as you spring on your right. Spring on both feet as they come back together. Repeat on the other side. Each time, extend the opposite arm out in front as you kick. Alternate kicks for the count of eight. (If you prefer, kick without springing.)

HOME EXERCISE VIDEOS
Some people find exercise videos a helpful way to keep fit. They have several advantages. They can be used at home whenever you have free time and they enable you to compare your efforts with expert exercisers. There is a wide range available illustrating a variety of styles – step routines, work-outs with weights, equipment-free exercises, basic aerobics. Be wary, however, of exercise videos compiled by celebrities as they may have been featured purely for their name rather than their knowledge of exercise. Make sure a video is endorsed by a recognised exercise body, or contact an exercise organisation for a recommendation.

Toning Routine

The following routine will improve your muscular strength and endurance while firming and toning your muscles. You will need weights, such as a set of dumbbells or a filled plastic water bottle, and an exercise mat. Initially, aim to complete two sets of ten repetitions, progressing to three sets of 15.

Triceps extensions

Works Muscles at the back of the upper arm (triceps)

Stand with your back straight and legs shoulder-width apart. Hold a dumbbell in your right hand above your head. Slowly lower the dumbbell behind and across the back of your neck, bending your arm at the elbow. Lift it above your head again but do not return it to the perpendicular (this will force the triceps to work harder).

Remember...
Pull your stomach in and keep your wrists straight but avoid locking the elbow when the arm is straight. Alternate arms to work in sets. Keep your movements smooth and flowing. Keep your weight balanced over your feet.

Lower back raises

Works Lower back muscles (erector spinae)

Lie face down with your hands by the side of your head, legs straight, feet together and toes resting on the mat. Pull your abdominal muscles in, breathe in and slowly raise your torso off the mat, breathing out as you do so. Hold for 2 seconds and then slowly lower again.

Remember...
Keep your head, neck and spine in line and your chin down. Keep your hips pressed into the mat.

Dumbbell lunges

Works Thighs (quadriceps and hamstrings) and buttocks (gluteals).

Stand with your feet shoulder-width apart. Hold weights by your sides. Step forward with the right leg, bending both knees and letting the back heel lift off the floor. Push with the right leg to get back to the start position. Repeat, this time leading with the left leg.

Remember...
Keep the upper body upright and centred over the hips and hold the abdominal muscles in. Bend your knees no further than a right angle. Keep the back knee clear of the mat. Toes face forwards at all times.

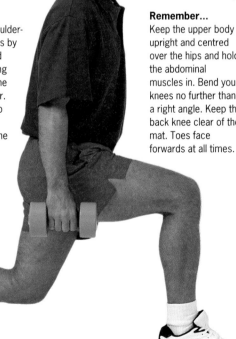

Abdominal curl with resistance

Works Abdominal muscles

Lie on your back with your knees bent and feet flat on the floor. Hold a weight on your chest. Pull in your abdominal muscles. Lift your head and shoulders up off the floor. Lower back down to the starting position.

Remember...
Exhale as you curl up. Keep your chin in a relaxed and neutral position and your lower back on the mat.

Three-quarter push-ups

Works Muscles of the chest (pectorals), upper arms (triceps) and shoulders (anterior deltoids)

Lie face down and place your hands below your shoulders with the palms flat on the floor. Lift your feet off the floor. Breathing out, push your chest off the floor. Hold for a count of two and then breathe out as you lower your body back to the floor.

Remember...
Keep your abdominals pulled in and your back straight. Avoid locking your elbows.

Dumbbell lateral raise

Works Shoulder muscles (deltoids)

Stand with your feet shoulder-width apart. Hold the weights in front of your thighs with palms facing inwards. Breathing out, lift the dumbbells out to the sides up to shoulder height. Breathing in, slowly lower the weights to the starting position.

Remember...
Keep the knees slightly bent. Pull your abdominals in and tuck your bottom under. Keep a slight bend in the elbows to relieve pressure on the joints. Move your arms smoothly without jerking. Don't let the wrists flex.

Inner thigh raises

Works Inner thigh muscles (adductors)

Lie on your right side with your head resting on your right hand and your left hand in front of you for support. Keep your right leg straight and place your left leg at right angles to your body. Breathe in, and then breathe out as you slowly raise your right leg as high as is comfortable. Hold for a count of two. Now breathe in and lower your right leg until it is 5 cm (2 in) above the mat. Hold for a count of two and then lower it to the mat. Repeat, this time lying on the left side.

Remember...
Keep your lower leg straight and your foot parallel with the floor.

Outer thigh raises

Works Outer thigh muscles (abductors)

Lie on your right side with your head on your right hand and your left hand on the mat in front of you to provide support. Bend your right knee back and keep your left leg straight. Raise your left leg as high as is comfortable. Hold the position for a count of two. Lower your leg until it is 5 cm (2 in) above the mat. Hold the position for a count of two and then lower your leg to the mat.

Remember...
Breathe in before starting the movement. Breathe out slowly as you raise the leg and then breathe in as you lower again.

EXERCISE AND YOUR LIFESTYLE

Working in a sedentary occupation, or having mobility problems connected with age or illness, may make exercise difficult to manage and lead to a decline in your general health and fitness.

Many people find that they lead a very sedentary lifestyle. This may be for a number of reasons – your job may offer you few opportunities for physical activity throughout the day, or you may suffer a condition that makes regular exercise problematic. Arthritis, for example, can make weight-bearing exercise difficult and painful and as a result many sufferers find themselves becoming increasingly inactive. However, being sedentary for long periods can cause serious health problems.

HEALTH PROBLEMS
Sitting for long periods can result in sagging muscles, poor posture and a sluggish circulation and lymphatic system so that the delivery of oxygen and nutrients to the body's tissues becomes less efficient. As lymphatic functioning declines, toxic by-products begin to accumulate in the body.

Your physical agility is also affected when constantly held in a flexed position. For instance, office workers who sit at a desk all day may find that their knee and hip joints gradually lose their range of motion as surrounding muscles shorten. Acids also build up in tissues as stress-induced muscular tension occurs. To make matters worse, as an office worker you may rush your meals, while stimulants such as coffee, chocolate bars and fatty or sugar-rich foods are consumed to pep-up the flagging body.

If you are suffering poor health, illness can also create a worsening spiral of immobility, which makes both exercise and the preparation of healthy meals more difficult, which in turn leads to a lack of energy and decreasing physical fitness.

However, a few simple adjustments to your lifestyle and environment can avoid this scenario. The most important point is to get moving and keep active in any way you can. The older you are, the more important it becomes to exercise regularly and to stay active to avoid gaining weight because of the increased health risks, such as heart disease, that this can cause (see page 16).

GET UP AND GO
Commuting does not have to mean standing still. Try walking down the escalators, taking the stairs instead of the lift, and standing while on the train or bus.

KEEPING ACTIVE
Lack of fitness can lead us to underestimate the body's capabilities, and the daily work routine likewise may teach us to rely too heavily on labour-saving devices. Developing an exercise habit can have a profound and positive effect upon your health, your enjoyment of life, and your productivity at work due to your enhanced mood.

A more active lifestyle can be achieved in a number of different ways, depending on your needs. For example, cycle to work instead of driving the car or taking the bus. Alternatively, leave home a little earlier and get off the bus one or two stops early and walk the rest of the way at a brisk pace.

Seated Exercises

Many people have to spend long periods of time in a chair, either because they work in a desk-bound job or because illness makes exercise difficult. However, there are a number of exercises you can perform while seated which will improve your circulation and flexibility.

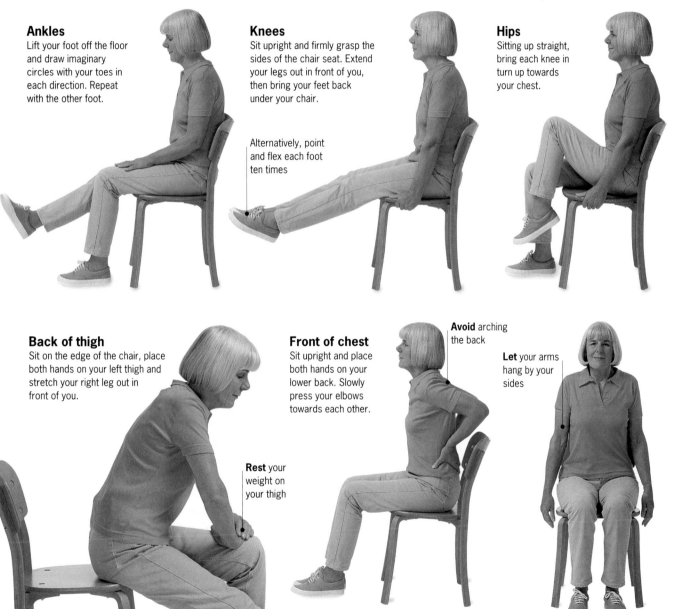

Ankles
Lift your foot off the floor and draw imaginary circles with your toes in each direction. Repeat with the other foot.

Knees
Sit upright and firmly grasp the sides of the chair seat. Extend your legs out in front of you, then bring your feet back under your chair.

Alternatively, point and flex each foot ten times

Hips
Sitting up straight, bring each knee in turn up towards your chest.

Back of thigh
Sit on the edge of the chair, place both hands on your left thigh and stretch your right leg out in front of you.

Rest your weight on your thigh

Front of chest
Sit upright and place both hands on your lower back. Slowly press your elbows towards each other.

Avoid arching the back

Let your arms hang by your sides

Neck and shoulders
Inhale and raise your shoulders towards your ears. Exhale and lower them. When you next exhale, drop your shoulders and lower your chin to your chest. Lift your chin as you inhale. Exhale and relax.

If illness means you spend much of the day in a sedentary position, this can cause your muscles to become stiff and sore. However, there are a number of gentle exercises you can do at home to improve the situation. If you have a condition such as arthritis or osteoporosis, ask your doctor or health care professional what exercises are best for you as they may be able to suggest specific movements to suit your needs.

The most common cause of muscle pain amongst office workers is immobility. Take a moment every 30 minutes to relax and avoid sitting for longer than one hour at a time. Find a reason to get up and move about for 5 minutes every hour. If you can't think of anything else, get up and go for a drink of water. Not only will this get you moving, it will also help to keep you hydrated throughout the day.

If you have to read a long document, try standing and stretching your lower body while doing so. By moving around and re-aligning your body position, you will give both your body and mind a welcome rush of blood that will stimulate all your muscles and nerve-endings.

OUTSIDE ACTIVITY

It is a good idea to get out of doors for some time every day. For office workers, breaks and lunchtimes offer the best opportunities for exercising outside during an otherwise sedentary day. Bring your own lunch and go for a walk during your lunch break; you will be surprised how much it enhances your concentration. The natural daylight and change of air and scenery will improve your health and mood and revitalise you for the rest of the afternoon.

If age or illness means you spend a lot of time indoors, a daily walk can be an opportunity for contact with other people. Joining a friend for a walk together can brighten up your day and boost your energy and health.

THE OFFICE GYM

With a little imagination it is possible to use many of the standard items of furniture or equipment in your office as props for a daily office exercise routine. So long as the objects are either fixed to the wall or floor, or placed against a wall for support, like a filing cabinet, or so heavy that you cannot move them, for instance a large desk, then they will generally be safe enough for you to stretch-off against.

Back stretch Stand with your right hand flat against a filing cabinet. Turn your left side to the cabinet and hold. Repeat with the other side.

Keep your back straight and feet a shoulder-width apart

STRETCH AS YOU WORK Some simple stretches can even be performed while checking through your work or reading reports.

Triceps dip Place a chair against a wall and sit on the edge. Ease forward off the chair and dip as low as you can comfortably manage. Hold briefly, and then sit back on the chair.

Calf stretch Stand with your hands on a desk and one leg back. Push against the floor with the ball of the back foot.

CHAPTER 8

MAKING THE MOST OF A HEALTH CLUB

The help, advice and range of facilities available
at a good health club can improve your chances of
sticking with an exercise programme. Whether it is the
financial commitment you have made, or the incentive
of working out with others, a health club can help
to sustain your interest and motivation.

CHOOSING AN EXERCISE CLUB

Once you have decided to start an exercise programme you will find that it's much easier to keep it up if you feel happy and relaxed in your surroundings.

With the growing popularity of exercise as a leisure pursuit, new health clubs are opening all the time and existing leisure centres are updating their facilities to attract new exercisers. With such a wide range of venues to choose from, it's worth while drawing up a checklist of services that you expect from a health club and then visiting different clubs and centres before deciding which one to join.

FACTORS TO CONSIDER

The first decision you must make is whether to join a health club or a leisure centre. Many leisure centres now offer exercise facilities that equal those of a health club. The main differences between the two types of facility usually relate to their membership rules and fee structures, but other factors such as customer care, additional facilities and staffing levels may also vary.

Leisure centres usually cater to a broad spectrum of the exercising public, while health clubs often appeal to particular sectors of society. This can create an air of exclusivity which some people may welcome but others find off-putting. When you visit each club, make a point of talking to members in the gym, the classes and refreshment area. You may find that you feel more comfortable being among people of a similar age and background to yourself.

Fees and membership options are also important considerations. Most health clubs are privately run, either by an individual owner or by a larger organisation. When you become a member of a health club you generally pay a one-off joining fee and then monthly instalments, often by direct debit. Once you've paid your money, you can use the facilities as often as you like. Some people like the commitment that this system involves, as well as the fact that the more often you exercise the more value you get for your money.

Leisure centres, even when owned by the local authority, may be run by a private management company which establishes the entrance fees in conjunction with the council. Fee structures tend to be more flexible as a result – you may be able to 'pay-as-you-go' or the centre may offer a monthly ticket allowing you to visit the centre as often as you like within the period. If you only plan to exercise a few times a week, a leisure centre may be a more cost-effective choice.

HISTORY OF THE GYMNASIUM

The word 'gymnasium' comes from the ancient Greek verb *gumnazein* meaning 'to exercise naked'. Exercises were originally performed without weights and were designed to enhance balance, strength and coordination. Although most closely associated with Greece, the ancient Persians, Romans, Indians and Chinese also exercised in this way. The modern sport of gymnastics evolved from calisthenics (from the Greek words *kallos* for 'beauty' and *sthenos* for 'grace') which developed in the 1800s in Sweden and Germany. Weights were introduced to prepare the body for gymnastic events. Today, however, most people who use gyms do so to get fit rather than to prepare for gymnastic competitions.

PERFECT FORM
In ancient Greece, men and women who were thought to embody perfect form and grace were encouraged to work out in the gym.

Club location

The location of the club or centre is an important consideration, depending on the time of day that you are planning to exercise. If you intend to exercise in your lunch break or immediately before or after work, for example, it would be best to choose a club that is close to your workplace. On the other hand, if you plan to exercise later in the evening or at weekends, or you have free time during the day, you might prefer to join a health club that is within a reasonable distance of your home. You should also check on the club's opening hours, which can vary widely between venues, and ensure that the club you choose is open at times that fit in with your lifestyle.

If you rely on your car to get to your place of exercise then parking facilities will influence your decision. Check that there is a sufficient number of parking spaces for the members actively using the club and that lighting and other security aspects are adequate. If you use public transport, consider which health clubs are close to a bus or train route. Alternatively, consider a health club within walking or cycling distance – this offers an ideal way to warm up before your exercise session.

Visiting the facilities

Most health clubs and leisure centres will be listed in the local newspapers and in the regional telephone directory, but advertising alone is not a reliable way to choose the club that is right for you.

You should listen to the comments of exercisers you know. If a club has been highly recommended by one of your friends, then it's well worth a visit. Health clubs

CHOOSING YOUR HEALTH CLUB

When looking for a suitable exercise venue you should draw up a list of the health clubs or leisure centres that match your particular needs and lifestyle. Before you make your final decision, arrange to look around the premises and feel free to ask the staff questions.

The tour should include a visit to the changing facilities which should be clean, fresh smelling, well ventilated and have an adequate number of showers and will provide a good indication of the general standard of the premises.

Costs
Enquire about the club's fee structure and membership scheme to help you decide whether to take out a subscription or pay per visit

Safety guidelines
Information on the safe use of facilities and machinery should be prominently displayed on or adjacent to the equipment

Qualifications
Staff qualifications and diplomas, including first aid certificates, should be clearly on show in the reception area

Children's facilities
Check whether facilities for children are available, such as a crèche or mother-and-baby swimming group

Gym equipment
Check that there is a wide range of gym equipment and that all machinery is well maintained and in good repair

Courses
Ensure that the courses available will suit your current needs and also fit in with your future aspirations

Public transport
Find out if the club or centre is close to main bus or train routes and that there are adequate services
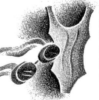

Parking facilities
Make sure that there are enough parking spaces at busy times and that the parking area is well lit for dark evenings

Opening hours
Check that the facilities you want to use will be available at the times you are most likely to need them, and not open, say, during office hours only

Additional services
Ask whether extra facilities are available such as swimming pool, sauna, sunbed or massage facilities

HEALTH CLUB CRÈCHE
Many health clubs have a crèche for members' children. Parents with young children often find it convenient to exercise during the day and take advantage of this facility. Check that the crèche is staffed by qualified child minders and that there is adequate space and equipment provided.

usually offer a tour of their facilities and it is advisable to make full use of this opportunity to ask as many questions as you can. A member of staff should also spend time with you to discover your goals and motivation in starting a fitness programme.

Try not to feel intimidated by the standard of members or the complexity of the equipment you see during the tour. A good health club will ensure that you are shown how to use each piece of equipment before you begin your training programme. This will usually be in the form of an induction course to new exercisers to enable the instructor to demonstrate how each piece of equipment works and which muscle groups it is designed to exercise.

You may be asked to attend a fitness assessment so that the instructor can draw up your training programme. These assessments can vary considerably between clubs but their main purpose is to establish your current level of fitness, strength and flexibility and to ensure that any training programme arranged for you will suit your particular requirements and abilities. It also provides a record of your initial fitness level so you can gauge your progress over the course of the programme.

You should also assure yourself that the staff are suitably qualified. Many health clubs put the qualifications of their instructors on display near the reception desk. These should include both exercise and first aid certificates or diplomas. If these qualifications are not evident, make a point of asking about them during your initial tour.

If you plan to take part in an organised course of exercises, you should ensure that the club or leisure centre offers a wide range of classes, catering for all levels of ability and at times of the day that suit you. The

range of equipment that health clubs provide varies considerably. A trainer will tailor fitness programmes according to the facilities available. You may prefer to use a wide range of exercise machines, however, so check that the venue has everything you are likely to need. These might include running machines, rowing machines, stationary bikes, strength-building machines, multi-gyms and free-standing weights.

Each club and centre should have guidelines for the safe use of their facilities and equipment. These should be explained to you during your initial assessment or induction and be available in either leaflet format or as posters prominently displayed on the walls that you can inspect when necessary.

Additional facilities

A small number of health clubs provide some form of weight management programme. If you want to exercise to control your weight, it's worth while joining a health club that recognises the close link between activity and nutrition and has qualified staff who can offer you sound and practical dietary advice.

Many clubs include facilities such as a sauna, Jacuzzi, or steam room which provide a good way to recover from a gruelling exercise session or to help you unwind after a stressful day at work. Sunbeds are also available at most health clubs but should be used with caution because excessive use can lead to skin damage, premature ageing and increased risk of skin cancer. A good health club will have safety guidelines clearly displayed and will be able to offer you practical advice on their use. Some health clubs also offer ancillary services such as massage, hairdressing and beauty therapies, at extra cost. Many people find this arrangement time-saving and convenient.

CAUTION
Sunbeds should always be used with care. They should be avoided altogether if you:

▶ *are under 16*

▶ *are prone to sunburn*

▶ *have a history of skin cancer in the family*

▶ *have a lot of freckles or moles*

GETTING STARTED

Your first session at a gym can be intimidating, but if you are clear about your goals and your needs then you will be able to get the most out of the instructors and facilities.

Once you have decided which health club or leisure centre you are going to join, the next step is to get yourself ready for action. Most health clubs will give you a fitness assessment, introduce you to the machines and prepare a training programme for you, but only you can know exactly what it is you want to achieve.

It is important to give this careful thought before your introduction so that you can explain your personal goals and ambitions to the fitness instructor (see page 59). The instructor can then tailor your programme to your specific needs, rather than making you follow a general programme that may be given to all new members. By keeping your final goal in mind you will be able to stay focused and motivated throughout your time at the club.

TRAINING REGIME

Unless you can establish clear goals the likelihood that you will abandon your fitness regime prematurely is very high. Research conducted by American exercise psychologist Dr Rod Dishman, on the other hand, shows a significant increase in frequency, intensity, duration and perseverance in fitness regimes if started and maintained for clearly understood and personal reasons.

Other important issues to consider are regularity and consistency. It is important to keep to your training regime and try to avoid skipping any sessions. You should also aim to set yourself a new target at each work-out. Given the correct exercise stimulus, your body will soon adapt to become, for example, stronger and more supple.

Finally, make as many changes as possible to your lifestyle that are going to assist your fitness programme. Integrating exercise with a healthy diet, adequate sleep and good working and social routines will achieve the greatest long-term results.

PLANNING YOUR ROUTINE

Your gym fitness adviser will help you plan a routine taking into account your goals, but as a general rule you will need to establish a routine that you can perform for at least 20 minutes three times a week. Try to include both cardiovascular training (exercise that increases your heart rate for at least 12 minutes at a time) and resistance work (strength exercises) in your routine. Your cardiovascular ability will be limited if your muscles are not strong enough to sustain exercise, and similarly your strength will be limited if you don't have sufficient stamina to keep you going throughout the session.

Most people begin their workout with cardiovascular training as this does not deplete energy reserves. Attempting cardiovascular exercise at the end of your routine may prove difficult as your resistance work-out may already have worn you out.

A positive approach
It is important to keep a positive attitude towards exercise classes. Decide on clear and realistic long-term fitness targets, and make up your mind to see the course through. Research shows that the highest drop-out rate from fitness classes occurs in the first two months among people who are unclear of their goals and have become dispirited because they do not feel they are making good progress.

COMBINATION EXERCISE

A machine such as a treadmill or rowing machine works all the major muscle groups at the same time and improves both strength and aerobic fitness. Rowing works the muscles and joints in the legs and back, while the arms have a resistance work-out and the overall action offers good cardiovascular exercise.

INCREASED GAIN
The resistance can be increased on a rowing machine, providing a harder work-out.

CARDIOVASCULAR TRAINING

Cardiovascular training options in the gym usually include aerobic, step and circuit training classes, and running, rowing, cycling, skiing and step machines. When starting a cardiovascular programme, it is worth trying out the low-impact alternatives as your first move. Too much unaccustomed impact through excessive jumping, bouncing or jogging is a primary cause of many limb disorders and injuries such as shin splints. Fortunately, most machines in

THE GYM: A BEGINNER'S GUIDE

When you first approach a gym it is important that you are fully aware of what you should expect. Don't be put off from asking questions about the gym and the instructors – if you aren't happy with your gym you may well give up on your exercise programme simply because you feel uncomfortable there. Take time to ensure that the gym is right for you, that it offers the facilities that you require and that the staff are professional, approachable and that they care about your fitness programme too.

1. Determine your goals
Decide what you want to achieve through the gym. Do you want to improve your all round aerobic fitness, do you want to improve muscle tone, or do you need to strengthen an injured or weakened muscle group?

2. Visit the gym Check out the centre, examine its facilities and have a fitness assessment. Discuss your fitness goals with the instructor and ask about the different classes and types of exercise equipment available that might suit your specific needs.

3. Decide how often you can visit
Establish a basic plan for how often you can exercise at the gym. Remember to build up the frequency and intensity of your visits gradually to avoid overstressing your body, but try to work towards the basic commitment of 20 minutes of exercise three times a week.

4. Plan your routine at the gym
Your particular routine should reflect the specific goals you have established, but as a general rule most people should include in their visit both aerobic activities, in order to increase heart and breathing rates for at least 12 minutes at a time, and resistance exercises that work specific muscle groups.

5. Begin with cardiovascular exercise
If you are planning a 20-minute session, devote 15 minutes to cardiovascular exercise. Options include aerobics, or running, cycling and rowing machines. Include muscle-building exercises in your routine as well.

7. Relax and unwind
Remember that your visit should be fun, so take advantage of the varied facilities offered at many clubs. For example, try a relaxing massage, or a sauna to soothe and relax tired muscles.

6. Decide on the type of resistance work
Resistance training options include weight machines and free weights as well as aqua aerobics and body sculpting. Your fitness assessment will help you to focus on the muscle groups that need most attention. As well as boosting the strength and endurance of the muscles, resistance exercises can also improve appearance by making muscles look tighter and more clearly defined.

clubs are low-impact by design for this reason (the exception being the treadmill, but even this provides more cushioning for the limbs than running on roads or pavements).

In aerobics classes, the formats and styles taught should vary according to the fitness levels of the class members. A competent teacher will be able to adapt most movements from low to high impact to suit the fitness of the participant.

Ideally the activities carried out in the class should be varied on a regular basis, or you could attend two or three different types of class (see page 149). As well as reducing the potential for boredom, and reducing the risk of repetitive-use injuries, this will create the necessary stimulus for constant adaptation by the body and ensure that certain muscle groups are not over-exercised while others are neglected.

FLEXIBILITY TRAINING

An exercise club can help you to develop flexibility through a number of different classes and forms of machinery. Aerobics, aqua aerobics and body sculpting will also help to develop flexibility; and many clubs also offer yoga classes which can be particularly helpful. Most exercise machinery is primarily designed for muscular or cardiovascular training, but machines such as the cross-country skiing machine will also help to develop flexibility.

MUSCULAR TRAINING

Strength training will primarily involve the use of weight machines, although aqua aerobics and body sculpting classes also help to develop the strength of specific muscles. Aim to develop a well-balanced routine. Muscles operate in pairs across most joints to provide balance and protection, so it is important that equal strength is maintained in each pair. An imbalance in the muscles is a common underlying cause of joint pain – neck problems may be the result of weak upper back and shoulder muscles, for example. A balanced routine will include an exercise for each muscle of the pair, such as chest with upper back muscles, shoulders with middle back muscles, abdominals with lower back, biceps with triceps, thighs with hamstrings, and calf muscles with shins.

It is not advisable to condition the muscles of the lower body, through stepping or running, for example, while neglecting the upper body. For optimal conditioning, it is best to select machines that utilise both upper and lower body function. The use of either a rowing machine or a cross-country skiing machine will accomplish this. What is more, greater initial gains can be made from exercising the muscles of the upper body which may quickly be noticed in everyday life. For example, you may find you're soon able to lift shopping or a young child without straining.

Correct exercise technique
For effective and safe exercising, make sure you use the correct technique for each exercise and take extra care when you are beginning to feel tired. Good technique should never be sacrificed for one extra lift with the same weight. Deviating from correct technique can present the greatest risk of injury to a muscle or the connective tissue in a joint. Lifting a weight without proper control threatens the integrity of other muscles or joint structures which try to cope with a sudden load that they are not prepared for, or do not have the strength to cope with. It also loses its purpose as the muscles originally targeted will not be exercised in the proper way.

MR UNIVERSE

The man who has become known as the 'Father of Modern Bodybuilding' was Oscar Heidenstam (1911–1991). His career in bodybuilding began when he became the first British bodybuilder to win the Mr Europe Contest in 1939. An exemplary sportsman, Heidenstam was internationally acknowledged as the foremost ambassador and expert in bodybuilding during its formative years. He became the publisher of the world's longest established physical culture magazine, *Health and Strength*, which had been founded in 1898. Continuing his close links with the sport, from 1956 Heidenstam organised the most famous and long-standing world bodybuilding contest, Mr Universe.

OSCAR HEIDENSTAM
A modest humanitarian, Oscar Heidenstam was famed for his motivational and inspirational skills and lived by his credo 'do good by stealth and blush to find it known'.

USING EQUIPMENT

Although many people think of exercise and weight-training machines as the domain of the serious athlete, gym machines offer many benefits for the more modest exerciser.

The machines available in a gym can be grouped into two main categories: cardiovascular equipment used to strengthen the heart, lungs and circulation, and resistance machinery, which strengthen the muscles. Understanding the equipment and deciding which pieces best meet your needs are integral to your exercise plan.

CARDIOVASCULAR EQUIPMENT

Cardiovascular machines not only improve your overall fitness level, but also provide a good warm-up exercise prior to a session on resistance machines. They include devices such as treadmills, rowing machines, step machines, aerobic bikes and cross-country skiing simulators. These different types of equipment will also tone specific muscle groups. For example, step machines and cycling machines tone the leg muscles, while rowing machines and skiing machines provide all-over muscle toning.

RESISTANCE EQUIPMENT

Whether you use exercise machines, free weights or your own body weight, resistance training is the most effective form of exercise for enhancing muscular strength, size and power. Most gyms and health clubs have a range of resistance apparatus available; but which type you choose will often be determined by personal preference. Some people enjoy the ease of use of machines and the fact that they require the minimum of training to master. They are also easy to adjust so that you make steady progress.

FREE WEIGHTS VERSUS MACHINES

There are advantages and disadvantages to both free weights and machines. Before you commit yourself to buying a piece of resistance exercise equipment, weigh up factors such as the cost, space available, ease of use, and your exercise goals.

FREE WEIGHTS	MACHINES
Inexpensive	Expensive
Need accurate technique to be effective	Easy to use
Minimal space	Substantial space
Using heavier weights may require help from a partner	Heavier weights easily controlled by machines
Changing weight plates can be time consuming	Increasing the degree of resistance is a quick process
Easy to target specific muscles	Best when used to work muscle groups
Good for toning and firming muscles	Best for building strength and bulk
Minimal maintenance required	Regular maintenance necessary
Work fixating (support) muscles that aid good posture	Little fixating work due to support provided by machine
Suitable for people of all sizes and builds	Some machines best for average sizes and builds only

Other people prefer free weights as they provide a greater range of movements while exercising thus giving individuals more control over which muscles they develop and how they develop them. However, resistance-machine training can be modified to help you focus on certain muscle groups. Whichever form of resistance training you choose, you must always make sure you exercise safely. If you have any doubts about how to use a particular piece of equipment, ask an instructor to show you.

Pin selected weight stack

This is the most common type of resistance machine and is characterised by a stack of weight plates with a central rod running through them to allow various weights to be lifted. Check if the machine you are using has adjustable training positions, so that you can alter it to fit your body size and shape. A major advantage of resistance machines is the ease with which each movement can be learned. You will also quickly recognise how the working muscles should feel when exercising properly to ensure maximum benefits with minimum risk.

Free weights

Free weights can either be dumbbells, which are available in a range of fixed sizes, or barbells (see page 123) which can be loaded with discs of varying weights. These discs are attached to each end of the bar and can be built up to make any weight desired.

As well as working the main muscle groups, free weights also utilise many of the minor fixating (support) muscles that help to control, balance and stabilise the body during resistance exercises. This exercises the body in a more natural way than is possible with exercise machines, and also enhances effective overall muscle strength.

The main disadvantage of free weights is that, although they appear easy to handle, a high degree of skill is actually needed to use them in a safe and controlled way and to ensure that the main muscle groups perform the lion's share of the work. Without sufficiently developed neuromuscular control, it is difficult to lift free weights correctly. As a consequence, excess stress may be placed on a joint or muscle that is too weak to cope with it, thus increasing the risk of serious injury. Like all new skills, controlling free weights should be learned properly.

MACHINE MONITORS

Many exercise machines have computerised gauges that enable you to check your performance. The read-outs from these machines help you to fine-tune your fitness routine for optimum benefits. On some machines the computation may include:

- ▶ *intensity of exercise*
- ▶ *duration of exercise*
- ▶ *distance travelled*
- ▶ *speed travelled*
- ▶ *heart rate*
- ▶ *total calories used during the session*
- ▶ *lung capacity*
- ▶ *changes in blood pressure*
- ▶ *recovery rate*

SIMPLE RESISTANCE EQUIPMENT

You don't need to use complicated machinery in the gym to improve your strength. There are some gym exercises – such as triceps dips – that involve the use of a workout bench and your body weight alone to condition and tone the muscles.

Many gym-goers also make use of simple props for resistance exercises. The most common non-weight props are lengths of rubber tubing or elastic bands, of varying degrees of resistance. These can be pulled between the hands, for example, or attached to a foot and stretched. As the resistance comes from stretching the rubber or elastic, rather than from the force of gravity acting upon a weight, imaginative exercisers can use these props to devise virtually any kind of resistance movement they choose. The effect of using an elastic band is similar to that of some resistance machines. Looking at how particular machines work can help you to devise elastic band exercises.

Other popular devices include wrist and ankle weights which increase the load that the arms and legs have to bear when performing resistance exercises. They can also be used during cardiovascular exercises such as aerobic step sessions. Some ankle weights contain individual weight bags so you can vary the load according to the type of exercise you are doing, and increase it as your muscular strength improves.

ELASTIC BANDS
Like free weights, elastic bands allow a natural range of movement, and can exercise both the assisting and stabilising muscles, as well as the major muscle groups.

Resistance Work

The resistance machines shown will develop your muscular strength and endurance and can be found at most gyms. Your trainer will advise you about the amount of resistance and number of repetitions, based on your exercise goals and fitness level.

Working your chest

The swinging motion when you bring your elbows together on the arm pads works your chest. As the pads meet, hold for a count of two before slowly letting the pads move back.

Remember...

Make the movements as smooth as possible. Make your chest and shoulder muscles do most of the work, not your forearms.

Working your legs

Extending your legs against the weights works the muscles at the front. The swinging motion makes the exercise seem deceptively easy. Make sure that your back is well supported throughout.

Working your shoulders

Pushing the bar up against resistance and then lowering it slowly and under full control strengthens the shoulder muscles and also firms and tones the muscles of the back, chest and upper arms.

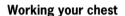

Remember...

Keep your back and neck straight and your feet flat on the floor. Avoid locking your elbows.

Remember...

Keep your movements flowing. Let your legs do the work, not your back and try not to favour one leg over the other. Keep the head and neck relaxed.

Working your back
Pull the bar on a high pulley down from above your head to behind it to work the muscles of the arms, shoulders and particularly the back. Don't overstretch by pulling the bar too low down behind you.

Remember...
Keep your wrists straight. Adjust the bar above the seat to secure your knees, keep your knees in line with your feet and your feet flat on the floor. Hold your abdominal muscles in and keep your back straight.

Working your arms
Pull down on the weighted bar until it is around chest height. Then raise and lower the bar, working your forearms below the elbow.

Remember...
Keep your movements fluid. Do not jerk your arms. Keep your back straight and your feet flat on the floor.

Working your abdominals
Lowering your torso slowly against resistance strengthens the abdominal muscles and also works the muscles of the lower back. Keep your abdominal muscles tight and breathe out as you lean forwards.

Remember...
Keep your neck and spine in line and make sure your feet are secured and held flat against the foot rest.

FOR BEST RESULTS
On completing the last set of resistance exercises, start to perform cool-down activities as soon as possible. Choose a full body aerobic activity to use all the muscles that have been used in the resistance work-out.

Straight after cooling down is the ideal time to enhance your flexibility because your muscles are at their most elastic. Permanent improvements in a muscle's mobility can be made with appropriate stretches. Stretch imbalanced muscles to increase your range of motion at the joint. The stretches will be the same as used in the warm-up, but more extensive. When you reach the point of initial stretch sensation, hold the position for 20–30 seconds, or up to a minute or more if comfortable in the position.

Exercise Relief from

Muscle Problems

Although the benefits of keeping fit outweigh any negative aspects, there may be times when you push yourself too hard and experience aches, cramps or stitches. There are, however, simple steps you can take to relieve these common problems.

HERBAL CREAMS
If muscles are prone to soreness or cramp you can often avoid the problem by applying a warming ointment or cream containing herbs, such as wintergreen, before exercising.

The sensation of pain as a result of injury, over-exercising, incorrect technique or other factors generally falls into three categories: instant, sharp and debilitating pain; nagging, chronic pain; and short-term pain.

Sudden sharp, debilitating pain generally signifies a serious injury which you should not attempt to treat yourself, but instead seek medical advice straightaway.

Chronic, or long-term, pain usually indicates a structural weakness of the body, joint inflammation, minor muscle tears, or stiff and imbalanced muscles which you may be able to treat yourself. The problem will usually be resolved with a period of rest, but if the pain continues then you should seek medical help.

Short-term pain that comes on during or shortly after exercise and gradually eases after a few hours is usually caused by intense fatigue and momentary muscle failure and is not usually a serious problem.

RELIEVING MUSCLE CRAMP

Cramp is characterised by very painful and violent localised muscle contractions. It usually occurs after a sustained period of exercise which involves intense muscular work, such as a hard game of football, a tiring aerobic work-out, or a long run. Cramp is primarily caused by an imbalance of two minerals, sodium and potassium, which regulate the electrical impulses that make the muscles work. Normally these minerals interact alternately to contract and relax the muscle, but when an imbalance occurs the muscle still contracts but then is not able to relax immediately afterwards.

Cramp can be relieved at once by massage and stretching the affected muscles as far as possible to relax them. For most muscle cramps you can do this for yourself, or ask an exercise companion to do this for you. As a preventative measure, make sure you drink some fluid prior to and during exercise.

SELF-HELP FOR CRAMP
If you develop painful cramp in your calf muscles, sit down and straighten your leg by resting your heel on the ground and pulling your toes towards you.

APPLY PRESSURE
To help relieve the pain of muscle cramp, press deeply into the centre of the painful area with your thumbs while you continue to stretch the muscle.

SALT AS A SOLUTION
To restore the mineral balance, add a teaspoon of salt to a glass of water, squash or fruit juice. Sip the liquid slowly, do not rush or gulp it.

RELIEVING A STITCH

A stitch is a dull, cramp-like ache normally experienced on one side of the abdominal muscles. The underlying cause of a stitch is not known for sure but it is thought to be due to a spasm of the diaphragm muscle or localised fatigue of the muscles that stabilise the hip and trunk. This usually occurs when athletes are out of shape or are pushing themselves too hard, for example by attempting speeds greater than they are normally accustomed to, or have not thoroughly warmed up before starting their exercise programme.

A stitch may also be a consequence of exercising too soon after eating a big meal or drinking large amounts of fluid. This is because the body diverts extra blood to the internal organs to deal with the digestive processes, leaving insufficient oxygen reaching the muscles to meet the extra demands imposed by exercise.

If a stitch develops, ease down on the intensity of the exercise and take deep breaths, holding each breath for as long as is comfortable before exhaling slowly. If the stitch becomes too painful you should stop exercising and slowly bend forward from the waist to flex the trunk while continuing to breathe deeply and slowly.

To reduce the risk of developing a stitch you should leave a minimum of two hours between eating a big meal

Lean slightly away from the painful side

and starting exercise. Develop a regular breathing pattern to match your stride rate and concentrate on good running technique – aim to keep your hips level and try not to overstride.

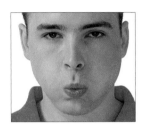

CONTROL AIRFLOW
To help control your breathing rate when suffering from a sudden stitch, make your mouth into a small circle as you slowly breathe out.

DEALING WITH THE PAIN OF A STITCH
To alleviate the pain of a stitch you should stop exercising and bend forward from the waist. Take deep breaths and exhale slowly until the pain diminishes.

RELIEVING MUSCLE SORENESS

Muscle ache 24–48 hours after exercise is very common and is usually part of the process of physical adaptation as your body adjusts to the demands of exercise. It is often a positive sign indicating that your muscles are expanding to cope with the increased workload you are placing on them. This delayed feeling of localised pain is called 'Delayed Onset Muscle Soreness', or DOMS for short (see page 77).

If muscle soreness develops after exercise it can be greatly eased by stretching the affected area, carrying out a series of light activities to flex the muscles, or having a massage to soothe away the tension within the muscle fibres. A warm bath that has been run through a herbal bath bag containing analgesic herbs such as rosemary can also help to soothe the pain of sore muscles. Alternatively,

essential oils, such as that of camomile or marjoram, can be added to the bath water.

Muscle pain is not an inevitable consequence of exercise, however. DOMS can be almost completely avoided by ensuring that the intensity of your exercising is not too

MAKING A HERBAL BATH BAG
Lay sprigs of thyme and rosemary on a square of muslin and draw the corners of the muslin together. Seal the bag with a piece of string or ribbon.

severe and by carrying out a thorough programme of warm-up exercises before each work-out, and a cool-down routine afterwards.

The warm-up and cool-down should include stretches to warm, loosen and oxygenate those muscles that do most of the work.

HERBAL RELIEF
Tie your herbal bag under the tap as you fill the bath to ensure the soothing ingredients are released. Both thyme and rosemary have relaxing and pain-relieving properties which ease aching muscles.

EXERCISE CLASSES

There are many different types of exercise classes, each designed to meet a particular need or standard of fitness. It is important to ensure that the course you choose meets your requirements.

Some clubs cater for a range of fitness levels by offering a variety of classes at different times of the day. Other clubs, and most leisure centres, prefer to offer a smaller number of classes aimed at more general ability levels. Ask for a brochure or leaflet explaining the classes on offer and don't be afraid to ask for more information about a class before trying it.

The facilities provided by different health clubs and leisure centres vary considerably. Some venues have purpose-built studios with sprung wooden floors, mirrors, and a sound system. Other classes may be held in a sports hall or a squash court, with a cassette player to play the music.

The quality of the class does not depend on the sophistication of the facilities, however, as a good instructor can create a good atmosphere in the most basic of venues. If a class is well-attended, it usually reflects the standard of the instructor.

PREPARATION FOR AN EXERCISE CLASS

Before attending an exercise class for the first time there are some important safety factors to consider. You should always wear well-fitting and supportive shoes, with a seamless pair of sports socks to avoid painful blisters.

Choose comfortable clothes, that are either loose or stretchable to allow you to move easily. Wearing several layers allows you to remove clothes as you gradually warm up during the class. Take a bottle of water with you so you can take frequent sips throughout the class.

Speak to the instructor before you start and tell him or her that this is your first time. The instructor may be able to offer some tips on how to adapt the exercises, if necessary, to make them easier for you. Always inform the instructor of any medical conditions you may have.

WARMING UP
The grape vine is a popular warm-up exercise used in many fitness classes. You can also incorporate it into your personal exercise programme. The grape vine is best done to music, the faster the tempo the more effective it is at warming muscles.

Keep the legs relaxed and the back straight

1 *Start with hands together. Place your left leg behind your right leg and put your weight on it, then step to the right with your right leg.*

2 *Cross your left leg in front of your right leg, put your weight on it, and raise your arms.*

3 *Step to the right with your right leg and bring your hands together. Bring your right leg behind your left and reverse the sequence moving in the opposite direction.*

COMPONENTS OF AN EXERCISE CLASS

A good exercise class should include a number of components, all of which can vary in length according to the type of class and the ability level of the participants.

Warm-up

The work-out starts with a warm-up lasting at least 5 minutes. This prepares the body for the exercises to come by loosening the joints, raising the pulse rate and increasing the blood flow to warm and oxygenate the muscles. The warm-up involves rhythmical movements of the larger muscle groups that start slowly and gradually build up in pace and intensity. These raise the heart rate, respiration, muscle temperature and elasticity. The warm-up also includes static stretches, each held for around 10 seconds.

Cardiovascular, or aerobic, section

These exercises are designed to increase general fitness by improving the strength and efficiency of the heart and lungs. They may be either low or high intensity, depending on the type and duration of the class. Popular low intensity moves include knee lifts and marching. High intensity moves include jogging, star jumps and squats.

Some exercise classes also refer to low-impact or high-impact moves, which should not be confused with high and low intensity exercises. The term low impact indicates that one foot stays in contact with the floor at all times during the move, thus limiting the impact on the joints. A high-impact move involves a jumping or jogging action where the weight of the body is in the air for a short duration. Low-impact moves are more suitable for those with joint disorders.

Muscular strength and endurance

This section is designed to increase both the strength and endurance of the muscles, improving body shape and making everyday tasks easier to perform. Exercises may be performed using body weight alone or with resistance equipment such as ankle weights, hand weights or rubber bands.

Stretching

The stretching section at the end of an exercise class is important and so should not be skipped. Static stretches involving the major muscle groups held for 10 to 30 seconds can

PROGRAMME

NAME					
DATE	PROGRAMME	FREQUENCY		INTENSITY	TIME
1/11	Muscle toner	2 x weekly		Low	6.30pm
EXERCISE		MAX WEIGHT	SETS & REP	SEAT NO.	TIME (min)
Warm up					10–15
Leg press		2 blocs	3 x 12–15	7	
Leg curl		1 bloc	2 x 10–12	7	
Chest press		1 bloc	3 x 12–15	3	
Shoulder press		1 bloc	3 x 12–15	4	
Lateral pull down		3 blocs	2 x 10–12	4	
Seated curl		1 bloc	3 x 12–15	2	
ADDITIONAL INSTRUCTOR ADVICE/ COMMENTS					

reduce muscular soreness and tension after exercise and increase the range of movement of both joints and muscles.

TYPES OF EXERCISE CLASS

There is a wide range of exercise classes available. Some mainly concentrate on cardiovascular fitness, while others aim to increase muscle size and definition.

Aerobics

An aerobics class includes elements such as muscular strength and stretches but puts most emphasis on aerobic or cardiovascular exercise. A session usually lasts from 20 to 50 minutes. In order to maintain the pulse rate within the training zone, a series of energetic movements are performed using a variety of foot and arm patterns. Some instructors teach combinations of movements that eventually build into routines.

Step aerobics

Originally developed as a rehabilitation exercise in Atlanta in the United States, step aerobics was introduced to the UK in 1990.

continued on page 152

TRAINING SCHEDULE
When you join a gym your instructor will fill out a training schedule for your personal optimum work-out. Your programme will be reviewed by your fitness instructor following a progress assessment, usually after a few weeks. This means that your training is always tailored to your needs.

The Aerobics Instructor

Choosing a good aerobics class means finding an instructor who is qualified, experienced and able to motivate the class. Whether you are in a modern exercise studio or the church hall, it is important that you find the class that suits your individual needs.

POWER BOOST
Wearing wrist and ankle weights, carrying dumbbells or using a step during aerobics can help with muscle toning.

Origins

Aerobic dancing originated in the USA in the 1970s and is credited to Jackie Sorenson, an exercise specialist and trained dancer. She aimed to make keeping fit more fun by combining exercises for stamina and stretches for suppleness with a background of music. The original 'high-impact' aerobics and the concept of 'No pain, No gain' have now been replaced with healthier forms such as low-impact step aerobics.

FITNESS BOOM
The aerobics classes devised by Jackie Sorenson quickly became an integral part of the exercise boom of the 1980s.

Joining an aerobics class can be fun as well as good for your health: you may even make new friends too. The combination of dance and keep fit means that you can exercise without feeling that it is all hard work. A session will leave you relaxed and in good spirits, ready to cope with the physical and mental strains of life.

How to choose an aerobics class?
The best place to start is by asking your friends and family if they have heard of a class which has had good reports. Most people find out about aerobics classes through word of mouth, often initiating friends after they have discovered the benefits and enjoyment of a good class.

You can also look out for posters in local halls and sports centres, or ask the people who work there. If you live in a small village, you may find that you have little choice without travelling to a local town. If you live in a town or city, however, you will probably find a wealth of classes to choose from.

Although you can tell a certain amount about each class from its poster, for example whether it is high, medium or low impact, you will need to go to the class itself to find out what it really involves and whether you will feel relaxed and well-exercised by the class. It is quite normal to turn up on the day and ask if you may watch the class without paying to judge whether it is the class for you. Alternatively, you can plunge straight in and see how you get on with the class.

What is high, medium and low-impact aerobics?
Low-impact aerobics is a gentle form of aerobics for beginners and for those who are unfit due to illness or injury. However, low-impact classes can be deceptively tough, so be ready to take a rest if it gets too hard.

Most people are seeking a medium-impact aerobics class which improves health, tones muscles and enhances fitness and body shape without pushing them beyond their own limits. Medium-impact classes aim to allow exercisers to stretch themselves as much as they can.

High-impact classes are generally for those who are seriously training for another sport or for those who are particularly keen to keep up their muscle tone and fitness.

Each instructor will describe their class in a different way and the only way to see how appropriate a class is for you is to go along and try it. If the type is not specified, then it might be a mixture of high, medium and low impact. Such classes are often found in centres that cater for small communities, such as local church halls, where numbers and available space are too limited to cater for each level of fitness.

In mixed classes, the instructor will attempt to offer a range of steps and exercises so that all levels are covered. This often works very well and can lead to an enjoyable and fun environment, although it may not be suitable if you are looking to really stretch yourself with a thorough work-out of high-impact exercises.

Are the steps easy to learn?

The first time you go to an aerobics class you might be baffled by the different steps which everyone else will appear to know. Don't worry: it will only take a few weeks for you to get to grips with the different movements. You might find that the instructor keeps to the same routine every lesson, and this can help you to learn the steps quickly.

What if I find it too hard?

Don't be embarrassed to sit down or even take a break if you need to rest, especially if you feel unwell. It is vital to know your limits and be able to judge when you are pushing yourself too far or you will put your health at risk. Experienced instructors are familiar with most problems associated with aerobics and will be pleased to offer you advice.

How long will the class last and will it be structured?

Most classes last an hour, but some high-impact classes take up to 2 hours. Ask about the duration of your class before you start. The class will begin with a warm-up and stretches to loosen the muscles, before going into the aerobic dance-exercise routine. The class may also incorporate muscle-toning exercises, often in a sequence of 12 exercises, with 2 minutes spent on each exercise. The class ends with a cool-down routine and stretches, plus deep breathing exercises to relax you. Afterwards you may feel tired, or even a little light-headed, but you should feel refreshed and satisfied with your efforts.

What should I wear?

Clothing and footwear for aerobics needn't cost a fortune. Your clothes shouldn't restrict your movements, but otherwise it does not matter what you wear – a leotard and leggings, or a T-shirt and shorts or track suit bottoms would be fine. It is important to feel comfortable at an aerobics class and you might prefer a relaxed style of class that helps you feel good about yourself whatever you wear. Footwear is important as shoes should be flexible, with good grip, and extra cushioning (see page 71). Your instructor can suggest the best type for your needs.

What makes a good instructor?

A good instructor should have a friendly and fun personality, encouraging participants to enjoy the session while benefiting physically. He or she should arrive well before a class is due to start. This allows time to prepare the music, be available to class members who have questions and meet new people.

EXERCISE CUES
An aerobics instructor uses visual or verbal cues to prepare the class for a change of movement or step in plenty of time for them to make the necessary adjustment.

What qualifications should an aerobics instructor have?

Aerobics instructors must complete an approved 80-hour training course. There are a number of courses available that have been validated by the Royal Society of Arts. A typical course includes basic anatomy and physiology, nutrition, choreography, music interpretation and exercise to music, and instructors must pass written, practical and oral exams.

Once they have qualified, most instructors go on to join one of the professional organisations that cater for exercise teachers. These provide regular newsletters including the latest research and choreographic material. Good aerobics teachers also attend seminars, conventions and workshops to keep up-to-date.

WHAT YOU CAN DO AT HOME

Creating your own aerobics music tape can be a great way to practise aerobics routines at home to your favourite music. Design your tape to last 20 minutes. Most pop songs are 3 to 4 minutes long so you'll need to select five or six songs.

Choose songs with a basic 4/4 beat (the classic rock/pop rhythm) as it will be easier to move in time. The tempo, or speed, at which this rhythm is played varies widely with different songs. Choose two slower songs for your initial 6 minutes while you gradually warm up. Make the middle 8 minutes from songs of a faster tempo to give you a good aerobic work-out. For the final 6 minutes choose songs once again with a slower tempo to allow your body to gently cool down as you bring your routine to an end.

PROS AND CONS OF EXERCISE CLASSES

There is a bewildering variety of exercise classes available. Each one offers benefits that may best meet your exercise goals as your fitness levels progress, so it is well worth taking the time to become familiar with everything that is on offer.

TYPES OF CLASSES	ADVANTAGES	DISADVANTAGES
Aerobics	Improves aerobic fitness in enjoyable social setting	May be intimidating for those who lack coordination
Step aerobics	Can be high intensity but low impact so limiting impact on the joints	Participants will need several sessions to learn foot patterns
Aqua aerobics	Ideal for pregnant women, and those with disabilities and joint ailments	Although swimming ability not essential, non-swimmers may feel uncomfortable
Cardio funk/dance aerobics	Enjoyable way to exercise, particularly for those who like dancing	May be intimidating for those who lack coordination
Power work-out	Ideal for regular exercisers who want a very high intensity work-out	Unsuitable for those who are just starting regular aerobic exercise classes
New body aerobics	Aerobic and muscle conditioning	Contains no high-impact moves
Body sculpting/body toning	Improves muscle tone and strength	Limited aerobics benefits

It is now a popular form of exercise that has led to the development of a number of different steps and home fitness videos. Each participant in a step class has his or her own step platform. The height is adjustable according to the individual's fitness level – the higher the step, the harder the work-out – so people of all levels can work out together. The instructor leads the class in stepping on and off the platform, using a variety of steps and turns. For safety reasons, the speed of music used for a step class is considerably slower than that of an aerobics class.

Aqua aerobics

The aqua aerobics class takes place in a swimming pool where the water should ideally reach mid-chest. This allows the water to support the lower body and to provide resistance during the exercises. The instructor stands on the side of the pool, to ensure adequate supervision of all participants, and a qualified lifeguard must be present during the session. An aqua aerobics class follows a similar format to that of a standard aerobics class, but adapted to allow for the slower speed of movement in water.

Cardio funk and dance aerobics

Following a similar format to a standard aerobics classes, cardio funk and dance aerobics classes incorporate disco dance movements during the warm-up and aerobic sections. The music is up-tempo, and instructors teach choreographed routines that involve more complex steps than those practised in standard aerobics classes.

Power work-out

A power work-out is a high intensity aerobics class that is more suitable for advanced participants. The aerobics section may be high impact and strenuous, possibly lasting up to 50 minutes, so it is advisable to inquire about the level and content of a power work-out class before attending.

Body sculpting/body toning

The emphasis of a body sculpting or toning class is on muscular strength and endurance components, and involves mainly resistance

*AEROBICS IN WATER
Because the water supports the body it eases strain on the joints. Aqua aerobics is therefore ideal for exercisers who are recovering from a back or joint injury. It also provides safe and effective exercise for pregnant women.*

exercise performed to music. Some exercises may be performed standing, such as squats and lunges, whereas others like abdominal curls and push-ups are carried out on the floor. Body toning classes often incorporate light weight-training equipment such as rubber bands or ankle weights to increase the resistance on the muscles.

New body aerobics

New body aerobics was originally developed in Australia. Based on the same format as an aerobics class, the participants perform low-impact moves to music during the aerobics section, while holding light hand weights. This allows the body to develop muscular strength and endurance while the pulse rate is raised and fitness levels are improving. New body aerobics is a good example of a class that is high intensity but low impact.

PLANNING YOUR OWN EXERCISE WORK-OUT

To supplement the formal exercise classes, you may want to plan additional exercise sessions on your own in the gym. When planning your first exercise workout it's probably best to aim for a session of cardiovascular exercise only, unless you are already quite fit and specifically want to improve your strength or flexibility.

As your confidence and fitness grow, try to add a selection of resistance exercises to your work-out. In this way you'll be maximising your fitness and making the best use

of your gym's facilities. Aim to vary the intensity of the workout so that you are training your body to work efficiently at different levels of energy exertion. You should try to keep a balance between the intensity of the different components of your exercise session and the time you take doing them. If the duration increases, the relative intensity must decrease to avoid premature fatigue. Conversely, if the intensity is to rise, the time spent must be reduced. The pyramid system (see below) provides an effective way of achieving this.

For an effective cardiovascular routine, the longest time should be spent at the lowest effective intensity – around 50 per cent of training time at level 1–2 (or 65–70 per cent of maximum heart rate – see page 61). As the intensity is increased the time spent is reduced. The shortest time is spent at the highest levels of intensity – no more than 10 per cent spent at level 4–5, or up to 80–85 per cent of maximum heart rate.

Circuit training

Circuit training classes consist of a series of exercise stations, some involving a piece of equipment, such as steps and skipping ropes, which are situated at various points around the exercise hall. Participants work their way around the circuit doing exercises at each station in turn. Circuit training classes start with a warm-up and finish with stretches, but otherwise vary greatly. The type of exercises included in the circuit will determine its aerobic and strength-building potential. Circuit training often includes weight-training equipment, and so may be held in a gym.

THE PYRAMID SYSTEM

The pyramid system is a structured way of varying training intensity within one work-out. In this system the intensity is increased to a predetermined level in gradual stages, and then brought back down again in stages.

For best results, use a treadmill and jog slowly for 5 minutes at low speed, then for 3 minutes at moderate speed, and then 1 minute as fast as you can. Then, slowing the pace, jog for 2 minutes at roughly between moderate and high speed, 3 minutes at moderate speed and finally 5 minutes slow.

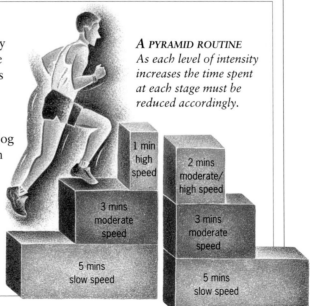

A PYRAMID ROUTINE
As each level of intensity increases the time spent at each stage must be reduced accordingly.

1 min high speed

2 mins moderate/high speed

3 mins moderate speed

3 mins moderate speed

5 mins slow speed

5 mins slow speed

The Menopausal Woman

As a woman's body changes with age, fluctuating hormone levels can cause distressing and debilitating symptoms, from headaches to disturbed sleep and irritability. When pressure of work and low self-esteem become a burden it can be very difficult to break the cycle of symptoms and depression. A supportive exercise class may provide the answer to these problems.

Marion is a 52-year-old teacher who has been suffering increasingly troubling menopausal symptoms for nearly a year. She has found that her fatigue, irritability, headaches and hot flushes are affecting her work and contributing to depression which is keeping her awake at night. She feels that she will not be able to face another term at school without help.

Her GP advised a course of HRT but Marion is nervous about the treatment because friends have told her about side-effects and related health problems that they have experienced. However, she feels she may have no choice if her work is not to suffer. She decides to visit her GP again to voice her fears and ask advice on alternatives to HRT.

WHAT SHOULD MARION DO?

Marion's doctor was able to allay many of her fears about HRT but was also willing to suggest certain alternatives, including dietary changes and an exercise programme. These will help overcome her symptoms of depression, anxiety and insomnia and improve her energy levels while also increasing her general well-being. Marion found a dietician who helped her to plan meals. She felt self-conscious about joining a gym because of her age and recent weight gain. A friend introduced her to a gym that runs women-only sessions and has instructors who tailor programmes to individuals and understand both the physical and psychological needs of older women.

Action Plan

HEALTH
Ask a GP about the conventional treatment and make sure all your questions are answered before either rejecting or agreeing to treatment.

EMOTIONAL HEALTH
Find a gym or exercise class that doesn't intimidate you. As you gain in confidence your self-image will improve.

FITNESS
Build up your strength, stamina and suppleness to help relieve symptoms and improve fitness and emotional health.

HEALTH
Horror stories from friends and relations can provoke a fear of conventional treatments. Don't dismiss medical help without professional guidance.

EMOTIONAL HEALTH
Age and physical changes, such as weight gain or water retention, can cause self-consciousness and lead to feelings of inadequacy and poor self-image.

FITNESS
Lethargy and general aches and pains may make forced or public exercise unappealing.

HOW THINGS TURNED OUT FOR MARION

Dietary changes coupled with mild and carefully monitored medication helped Marion in the first few weeks, but she felt that long-term relief came from her regular exercise class.
At the gym Marion met other women in her position and gained support from them. Her symptoms subsided and her fitness improved. She now feels more confident about work, her energy levels are higher and she is looking forward to the new term.

BEFORE AND AFTER EXERCISE

To get the most from your health club, take advantage of its various facilities to help you to prepare for – and recover from – your exercise programme.

Taking time to prepare your body physically and focus your mind before a work-out will enhance every aspect of your training. Physically you will be in the best possible condition – your body will be fuelled and ready to go – and mentally you will be prepared, with your mind focused and motivated on the immediate task ahead.

Just as conditioning yourself beforehand will set you up for a productive work-out, spending time afterwards can help your body to recover from the recent increased effort demanded of it. This can be accomplished by stretching the muscles thoroughly and then encouraging increased blood flow through the body by, for example, using various forms of hydrotherapy.

PRE-EXERCISE

To ensure an effective work-out, you should prepare both physically and mentally for exercise. About 2 hours before a session eat a light, carbohydrate-rich snack: about 50 grams (1¾ ounces) of carbohydrate-packed foods, such as dried fruit, muesli, cereal, or bagels with a light coating of jam or preserve are all ideal. This allows time for adequate digestion, and will provide around 200 calories of energy. You should also drink about 225–300 millilitres (8–10 fluid ounces) of pure water to provide adequate hydration for absorbing and metabolising the food. Many health clubs provide café or even restaurant facilities where you can enjoy a healthy snack before your routine.

It's important to prepare yourself mentally before your session. To avoid rushing allow plenty of time to get to the venue. If you find your mind is preoccupied with work or home problems, set aside 5 minutes to sit down and unwind before you begin.

Clearing your mind of distracting thoughts will help you to unwind from everyday stresses and pressures. If high levels of stress are left unchecked and are allowed to develop, they can activate unhelpful and potentially damaging hormones, such as cortisol, that interfere with energy metabolism and inhibit efficient neuromuscular action. This can then cause symptoms such as lethargy and poor concentration. If your levels of stress or tension are of particular concern, and a short spell of quiet contemplation is not sufficient, you could have a sports massage before your exercise session. This will loosen tight muscles, increase blood flow through the tissues to relax you and counteract the effect of the stress hormones.

BANANA CINNAMON SMOOTHIE

Many health clubs offer re-energising snacks and drinks – smoothies are particularly popular as they pack a lot of nutrition into an easily digestible form of food. Here's an energy-boosting recipe you can try at home.

250 ml (9 fl oz) semi-skimmed milk
115 ml (4 fl oz) low-fat plain yoghurt
1 tbsp honey
1 banana, cut into chunks
¼ tsp cinnamon

■ Put all the ingredients into a blender or food processor and blend at high speed for about 10 seconds until the mixture is smooth.
■ Chill for at least half an hour before serving. Alternatively, pour the mixture into moulds and place in the freezer to make a delicious frozen yoghurt.
■ To serve, decorate with extra cinnamon sprinkled over the top.
Makes 3–4 glassfuls

CREATING A SAUNA EFFECT AT HOME

The benefits of a sauna in relieving sore and tired muscles can be achieved by alternating hot and cold water in your shower at home (see caution, right).

▶ *Stand in the shower and run the water as hot as is comfortable until your skin develops a pleasant pink flush.*

▶ *Quickly lower the water temperature to cold, causing the blood to be shunted to the core of the body again.*

▶ *Run the water hot again and repeat the process of temperature fluctuations as often as desired. Sessions of 30–60 seconds are usually sufficient.*

SAUNA RELIEF
Having a sauna after a vigorous exercise work-out can speed the recovery of the muscles.

POST-EXERCISE

A thorough post-exercise routine including cooling-down exercises (see page 70) and extra stretches will improve the suppleness of your muscles and joints and help to avoid muscle soreness. An enhanced cool-down might include a 5–10 minute swim. This light activity will aid blood circulation without placing great stress on the working muscles. Improved circulation helps in the breakdown of any lactic acid that has accumulated in the muscles through anaerobic exercise. This will help to avoid muscle soreness and also facilitate the repair of any damage to the muscle fibres that might have occurred during the work-out.

Hydrotherapy

You can also help to cleanse your muscles with hydrotherapy techniques, such as taking a hot bath or shower. The hot water raises the body temperature and causes the blood to move from the muscles within the body and spread out towards the surface of the skin, giving rise to the pink, flushed look of the skin. This process is called 'flushing', and is also known as a 'blood shunt'. It is an effective method of getting the blood moving through the worked muscles, so aiding the removal of lactic acid and other waste products of the metabolism.

The effect on the bloodstream caused by the flushing process is reversed by applying cold water, which causes the blood to be shunted to the core of the body again, so creating another opportunity to flush waste products out of the muscles. This is the basis behind the practice of alternating hot and cold showers (see left).

If your gym has a sauna, before entering it, take an initial cleansing shower after the work-out. Run the water down to a cold temperature and then enter the sauna and sit down on the lowest, and therefore the coolest, level until you have acclimatised to the high temperatures. After 5–10 minutes, move to a higher position to raise the body temperature. Do not spend more than 15 minutes at a time in the sauna.

When you leave the sauna, take a cold shower as before for 1–2 minutes, then return to the cool area of the sauna for 2 minutes to assist flushing. This is considered in most clubs as a single use of the sauna; up to five visits to the sauna will be enough to assist your recuperation.

Muscle soreness

If any symptoms of muscle soreness appear in the days following a work-out, the best remedy, in addition to the self-help techniques described on page 148, is to make the muscles perform light activities that are as similar as possible to the exercise movements used in the workout that led to the soreness. This ensures that the sore muscles or regions are being flushed with blood to aid recuperation.

The intensity of such activity must be kept below the thresholds of aerobic activity or else it will generate more muscle fatigue and potential soreness. Between 55 and 65 per cent of your maximum heart rate (see page 61) is considered the ideal level. This strategy, called active recovery, is far more effective than just resting and doing no activity after exercise, which is known as passive recovery. Active recovery can dissipate muscular soreness in less than half the time needed for passive recovery.

> **CAUTION**
> *When alternating hot and cold showers, avoid wetting your head as the temperature fluctuations on the brain can cause dizzy spells or fainting. Those suffering from a heart disorder or high blood pressure should avoid this technique altogether.*

INDEX

ACKNOWLEDGMENTS

Carroll & Brown Limited
would like to thank
Budo Store
Chartered Society of Physiotherapists
Chartered Society of Sports
    Physiotherapists
Hales Sports Shop
Holmes Place Health and Fitness Club
Obesity Resource Information Centre
Porcelli Dance Shop
Sports Council
Malcolm Whyatt, Oscar Heidenstam
    Foundation

Editorial assistance
Sharon Freed
Jennifer Mussett
Nadia Silver
Simon Warmer

Design assistance
Evie Loizides
Gilda Pacitti

DTP design
Elisa Merino

Photograph sources
9   (Top) Hulton Getty Picture
    Collection
10 (Top) Hulton Getty Picture
    Collection
11 (Top) Tony Stone Images
16 Juan Alvarez/Image bank
19 *and front cover* (Bottom left)
    Angela Hampton/Family Life
    Pictures
21 (Top) CNRI/SPL;
    (Bottom) All Action
22 (Top) The Post Office
23 Museum of Fine Arts/Bridgeman
    Art Library
28 (Bottom) Sporting Pictures UK
    Ltd

33 (Left, centre and bottom)
    Sporting Pictures UK Ltd
34 The Stock Market
35 Sporting Pictures UK Ltd
36 (Left) Rex Features
39 The Stock Market
41 The Stock Market
42 Robert Harding Picture Library
45 Alain Deniz/Frank Spooner
    Pictures
53 Will and Deni McIntyre/SPL
60 Larry J. Pierce/Image Bank
64 Mary Evans Picture Library
67 (Top) Sporting Pictures UK Ltd
73 Rex Features
78 (Top) Philips Domestic
    Appliance and Personal Care
81 (Top) SPL; (Bottom) John
    Greim/SPL
82 (Top) D. Mossiat/Frank Spooner
    Pictures; (Bottom) The Dame
    Rosalind Paget Trust
84 (Bottom) The Stock Market
86 The Stock Market
89 The Stock Market
92 (Top) Tony Stone Images
93 Collections/Anthea Sieveking
95 (Left) Rex features; (Centre and
    right) Sporting Pictures UK Ltd
96 (Top) Rex Features
97 (Top) Popperfoto
98 (Top) Angela Hampton/Family
    Life Pictures
100 (Top) Telegraph Colour Library;
    (Bottom) Rex Features
102 Telegraph Colour Library
103 (Right) Tony Stone
104 Sporting Pictures UK Ltd
105 (Top) Brylak/Frank Spooner
    Pictures
106 (Top) The Hutchison Library
107 (Top) Tony Stone Images
108 (Top) The Telegraph Colour
    Library
109 Rex Features
110 (Top) Tony Stone Images
111 (Top) Rex Features

112 (Top) Rex Features
114 (Top left) The Telegraph Colour
    Library; (Right) Rex Features
115 (Top) Rex Features
116 Simon Grosset/Frank Spooner
    Pictures
117 (Top and bottom left) The
    Stock Market
118 (Top) Rex Features
120 The Stock Market
132 Telegraph Colour Library
136 Mary Evans Picture Library
138 The Stock Market
141 The Oscar Heidenstam
    Foundation
150 (Bottom) Corbis-Bettman/UPI
152 Tony Stone Images
156 The Stock Market

Illustrators
Debbie Hinks
Conny Jude
Alan Nanson
David Stevens
Josephine Sumner
Paul Williams

Photographic assistant
Mark Langridge

Hair and make-up
Kim Menzies
Jessamina Owens

Picture research
Sandra Schneider

Food preparation
Maddalena Bastianelli

Research
Steven Chong

Index
Richard Emerson